MINNIE DEAN

HER LIFE & CRIMES

MINNIE DEAN

HER LIFE & CRIMES

LYNLEY HOOD

PENGUIN BOOKS

PENGUIN BOOKS

Penguin Books (NZ) Ltd, 182–190 Wairau Road, Auckland 10, New Zealand
Penguin Books Ltd, 27 Wrights Lane, London W8 5TZ, England
Penguin USA, 375 Hudson Street, New York, NY 10014, United States
Penguin Books Australia Ltd, 487 Maroondah Highway, Ringwood, Australia 3134
Penguin Books Canada Ltd, 10 Alcorn Avenue, Toronto, Ontario, Canada M4V 3B2

Penguin Books Ltd, Registered Offices: Harmondsworth, Middlesex, England

First published in 1994
1   3   5   7   9   10   8   6   4   2

Editorial services by Michael Gifkins and Associates
Designed by Richard King
Typeset by Egan-Reid Ltd, Auckland
Printed in Australia

This book is dedicated
to the memory
of Jennet Mitchel

Contents

―――― ~ ――――

Chapter VII
A GREENOCK CHILDHOOD
Problems of non-fiction — Minnie's childhood — her dead sisters — infant
mortality in Victorian Britain — opium — railways — Minnie's father — her
education — her mother's death — Minnie vanishes

Chapter VIII
THE PARISH MINISTER
The Reverend McCulloch — history & practices of the Church of Scotland
— the children of the manse

Chapter IX
TERRA AUSTRALIS / TERRA INCOGNITO
Minnie's mysterious Australian sojourn — the birth of her 1st daughter

Chapter X
NEW ZEALAND, THE EARLY YEARS
Minnie arrives in Southland — her 2nd daughter is born — she marries Charles
Dean — Dr John McCulloch dies — Minnie's daughters marry —
1 daughter & 2 grandchildren drown — Minnie adopts Maggie Cameron — Maggie's
childhood — Charles Dean's bankruptcy — Charles & Minnie attacked in bed, &c

Chapter XI
PRIVATE TRAGEDY AND PUBLIC SCANDAL
Newspaper clippings illustrating nasty, brutish & short aspects of
New Zealand colonial life

Chapter XII
A NEW START AT WINTON
The Deans move to Winton — house fire — financial problems — Minnie becomes a
child care worker — colonial illegitimacy — Minnie's infant mortality rate —
adoption arrangements — the Deans move to a shack — 1st infant dies — more &
more children — Minnie's extravagances, &c

Chapter XIII
RUNNING DOWNHILL AND GATHERING STEAM
Police surveillance begins — more babies — 1st police list — 2nd infant dies —
inquest — Minnie exonerated but tarnished — her relationship with police
deteriorates — more babies — 2nd police list — 2 infants disappear — financial
problems — she neglects a baby in Christchurch — she spends a night in the open —
3rd infant disappears — a mother visits — Infant Life Protection Act — Minnie fined
1d — 4th infant disappears, &c

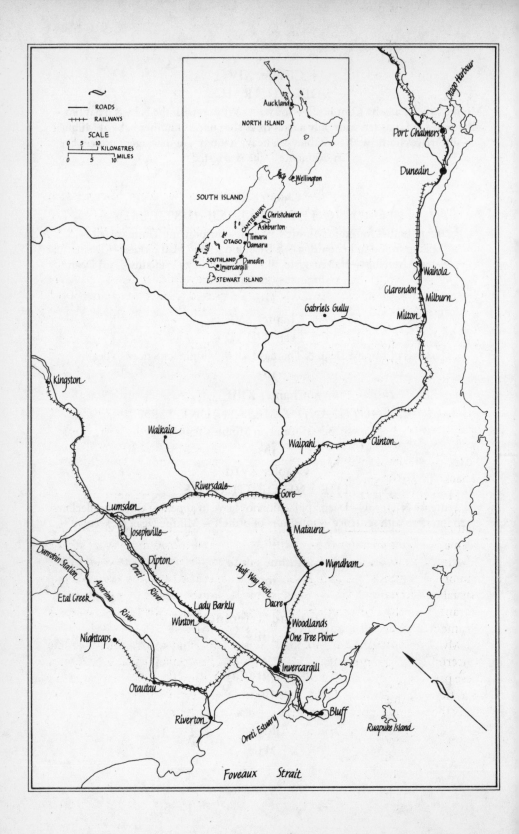

ROADS
RAILWAYS

SCALE
0 5 10
KILOMETRES
0 5 10
MILES

Auckland
NORTH ISLAND

Wellington

SOUTH ISLAND

CANTERBURY
Christchurch
Ashburton
OTAGO
Timaru
Oamaru
SOUTHLAND   Dunedin
Invercargill
STEWART ISLAND

Port Chalmers

Otago Harbour

Dunedin

Waihola

Clarendon
Milburn

Gabriels Gully

Milton

Kingston

Waikaia

Waipahi
Clinton

Riversdale

Gore

Lumsden

Mataura

Josephville

Dunrobin Station

Dipton

Wyndham

Half Way Bush

Dacre

Etal Creek

Oreti River

Aparima River

Lady Barkly

Winton

Woodlands
One Tree Point

Nightcaps

Invercargill

Orautau

Riverton

Bluff

Ruapuke Island

Oreti Estuary

Foveaux   Strait

Prologue

———— ∿ ————

Though almost one hundred years have passed since her death, Minnie Dean remains Southland's best-known citizen. Early in this project I visited the Deep South in search of community memories and memorabilia of the Winton baby farmer and was rewarded with a barrage of bizarre and gruesome stories. I was told that she killed babies with hat pins (or knitting needles, or rusty nails) and that she stuck pins into dolls. I was told that the bodies of her victims were thrown into waterways, left in railway sheds, buried along country roadsides or chopped up and fed to pigs. There were legions more stories about her hat box, her train journeys, her hanging and her burial ('Nothing will grow on her grave'). Many of the stories were demonstrably untrue; most of them carried a whiff of folklore and superstition. Their core motifs were the stuff of legends: sex, infanticide, tragedy and scandal.

These stories came from policemen, lawyers, journalists, farmers, doctors, social workers, housewives and school teachers. All around me intelligent, well-educated people kept telling and retelling the stories and equally intelligent people kept believing them. It seems that contrary to popular belief, the transmission of folklore and superstition is not confined to ancient crones in backblocks villages.

Most books on famous New Zealand crimes carry a chapter on Minnie Dean, as do most works of Southland history. Invercargill journalist J. O. P. Watt compiled a whole book on her trial. These authors presented Minnie Dean as a freak and a monster. In 1985 Ken Catran took a more sympathetic view. In his book and television series on Minnie Dean's defence counsel, Alf Hanlon, he presented her as high-born victim of circumstance, a well-meaning lady fallen on tragically hard times. He raised a question mark over her guilt. Catran's work sparked a controversy in Southland. Voices were raised. Tempers became frayed. People stormed out of dinner parties.

My aim in writing this book is to establish, as far as possible, the facts concerning the life and death of Minnie Dean. The woman who emerges from these pages was not a freak or a monster, nor was she a gentlewoman fallen on hard times. So who was Minnie Dean? And was she guilty? Reader, you must study the evidence and answer these questions for yourself.

Chapter I

———— ❧ ————

THE LAST WORDS AND CONFESSION OF JENNET MITCHEL

A Brief Account of the last Words and Confession of Jennet Mitchel,
Parishioner in Saline, who was Executed at Dumfermling on the
8 of Sept 1709, for the Crime of CHILD Murder.

Reader, it being generally desir'd, by the most Judicious Eye and Ear Witnesses of what past at this Womans Death, that the Following Account thereof should be published, You have it therefore in the very same words as they dropt from her own Mouth, without Alteration of one Sentence, to the best of my Remembrance, but with some change of the Order in which they were Spoken; because thro the Fervency of her Spirit, she some times came over the same Petitions and Warnings, which were gathered afterwards upon serious Reflection, not being Marked at the time. And it's thought the publication hereof may be Expedient and usefull, as an awfull Document and Caveat against the crying Abominations of the times, particularly, that unnatural and Atrocious Crime of Infant Murder . . .

The first time that I began to be concern'd about Religion, a Word that gripped my Heart, was at Fossua Communion, in the close of the Sabbath, the Minister who came forth to the Tent, said, That the Lord Jesus had been kindly offering Himself to the Multitude, there that Day, and was now to take his farewell that night: and it may be it would be His last Farewell to some there. I found that word follow me home, and it set me to my Knees, and for a while I was afraid to Sin, and I waited on the Ordinances diligently long after, but I forgate that and others.

Thereafter at the first Communion, (given by Mr. Plenderleith) at Saline, I Communicate at the third Table, I think, a Word the Minister had there, was, Now I see some young Communicants here the day, remember ye have now professed your selves to be the LORD's; Satan will be upon you afterwards to tempt you to Sin, but let this be your Answer, I am not mine own but Christ's, and have given my self away to him. This had weight with me for a time, but when I began to leave him, the LORD justly left me, and gave me up to my self: So that afterwards I fell into the Sin of Fornication, and did hide it, till I had born the Child, because of the weary Fee, that I might serve out my Service the Terme. I blame not either Minister or Session, for not inquiring after me, for it was not heard of in the Parish till all was over; as to the Child. And upon a Sabbath I went carelesly out of the Church, in the Afternoon, with my Pains upon me I called for no help, but in the open Fields, in my way to Muckhart. I brought forth a living Child, and carried him about two or three Miles in my Lap, and then he died, and I hid him under Ground, thinking the Business was over, and hidden from Man, and that I would have no more Trouble. Within a few days I returned to my Service, and in all this I confess, O! what an Unnatural Mother was I, and justly deserve this death this day, for my Neglect and Carelesness of the poor Infant, tho' I did it through much Ignorance and Unskilfulness.

When I was returned to my Service, it being reported that I was guilty of Fornication, the Minister came to me on a Fridays night; and tho' he prayed thrice with me, and earnestly enquired if I was guilty, I stifly denied that Night: but thereafter confessed to the Women, who found Milk in my Breasts, and to the Session, that I was guilty of Fornication, and upon the Monday Morning I thought I saw mine own Minister praying for the Discovery of my Sin, and I thought I knew as well when he went to Prayer, as if I had been with him; and as I was sitting by the Fire side, I thought the Arrows of the Almighty went through my Heart, and that I would not be able to cover it longer whereupon I longed as much to see him as he could to see me, and when he came with some others to the House where I was, I freely acknowledged, that I had brought forth the Child, and left him hid in a place under Ground, but there was no Wound or Bruise upon him, and that I should go my self, and bring him to be seen at the Kirk, which I did, and that Day I found my natural Conscience greatly eased with my Confession . . .

I confessed no other things before the Sentence of Death past, except that one word, That the Child had Life, and after the Sentence I freely acknowledged he had Life, and none was the cause of his Death but my self . . .

When she was going up the Ladder, she said to the People, O take Warning now Sirs, and pray much for me, for you know not what Death you may die your selves. Then she Sang upon the Ladder Psal. 51. two double verses from the beginning, and gave out the Line her self; And then kissing the Bible, and gave it to her Brother, saying, Farewel Sweet Bible, but I hope I am going where there will be no need of a Bible, and Prayed Appositely and Ardently for all; and particularly for the Minister and Paroch she came from, that the Lord would comfort him, and send days of his Power there: I have been the greatest Grief of Heart to him that ever he had, and he hath been at much Pains, and oft creeping about the Throne of Grace to gain my poor Soul, but I hope the Lord will comfort him for all when I am gone. And she prayed that the poor worthless Wretch (for so she named him) who hath been guilty with me, that the Lord would take away the Guilt from him, and the place where it was committed, that the Scales of Ignorance might be made to fall from his Eyes; for (said she) he is not free of this, tho he come not to such an untimely Death as I have done; O that the Lord would awaken him, and this Sleepy Generation, before the Flames of Hell awaken them . . .

And with many moe Significant Expressions, she gave a Sign, saying, Into thy Hands I Commend my Spirit.

FINIS

Chapter II

———— ~ ————

SOUTHLAND, RELATIVELY SPEAKING

*T*endrils of interlacing people-nets twine through the time and space of Southland; puritan and sinner, observer and observed: all are knotted into the web.

'Is Lynley Hood a local girl? What was her maiden name?' the caller demanded of my Southland host. ('Who is this stranger?' she seemed to be saying, 'digging under the neatly raked surface of our lives, unearthing skeletons.')

'She was born in the North Island. I think that her maiden name was Preston.'

As it happens Preston was my mother's maiden name, but it was a good answer. The name Preston has its place in the southern genealogical matrix. As I pass among them, researching the life of Minnie Dean, canny Southlanders weigh my local roots against the deviancy of my birthplace — and for the time being suspend judgement.

One hundred and forty years before I began writing this book my great-grandparents, Robert and Sarah Preston, left their Yorkshire village and sailed around the world. They went first to South Africa and then to Australia before joining Robert's three brothers in New Zealand in 1860.[1] For the next two decades Robert and Sarah's dairy farm supplied milk to the fledgling town of Invercargill. Every day after milking, the younger members of their large family drove a three-horse dray around the deeply rutted streets, stopping at each house and carefully measuring each order from a ten-gallon can. In winter the mud was axle-deep. Barely two thousand people lived in Invercargill in the 1860s but in winter the milk delivery took all day.[2]

At that time one of the town's most famous residents was Granny Kelly, the first white woman in Invercargill. Four years after her death Granny Kelly achieved unwelcome fame-by-association when her niece Minnie Dean became the only woman hanged for murder in New Zealand, but during her lifetime Granny Kelly was famous in her own right as a pioneer. Through the wide-angled lens that spans the adventurous lives of Granny Kelly and her late husband John one can survey the colourful history of Southland during the early years of European settlement in New Zealand.

§ *A note concerning the life history of Granny Kelly*

Granny Kelly was born in 1808 as Christina Swan, the eldest daughter of a Scottish farmer from the village of Cardross, a huddle of grey stone cottages on the banks of the Clyde. During her childhood a forest of industrial smokestacks grew where once there were trees and the white river mists turned grey. Waves of work-hungry strangers poured in from Ireland and the Scottish Highlands; picturesque fishing villages sprawled into ugly slums; cholera, typhoid, smallpox, malaria, tuberculosis and typhus stalked the land; emigration to the colonies seemed the only answer.

In 1847, after fifteen years of marriage and seven children, Christina and her first husband Dugald Niven set sail with their three surviving children on the *Philip Laing* — one of the founding ships of the Free Church of Scotland settlement in Otago. During the stormy five-month voyage Christina gave birth to a healthy baby boy; in the new colony she cooked on an open fire outdoors while Dugald built their home. Along with the other new arrivals their first shelter was a dismal barracks:

> . . . the long windowless room in almost total darkness, the rain pouring through the roof, the floor in a miserable condition and women with young children on their knees and mid-leg deep in mire and puddle, huddled in many instances under an open umbrella.[3]

As the weeks passed more and more settlers moved into their own homes and Dunedin — 'the Edinburgh of the South' — took root. There were Maori in the district but that was almost irrelevant; the Otago colonists were convinced that their future lay with their fellow Scots, and that future looked bright.

Then for the Nivens tragedy struck. In 1849 Dugald was killed by a falling tree.[4]

At the end of the following year Christina met and married John Kelly, a twice-widowed Englishman of Irish descent. Together with her three youngest children she exchanged the familiarity of the Scottish settlement for life with her new husband among the Maori of Foveaux Strait, and she accepted Kelly's half-caste family as her own. She was, in the words of the missionary Wohlers, 'an excellent and kindhearted woman'.[5]

In 1856, just before their second child was born, John and Christina Kelly made history. In March of that year they became the first residents of another new town — Invercargill.

Founding Invercargill was not John Kelly's only claim to fame. In his early twenties he had been one of southern New Zealand's earliest European settlers, one of the first of the sealers, whalers and flax merchants to abandon seafaring for a shore-based life at one of the whaling stations scattered along Foveaux Strait.[6] For more than twenty years he flourished as a whaler, trader and boatman on remote, windswept Ruapuke Island, stronghold of the great Southern Maori chief, Tuhawaiki.[7] Kelly fathered one son by a woman named Hine Tuhawaiki and adopted another, and had two daughters by a second Maori wife whose name is unknown.

By early 1850 both Kelly's Maori wives and his natural son were dead, but when the survey ship *Archeron* called, Kelly was thriving:

> The Englishman came off next morning in a large boat manned by natives, bringing with him a supply of vegetables, a grisly black pig and a firkin of very questionable looking butter. He was regarded with a degree of interest, being thus secluded from his countrymen, amidst a half savage race — in this most dreary climate — dreary to the eye but probably not insalubrious, since our Robinson Crusoe was a burly-looking subject; his snow-white locks and wholesome ruddy countenance bespoke an age 'Frosty yet kindly.'[8]

During a stay in Dunedin at the end of that year John Kelly met and married the widowed Christina Niven. For the next five years the couple made a home for their families (his, hers and theirs) on Ruapuke Island.

By 1855 it was clear that the future of the colony lay on the mainland: Tuhawaiki was dead, the whaling industry was in decline and settlers were spreading across the southern plains.

In January 1856 Governor Gore Browne announced that a town to be called Invercargill would be located near Bluff. Surveyors were sent to find a site but such formalities were of no interest to John Kelly. In March 1856 he rowed up the Oreti Estuary and built a whare and stockyard at the edge of the bush. His garden flourished in the deep alluvial soil, his cattle thrived on the lush grass. Within months other settlers moved in. By the time the site for Invercargill was proclaimed in October 1856 the new town had taken root. On 6 July that year Christina and John Kelly's second son became the first white child born in Invercargill.

The Kelly family had been in Invercargill for less than a year when the normally robust John fell ill. On 16 May 1857 he died in his Invercargill home.[9]

§ *The story of Minnie Dean resumes*

After her husband's death Granny Kelly stayed in Invercargill. Around the end of 1863 she was living in a six-roomed house at 115 Princes Street with her four youngest children when a near-stranger, a niece she had farewelled as a three-year-old in Scotland sixteen years earlier, came to stay. She was accompanied by one small girl and gave birth to, or otherwise acquired, another on arrival. Her name was Williamina McCulloch.

Williamina was a clergyman's daughter who had come to New Zealand via Tasmania, where her physician husband had died and her first daughter was born — or so her Invercargill neighbours believed.[10] Williamina McCulloch was also a woman destined to pass into history as Minnie Dean, the Winton baby farmer — the only woman hanged for murder in New Zealand.

My Southland host knew none of this history. She did not know about John Kelly who spent more than half his life among the Maori on Ruapuke Island and later founded Invercargill, or about Robert and Sarah Preston who pioneered the Invercargill milk supply. She did not know about John Kelly's kindly third wife, or about her niece Williamina McCulloch who stayed with her in Invercargill; who in fact stayed with her at the very time that the Preston children were delivering milk around the Invercargill streets. Nor did she know that Williamina McCulloch later became the infamous Minnie Dean. Had she known she could have woven their lives into a story. Had she known, in this community where relationships matter, she could have told her caller 'Lynley Hood's great-grandfather was Minnie Dean's milkman.'

Chapter III

———— ∽ ————

SOUTHLAND DAILY NEWS
12 AUGUST 1895

EXECUTION OF MINNIE DEAN

FIRM TO THE LAST

SHE PROTESTS HER INNOCENCE

The last act in the tragedy surrounding the life of Minnie Dean, the Winton baby murderer, was performed in the Invercargill gaol this morning. The facts of her crime are too familiar for recapitulation. Her business, as everyone knows, was to receive young children ostensibly for adoption, but actually to traffic in the lives of the little ones entrusted to her for gain. It was built on lying and deceit, and was carried out with appalling callousness. To those in trouble she represented herself as a childless wife, pining for the orange blossoms nature had denied her, upon which to bestow her affections, and not unnaturally there were numbers who readily availed themselves of the chance of getting rid of a burden that meant social ostracism, confidently believing that their unfortunate offspring would be under the charge of one who would, in every respect, prove a kind and exemplary mother.

Minnie Dean brought education and intellect to bear in her hideously cruel business, which would long ago have been brought to a close but for her adroitness. When her real character was revealed in the recent court proceedings it was but too apparent that the crime she expiated this morning, the killing of Dorothy Edith Carter, was not the only murder to be laid to her charge. How many helpless infants met their doom at her hands is known only to herself, but there was sufficient evidence forthcoming to justify the belief that at least six children were unaccounted for.

Since the death sentence was passed an effort was made to quash the conviction on the ground that evidence had been improperly admitted, necessitating a delay of seven weeks in carrying the sentence into effect. During this period the condemned woman has borne up remarkably well. Singular to say, though it was in evidence that she occasionally drank to excess, since incarceration she has sternly refused to take any ardent spirits, though allowed to do so by the regulations, and has taken nothing more than a little stout daily. She fully realised all through her terrible position,

and though always self-possessed in conversation, was clearly much agitated when
left to herself.

For the last two or three weeks she has
not left her cell. Yesterday her husband had
a last meeting with her. She slept from half
past eleven till three this morning, but took
no breakfast. The Rev. Mr Lindsay, who has
been in constant attendance since the time
of her conviction, arrived at the gaol at 7.30,
and engaged in prayer with her up to the
last.

The execution took place at eight o'clock,
the only persons present besides the gaol
officials being the Sheriff (Mr W. Martin),
the Chaplain, the Surgeon, and the Press
reporters. At three minutes to eight o'clock,
the Gaoler, accompanied by the Surgeon,
the Sheriff, and the Executioner, proceeded
to the condemned woman's cell, a comfortable apartment into which the sun
shone, and a fire slowly burned. Here Mrs
Dean had spent the last seven weeks
awaiting the judgment of the Appeal Court,
and the final decision of the Executive. On
the mantelpiece was a glass of spirits, which
she had left practically untouched, and a
neat bouquet of violets and snowdrops.

The Sheriff then formally demanded the
body, and commanded the hangman to do
his duty. Mrs Dean's arms were then
pinioned with a strap round the wrists and
biceps, and the procession started, the
Gaoler (Mr Bratby) and the Surgeon (Dr
McLeod) leading, followed by the chaplain
(Rev. G. Lindsay), the condemned woman
— supported on either side by a warder —
the hangman and the sheriff.

As the bell tolled she marched erect,
and with a firm step to the stairs leading to
the platform of the scaffold, womanlike,
lifting with her pinioned hands her skirts as
she walked up the fourteen steps. With
amazing calmness she stood on the drop,
facing the west, a small black board against
the high brick wall directly in front of
her marking the spot where Walsh, the

Waikawa wife murderer was buried in
February 1879.

Then the Sheriff asked, 'Do you wish to
say anything before you leave this world?' to
which the unhappy woman replied in a
subdued tone, 'No, except that I am
innocent.' The hangman then adjusted the
rope, Mrs Dean calmly holding her head to
one side, apparently to facilitate the tying of
the knot, and placed on her head the white
cap.

Her last words, in almost inaudible tones,
were 'Oh; God, let me not suffer!' and she
momentarily swayed to and fro, though
supported by the warders who held her
hands.

Just as she uttered the final syllable the
executioner, who was standing immediately
behind her, drew the lever, the trap door on
which she stood opened out and instan-
taneously all was over, not a tremor being
visible. From the time the sheriff entered
the condemned woman's cell until the fatal
drop, at two minutes past eight o'clock, only
five minutes elapsed. The body was left
hanging for one hour, when it was removed
from its ghastly position, and the doctor,
having, in accordance with the require-
ments of the law, satisfied himself as to the
cause of death, it was placed in a plain coffin
for removal for burial at Winton by the
deceased's husband.

The scaffold used was built for the
execution of Captain Jarvie, who was
engaged in the coastal trade between Invercargill and Dunedin, over a quarter of a
century ago, and who, forming a *liaison*
with another, poisoned his wife. It had
remained in Dunedin ever since. It is
understood that Mrs Dean has left a long
written statement regarding her life in
which she places a different construction on
her later acts from that to be inferred from
the evidence led at the recent trial. The
contents of the document will not of course
be disclosed by the officials, but it will be
forwarded to the Government.

The scaffold stood sixteen feet high, and the drop allowed was seven feet eight inches. The structure was covered in by tarpaulins to obscure the view from any of the buildings in the vicinity, upon which quite a large number had taken up a position, though it was impossible for them to see anything of what was taking place within the gaol.

In this connection an unfortunate accident occurred. A youth named Edward Donoghue had managed to climb to the top of W. H. Mathieson's carriage factory and whilst there was seized with a fit. A companion tried to hold him but fearing that both would fall let go and Donoghue fell to the ground — a distance of thirty feet. He was taken to the hospital where he was promptly attended to by Drs Hogg and Fullarton. In addition, a large number gathered outside the walls, though they must have known that nothing could either be seen or heard.

The executioner, who came from the North, is a man of between fifty and sixty years, but of very athletic build, and to his promptness in the awful last extremity was probably due the fact that there was no 'scene' on the scaffold.

It is worthy of note that Mrs Dean is the first woman who has met her death at the hangman's hand in New Zealand. Others have been sentenced to be hung, but in their cases the Government has hitherto granted a reprieve.

The usual formal inquest was held this afternoon at the gaol, before Mr Poynton, S. M. Evidence was given by Walter Martin, sheriff, J. H. Bratby, gaoler, and Dr McLeod. The medical evidence was to the effect that the neck was completely broken and that death was due to pressure of the bone on the spinal cord and a verdict was returned accordingly.

Chapter IV

——— ❧ ———

MYTHS AND MONSTERS

The Editor
The Southland Times
INVERCARGILL

Dear Sir
I will be visiting Southland between 27 September and 13 October for the purpose of researching a biography of Minnie Dean. My aim is to thoroughly research her life, and to write about it in a way that is fair, accurate and sensitive to the motives and actions of all the people involved.

I would be interested in hearing from anyone who may have official or family memories or memorabilia (letters, diaries, photographs and so on) of Minnie Dean and her times. I would be happy to respect the confidentiality of anyone who does not want their identity revealed.

My Invercargill contact number during my stay will be 487-768.

Yours sincerely
Lynley Hood

Folk tales swarm like flies around the life and death of Minnie Dean, carrying with them the recurring motifs of hat pins and hat boxes, dead babies, trains, plants and graves. They're old stories, most of them, echoing ancient lore. Russia has Baba Yaga; Britain has Black Annis; Germany has the witch in 'Hansel and Gretel'. Throughout the world that terrible archetype, the woman who kills children, lurks in the collective unconscious. New Zealand has the Winton baby farmer and her name is Minnie Dean.

'My grandma used to say — you kids behave yourselves or I'll send you to Minnie Dean!'

'Minnie Dean'll get you! Minnie Dean'll get you! I can remember kids chanting that at school.'

The Minnie Dean story is a bloated carcass from the past, fly blown with legends. It moves; it glows. But its movement is the writhing of maggots beneath a dried and brittle skin; its glow is the dull green light of reflected terror. Only the bones are real.

'Mum told me that Minnie Dean used to kill babies by sticking a hat pin through the fontanelle.'

'She did some terrible things. My father told me she used to kill babies by sticking hat pins through their eyes. You wouldn't credit it would you?'

'A man who grew up in Invercargill told me that she used to stick pins into dolls.'

'I can remember kids at school talking about how Minnie Dean used to hide babies inside hat boxes. She used to torture them by sticking hat pins through the sides.'

'My parents told me that she used to kill babies by stabbing them with rusty nails.'

'She used a knitting needle. I grew up with the story that she killed babies by sticking a knitting needle through that soft spot on the top of their heads.'

Reader, these are witch stories, aeons old. In the seventeenth century Reginald Scot reported that witches were said to 'sacrifice their owne children to the divell before baptisme, holding them up in the aire unto him, and then thrust a needle into their braines'.[1] The roots of such stories creep and twist deep into the human psyche — down through the foundations of adult rationality, down through the crumbling insecurities and guilts of ourselves as parents — to touch that most elemental human fear: that grandmother will turn into a wolf, that the giant will eat Jack, that the stepmother will poison Snow White — that in the helpless vulnerability of our infancy, mother will turn murderer.

In reality, hat pins did not appear in New Zealand until after Minnie Dean's arrest, and knitting needles were used to deal with unwanted babies before birth, not after. In fact there is no evidence that Minnie Dean ever stabbed anyone with anything.

'She had an arrangement to pick up a baby at Bluff that had been born out of wedlock. The guard saw her getting on the train with it but she didn't have it when she got off at Winton — she must have thrown it out along the way.'

'She murdered babies on the train and threw their bodies into passing streams.'

'You know where the railway line from Dunedin to Invercargill crosses an arm of lake Waihola? Well that's where she used to throw the bodies off the train.'

'I well remember my parents talking about Minnie Dean. In those days the express train stopped at Clinton for refreshments. Minnie Dean was seen leaving the train carrying a brown paper parcel, but was without it when she returned. Later the parcel was found at the engine sheds. A baby's body was in that parcel.'

Maggots! These stories are nothing but maggots!* There is no evidence that Minnie Dean ever threw dead babies off trains — into streams or lakes or anywhere else — or left them in engine sheds.

'Dad knew the guard on the train. Apparently he saw her getting on with a baby and a hat box and getting off on the wrong side of the train at Winton, with just a hat box.'

'When she got off with the hat box she didn't get off at Winton. She got off at Gap Road.'

'Do you know how they caught her? They saw *blood* trickling out the bottom of her hat box. That's how they caught her.'

'The original hat box she hid the baby's body in is in the Riverton Museum.'

'The family that moved into "The Larches" after Minnie Dean was hung has got the original hat box.'

'We had the original tin hat box in our family for years. It was bigger and more oval than the one in the Riverton Museum.'

'Mother would never have a tin hat box in the house because that was the sort that Minnie Dean used.'

'Our mother had a round leather hat box which had been in almost universal use with women. It went suddenly out of fashion when they became known as "Minnie Deans".'

'I touched Minnie Dean's hat box! It was the bravest thing I ever did as a child. One time when we went to the Riverton Museum I screwed up all my courage and reached out and touched it.'

'I still have in my possession my mother's old oval tin hat box which has always been referred to as the Minnie Dean hat box.'

See how the maggots move, see how the carcass changes. Consider this: if all the Minnie Dean hat boxes in Southland were laid end to end they would reach halfway to Dunedin.

'She buried the babies' bodies under that tree with the dark blue flowers.** Mother would never have it in our garden because it was the Minnie Dean tree.'

'I heard that she put ordinary lime instead of quicklime on the bodies. That's why they were still there when the police dug over her garden.'

'Minnie Dean lived in our district before she moved to Winton. There's said to be a baby buried under a certain tree in the area.'

---

*   *Maggot n. 1.* The soft limbless larva of dipterous insects, esp. the house fly and blowfly, occurring in decaying organic matter. *2. Rare.* a fancy or whim. (*Collins English Dictionary*, Collins, London, 1979.)

** Ceanothus.

[25]

'She used to bury babies along the roadsides and plant clumps of that little orange lily* on top. That's why you see it growing wild all over Southland. If it came up in our garden Grandma used to say — Pull it out! Pull it out! That's a Minnie Dean!'

'You know that photo of the policemen digging over her garden? Well my grandfather is the one with the beard.'

'If the people of Winton saw lights at the cemetery at night after a burial they knew it was Minnie Dean burying one of her babies in the soft earth.'

Maggoty legends old as Albion hatch anew in colonial Southland. Legends of dead souls dwelling in the plants that grow on their graves. Legends of witches pulling up mandrake root in churchyards by moonlight. Mandrake root: pale and lumpy as a dead baby, forked like a baby's legs (and they say it screams like a baby when it is wrenched from the earth).

And then there are the hanging stories. Nothing attracts blowflies like a jolly good hanging.

'Is it true that the gaol used to be on the site of the old Macalister building in Invercargill? I was told that the toilet block of Macalister's was the actual cell where she spent her last night.'

'I do know that she was hung in Invercargill. I think the gaol used to be where the railway station is now.'

'My cousins used to play under the tree in Winton from which Minnie Dean was hung.'

'My great-grand-uncle went to Invercargill to watch the hanging.'

'My father climbed over the wall and watched Minnie Dean hang.'

'My parents told me that she was hanged wearing a red frock, and that New Zealand women for years afterwards would not wear anything red.'

'Apparently the hangman went through the train to Dunedin the day after the execution selling off Minnie Dean's shoes as souvenirs.'

'One of my Winton relatives told me that the day after the hanging Minnie Dean's husband was selling off pieces of the hangman's rope in Invercargill as souvenirs.'

James Joyce knew the hangmen stories. 'They . . . would hang their own fathers for five quid down and travelling expenses . . . and then they chop up the rope after and sell the bits for a few bob,' he wrote in *Ulysses*. The roots of such stories run deep. The custom of giving the hapless felon's clothes to the executioner had its origins in a belief, dating from Roman times, that the soul was retained in the body of a person who suffered an unnatural or premature death. The clothes of executed criminals and pieces of the hangman's rope, like the garments of martyrs and fragments of the true cross, were believed to be imbued with magical powers through their association with the living soul.

---

* Montbretia.

Such relics might ward off tuberculosis, cure infertility, bring good luck.[2] Though I can find no hard evidence to support the claim, rumours abound that New Zealand hangmen were given their victims' clothes as part of their payment until the early years of the twentieth century. All we know about the arrangements made for the impoverished drunkard who hanged Minnie Dean is that he was brought from Wanganui to Invercargill in police custody and was not released until the hanging had been performed. His return travel and accommodation were arranged by the Justice Department and he did not get paid until he reached Wellington. Yet several newspapers reported that he was arrested for drunkenness at Ashburton en route to Wellington. Where did he get the money from for the alcohol if he had not been paid? Perhaps he really did sell off Minnie's clothes on the train?

Minnie Dean's final journey from the scaffold to the grave is obscured by black swarms of stories. The thickest swarm conceals in its midst Winton's three hotels — known to locals as the top, the middle and the bottom pub.

'My friend Nan who is eighty-four says that Minnie's husband claimed her body at the Invercargill gaol, which was somewhere about where the gasworks are now. He loaded the coffin onto a four-wheeled spring cart and drove out to Winton. He hitched the horse to the hitching rail at the bottom pub and went in and got roaring drunk. He then continued out to the cemetery and, all on his own, buried Minnie. There her unmarked grave is still to this day.'

'Mr Butcher the carter brought the coffin out from Invercargill on his dray. It was a really hot day and when he got to the top pub he stopped for a drink on his way to the cemetery.'

'Apparently they wouldn't allow her coffin on the train so Hugh Taylor — he was a carter who carried goods between Invercargill and Winton — he carried it out on his dray. The story goes that he stopped at the bottom pub for a drink on the way.'

'One story I heard was that Fred Taylor brought her coffin out to Winton on his cart and stopped at the middle pub for a drink on the way to the cemetery.'

'My dad used to tell a story about Charles Dean picking up the coffin from the train and putting it on the back of his dray. On the way to the cemetery he stopped at the top pub for a drink. While he was inside some urchins pelted the horse with stones and it bolted with the coffin.'

'Grandma used to talk about how Minnie's husband carried her body all the way from Invercargill to Winton in a handcart.'

Once the unfortunate woman's coffin arrived at the cemetery her problems were not over.

'Of course she's buried outside the cemetery. They wouldn't bury her in consecrated ground.'

'They buried her in the middle of the main road so that she could never rest in peace.'

Another maggoty folk-memory here: the custom of burying criminals and suicides at crossroads, often with a stake through the heart, continued in England until 1823 when, as a result of the delay caused to the carriage of George IV by the crowd watching a crossroads interment, an Act was rushed through Parliament ordering parishes to set aside unconsecrated ground for burials.[3] But this is one place where the maggots can be scraped away to let the bones show through: the day after Minnie Dean's funeral, which was conducted by the Reverend Baird of Winton and attended by about six people, the *Southland Times* reported:

> A number of outrageous rumours are current about the interment of Minnie Dean . . . Everything was done quietly and in order from the time of the arrival of the remains on Monday's evening train to the time of interment. I am informed that one of the reports in circulation is that Winton cemetery authorities refused to admit the body, but there is no truth whatever in that rumour. Section 83 of the Cemeteries Act 1882 makes anyone liable to a penalty of £50 for burying 'any body upon any land whatsoever not being a cemetery.' The report that the body had to be taken on and buried at the 'Larches' is a pure fabrication.

But of course mere facts can never match the timeless power of myth.

'Is it true that they buried her eight feet deep, instead of six feet deep, in case . . .'

'She's buried under a tree in the Winton cemetery. It's called the Minnie Dean tree.'

'Nothing will grow on her grave.'

'There's a story that no grass will grow on her grave. I reckon if any does, someone goes and grubs it out.'

'Nothing will grow on her grave except the Minnie Dean plant.'

'She's got white daisies growing on her grave hasn't she? That's what I was told.'

'My father said that old Mrs Gill used to keep Minnie Dean's grave tidy. That's where the story came from that nothing would grow on it.'

'My mother told me that the local children used to go and jump on Minnie Dean's grave — that's why nothing would grow on it.'

Winton local historian Vince Boyle takes me to the cemetery. 'Weedkiller,' he explains, pointing to the ring of dead grass surrounding her bare unmarked plot. And it's true. When I go back the following winter the weed sprayers have not been near for a long time; Minnie's grave is covered with a thick mat of grass. It is also true, I discover when I consult the cemetery register, that Minnie Dean was buried eight feet deep, but there was nothing sinister about that; in every plot in the cemetery that was expected to accommodate more than one body the first was buried eight feet deep. And as it happens the Dean plot does contain two bodies; Minnie was buried eight feet deep in 1895, while her husband Charles was buried six feet deep in 1908.

Mythology builds on mythology — but for Southlanders the fascination never wanes.

'I read somewhere that the number of babies she killed may never be known. Well my father told me it was twenty-two.'

'I was brought up on the story that she killed 140 babies!'

'She murdered babies and fed their bodies to the pigs!'

'She was so *evil*, wasn't she? Why did she do it? For the money! And the more babies she killed the more she could take in!'

MINNIE DEAN

At Winton's Larches vile and mean,
There lived the wife of Charlie Dean,
Who gathered babies to adopt,
No questions asked a daughter's lot.

An intellectual through and through,
She taught at many Southland schools,
A doctor's widow she had been,
Until she married Farmer Dean.

With two room and a small lean-to,
And kids in boxes quite a few,
But as two deaths had drawn the law,
There really was no room for more.

She came from Edinburgh town,
Her usual fee was just ten pounds,
But when from business she arrived,
Her hatbox had a corpse inside.

When as the talk and rumour flew,
A train-guard more suspicious grew,
And when they dug her garden ground,
Some corpses and some bones were found.

O baby farmer Minnie Dean,
A dreadful creature you have been,
You stifled babies all forlorn,
And put them down with laudanum.

Minnie Dean

Some say your score was twenty-two,
They changed the laws because of you,
And on your grave no growth is seen,
Except the plant called Minnie Dean.

— *W. G. P.*

Though nearly one hundred years have passed since her death, there can be no doubt that Minnie Dean remains southern New Zealand's most celebrated citizen. But despite all this research I don't think I've unearthed a single verifiable fact. I need facts. Plain, incontestable facts. Starting with Minnie's childhood.

Chapter V

────── ∾ ──────

A BRIEF ACCOUNT OF THE LAST WORDS AND CONFESSION OF MINNIE DEAN

A Brief Account of the last Words and Confession of Minnie Dean, Parishioner of Winton, who was Executed at Invercargill upon the 12th of August 1895, for the Crime of Child Murder.

*I*n southern legal circles it's known as 'Minnie Dean's confession', but it isn't really. The fifty-three-page statement she wrote while awaiting the scaffold is Minnie's response to the evidence presented at her trial, a response that she was unable to make in court because she was never given the opportunity to enter the witness box in her own defence. The statement, which begins with a verse from an appropriately morbid hymn used in the Church of Scotland until the mid-nineteenth century, also contains references to her childhood:[1]

I Minnie Dean awaiting death

The hour of my departure come, I hear the voice that calls me home. At length Oh Lord let troubles cease and let thy servant die in peace. Not in mine innocence I trust, I bow before Thee in the dust. And through my saviour's blood alone. I look for mercy at thy throne. I leave this world without a tear save for the friends I held so dear. To heal their sorrows Lord descend, and to the friendless prove a friend.

Who my parents were or what they were concerns no one, although I have no doubt that problem has been already solved by the public to their own satisfaction. That I came from respectable parents and in a comfortable position none more so. A truer more earnest or devout Christian than my mother I have never met. She died from cancer when I was in my eleventh year. She was confined to bed for some eighteen months before her death. In all her sufferings which was sometimes

Minnie Dean awaiting death

hour of My departure come I hear the voice
that calls me home. At length Oh Lord Let
Troubles cease And let Thy servant die in peace
Not in mine Innocence I trust I bow before
Thee in the dust. And through My Saviours
Blood Alone. I look for Mercy at Thy Throne
I leave this World With out a tear. Save for
The friends I held so dear to heal their
Sorrows Lord descend And to the friendly
Prove a friend — Who My parents are
Or what they were concerns. No One. Although
I have no doubt. That Problem has been
Already Solved. by the public to their own
Satisfaction — That I came of respectable
parents and in a comfortable position none
have so — A truer more earnest or devout
christian than My Mother I have never Met
She died from Cancer when I was in My
Eleventh Year — She was confined to bed for
some eighteen Months before her death. In
all her Sufferings which was sometimes Intense
She bore Without a Murmur. The Doctor said
her patience kept her alive. Her last words
In life were come Lord Jesus Come quickly
And I her daughter is lying here. to die an
Ignominious death charged With the cowardly
crime of Infanticide. Its little did My
Mither think the day she cradled Me that
I would travel say far from home or hang
On a gallows tree — If I had never troubled
With other peoples children I would not now
be where I am. They Made Me a Social Pariah

First page of Minnie Dean's last statement.
National Archives, Wellington

intense she bore without a murmur. The doctors said her patience kept her alive. Her last words in life were come Lord Jesus come quickly. And I her daughter is lying hear to die an ignominious death charged with the cowardly crime of infanticide. Its little did my mither think the day she cradled me that I would travel sae far frae hame or hang on a gallows tree*. If I had never troubled with other people's children I would not now be where I am. They made me a social pariah estranged me from my husband beggared me in pocket and repute and has now brought me to the scaffold. Every morning before my sister and I left for school we knelt at mother's bed while she offered up a fervent prayer for our care and guidance during the day and this is the end . . .

Over the years loose strands of research, speculation and gossip have been collected up, knotted into long drawn out stories and wound into a tight ball around the meagre information about Minnie Dean's childhood supplied in her last statement.

In 1985 Ken Catran summarised all the previously published information about her past in *Hanlon — a casebook:*[2]

> She was born in Edinburgh, Scotland, in 1847, one of two daughters. Her father is thought to have been McKellar, a clergyman of the First Church of Scotland . . .
>
> She married early, after an excellent formal education, and with her husband, a Dr McCulloch, emigrated to Tasmania. There were two daughters to the marriage and, when her husband died in Tasmania Minnie went with them to New Zealand to join her aunt, 'Granny' Kelly.

Reader, this story is untrue. After an intensive search of the official records of Scotland, Australia and New Zealand I have found no Minnie or Williamina McKellar born anywhere in Scotland around 1847, or married anywhere in Scotland, Australia or New Zealand prior to 1872. I have found no Reverend McKellar in Scotland who could have been her father, and anyway, although Scots of a Presbyterian persuasion around the time of Minnie's birth could choose between the Established Church of Scotland, the Free Church of Scotland, the Scottish Episcopal Church, the Reformed Presbyterian Church, the Auld Lichts, the United Secession Church and the Relief Church — there was no such thing as the First Church of Scotland.

To make matters worse I have found no Dr McCulloch in Scotland, Australia or New Zealand who could have been Minnie's husband, no likely births to a Minnie or Williamina McKellar or McCulloch in Scotland, Australia or New Zealand, and no likely deaths of a Dr McCulloch (or any other male

---

* A couplet from a Scottish ballad, 'The Four Marys', about the four women (all named Mary) who accompanied Mary Queen of Scots to France. One of the Marys in the ballad was hanged for child murder.

McCulloch who could have been Minnie's husband) in Scotland, Australia or New Zealand.

So who was Minnie Dean? Granny Kelly must have been one of the few people in New Zealand who knew. Granny Kelly must have known that her niece Williamina McCulloch, the mother of two small girls, was not the daughter of a clergyman or the widow of a doctor from Edinburgh. She must have known that Williamina McCulloch was really the unmarried daughter of a railway engine driver from Greenock.[3] But Granny Kelly kept that secret to herself.

Chapter VI

———— ❧ ————

VICTORIAN GREENOCK

A GREENOCK POET DESCRIBES HIS TOWN

. . . this grey town
That pipes the morning up before the lark
With shrieking steam, and from a hundred stalks
Lacquers the sooty sky; where hammers clang
On iron hulks, and cranes in harbours creak,
Rattle and swing, whole cargoes on their decks;
Where men sweat gold that others hoard and spend,
And lurk like vermin in their narrow streets,
This old grey town, this firth, the further strand
Spangled with hamlets, and the wooded steeps
Whose rocky tops behind each other press,
Fantastically carved like antique helms
High hung in heaven's cloudy armoury
Is world enough for me.

— *John Davidson, 1894*

*I*n the middle decades of the eighteenth century the industrial revolution brought a new, dynamic rhythm to the life and landscape of Scotland; by the time Williamina McCulloch was born in 1844 it had grown into a runaway juggernaut.

In 1776 Scotsman Adam Smith proclaimed in *An Inquiry into the Nature and Causes of the Wealth of Nations* that a country's prosperity was the direct result of the diligent pursuit by each of its citizens of his own self-interest, and his fellow capitalists saw no reason to disagree. They harnessed their self-interest to the steam engine and the spinning jenny, the iron smelter and the shipyard, and brought unprecedented fortunes to the few — and long working hours, low wages, ill health and squalor to the rest.

Throughout the nineteenth century the living conditions of Scottish workers were among the worst in the industrialised world, and the living conditions of workers in Williamina McCulloch's home town, Greenock, were among the worst in Scotland. With a population of 36,000 in 1841 Greenock was one tenth the size of the great cities of Glasgow and Edinburgh, and little more than half the size of Aberdeen, Dundee and Paisley, but per head of population more people died in Greenock each year than anywhere else in Britain.[1]

Greenock first made a mark on history in the late sixteenth century when a man named 'John Schaw of Grenok' held feudal sway over the inhabitants of a sheltered north-facing bay on the gravelly bank of the Clyde. In 1589, when the reformation was drawing to a close and standard spelling had yet to be invented, John Schaw wrote to the king. He was, he explained: 'movit wt the ernest zeill of grite affection to goddis glorie and propogation of the trew religioun' and he wanted the king to grant him a Royal Charter to build a church, 'Sua that the puir pepill duelling opoun his lands and heritage quilkis are all fischers and of a reasonable nowmer dualland four myles fra thair parroche Kirk and having ane greit river to pas over to the samyn, May haif ane ease in winter seasoun and better comoditie to covene to goddis gruice on the sabboth day and rest according to goddis institution.'[2]

A few years later the worthy laird made two further contributions to the future of Greenock; he petitioned the king to have the town made a burgh of the barony, and he built a dry stone pier for the convenience of fishermen and passenger boats from Ireland.[3]

Greenock was strategically located just where the deep, wide Firth of Clyde narrowed to a shallow river. During the seventeenth and eighteenth centuries, as Scotland's trade with the world expanded and nearby Glasgow burgeoned into a great city, Greenock became a major port. To the burgh's bustling docks came shiploads of raw sugar, molasses, rum, mahogany, cotton and coconuts from the West Indies; wine and fruit from the Iberian Peninsula; timber from Canada; fish from Nova Scotia and Newfoundland; tobacco from America; tea from China and Ceylon. For their part the merchants of Greenock exported textiles, ships, industrial machinery, refined sugar, cured herrings and straw hats to the world.[4]

During the second quarter of the nineteenth century Greenock's more prosperous citizens (the superior ranks, as they were known to contemporary commentators) deserted the congested town centre and moved west along the Clyde. There they built gracious mansions, installed water and sewerage systems, and paved the roads. In 1921 Greenock historian R. M. Smith wrote this paean to their industry:[5]

If by any chance, through the intervention of adverse atmospheric conditions or of overhanging smoke from a hundred stalks that mark the hives of industry, the working town should be blotted out or lie blurred in a mist of its own begetting, one can with a less distracted eye admire and linger upon the loveliest West-End in the world ... Mansion, villa and church are virtually embowered on the wide front of the sweeping hill, the broad mile-long roadways and their intersections lying fair and wholesome, the air redolent of the odours of flower and tree. The shipping merchant princes of over half a century ago did much better for posterity than merely amass riches. Whether designedly or by happy fortune, they founded a new and more admirable town side by side with the dingy and congested old.

The old town of Greenock — Williamina McCulloch's childhood home — was neither fair nor wholesome. It was overcrowded and filthy. It did not smell of flowers.

When Victoria ascended the throne in 1837, eighty years of industrial and agrarian change had brought a four-fold increase to the population of Britain and a surge of migration to the cities and towns. In 1791 the population of Greenock was 15,000. By 1841 it had risen to 36,000. All those extra people had to fit in somewhere. The result in Greenock, and throughout urban Scotland, was overcrowding.

According to the 1861 census more than seventy-two per cent of Scottish families lived in one or two rooms.[6] By 1911 that figure was down to fifty per cent — but the comparable figure for England and Wales that year was only seven per cent.[7] The Scottish figure reflects more than a shortage of housing. Throughout the years of rapid urbanisation the Scots were very much poorer than the English and their incomes were far less secure.[*] Because of the savings to be made on candles, coal and rent by living in two rooms rather than three, or in one room rather than two, squeezing together into the smallest possible space made a lot of sense to the Scots.

Dr Lawrie of Greenock, in his contribution to the 1842 Poor Law Commission *Reports on the Sanitary Conditions of the Labouring Population of Scotland*,[8] estimated that where poor families occupied two rooms in his town '... the average size of each room I should think would be from eight to nine feet square, and about the same measure in height'. The inhabitants of such rooms had nowhere to work in peace, nowhere to play, nowhere to think, nowhere to relax, nowhere to escape from the tensions of family life; but for most nineteenth century urban Scots one or two overcrowded rooms in an overcrowded tenement was home.

In the course of investigating the causes and results of a typhus epidemic in Greenock in 1864–65,[9] Dr Buchanan discovered that the population density

---

[*] Unlike England and Wales, Scotland lacked any nineteenth-century poor law provisions to tide able-bodied men over periods of unemployment.

of the town's middle parish was an astonishing 470 people to the acre. He attributed this swarming mass of humanity not only to 'the huddling of persons into too confined rooms' but also to 'the packing together of dwellings too closely upon area and bad construction of dwellings'. He went on to explain:

> . . . the system prevails here, as in other towns of Scotland, of constructing dwelling-buildings with a common stair, from which separate rooms or sets of rooms lead off. These rooms or sets of rooms are called 'houses', and the whole pile of houses is called a 'tenement' or a 'land'. In the old town, the houses are so closely packed that every particle of ground (that is not a street) is covered with buildings . . .
>
> Houses . . . are piled one over another three or four high, and two or more up to six of them lead off a common stair at each floor.

The merchant princes of the West End may have been driven from the old town by congestion alone, but for the less wealthy of Greenock lack of space and absence of privacy were the least of their problems.

The narrow streets of old Greenock were unpaved and undrained. All the drinking, cooking and washing water for the town came from a chain of polluted wells supplied by an inadequate reservoir. There were no sewers for the removal of liquid waste, and only a token disposal service for solid garbage. The debris of urban living simply accumulated in the streets. In his 1842 Poor Law Commission report[10] Dr Lawrie wrote:

> Behind my consulting rooms, where I am now sitting, there is a large dunghill with a privy attached; to my knowledge that dunghill has not been emptied for six months; it serves a whole neighbourhood, and the effluvium is so offensive that I cannot open the window. The land is three stories high, and the people, to save themselves trouble, throw all their filth out of the stair-window, consequently a great part of it goes on the close, and the close is not cleaned out until the dunghill is full: the filth in the close reaches nearly to the sill of the back window of the shop in front, and the malarious moisture oozes through the wall on the floor.

Twenty-three years later some cosmetic changes had been made to the cleanliness of the streets, and sewer pipes had been laid. But few dwellings were connected, and anyway a sewerage system can't function without an adequate water supply. Dr Buchanan reported:[11]

> . . . out of the 50,000 residents of Greenock 35,000 are estimated to be unprovided with any water but such as they carry up from the public streets, and that the great bulk of the poor houses have no privy or ash-pit accommodation whatever . . . The common method of getting rid of refuse in houses thus deficient is by depositing the contents of chamber

vessels with ashes and other filth in the roadway between the hours of 10 p.m. and 8 a.m. For the 14 hours of daytime such matters have, for want of any other means of disposing them, to be voided and retained inside the close and crowded rooms . . .

The scandalous state of Greenock sanitation was repeatedly pointed out to the authorities by a succession of distraught physicians, and though local bodies were required by the Police Act of 1773 to provide the people with 'clean wholesome water' and to pave, light and wash the streets, the problems persisted, with only spasmodic and inadequate improvements, beyond the end of the nineteenth century.

The greatest obstacle to sanitary reform in Greenock, and throughout Victorian Britain, was the composition of civic authorities. The property-based franchise system ensured that less than ten per cent of the population was eligible to vote in local body elections — and those privileged few were wealthy, land-owning men.[12]

All good Victorians knew that cleanliness was next to godliness, and most of them believed that diseases arose spontaneously from the effluvia emanated by putrefying matter, but when it came to public works the merchants and landowners who held the purse strings of Greenock had their own priorities.

Over the 175 years following the completion of the West Harbour in 1710 the burghers of Greenock spared no expense in building new docks and creating wider, deeper and more sheltered harbours. The only other major public work undertaken in the first half of the nineteenth century was the Shaw Water Scheme. This was intended to supply drinking water and 'to power all the machinery in Greenock which was presently run on steam', but by the time flax mills, saw mills, paper mills, flour mills, dye works, sugar refineries, foundries, distilleries, chemical works, rope works and woollen mills had been built along its chain of falls, and water had been piped to the homes of the wealthy, there was nothing left for the townsfolk to drink. Most of the residents of Greenock continued to draw their domestic water from the old wells, which in summer were inclined to run dry.[13]

Inevitably, in this town known throughout the west of Scotland as 'Old Dirty',[14] the worst diseases of the Victorian age wrought a terrible toll. The full extent of the problem was revealed when registration of births, deaths and marriages became compulsory in 1855:

> The death-rate in Greenock was so high as 336 deaths in every ten thousand people. Glasgow followed next, giving the proportion of 303 deaths in the same number of persons.[15]

Statistics from the 1850s[16] and 1860s[17] indicate that tuberculosis and other respiratory diseases were the main killers, but to nineteenth century Scots such deaths were inevitable — only the great epidemics alarmed them. When cholera first struck in 1831–32 two thousand inhabitants of Greenock died within a few months. Fears that the newly established fever hospital was supplying the Glasgow medical school with bodies for dissection provoked riots in the streets.[18]

A smallpox epidemic, which claimed 431 lives, broke out at the same time as the cholera. Sixteen years later, in 1847, 353 people died from typhus. Later that year another 1400 died of an ill-defined 'fever'. Cholera returned in 1851 to claim 1300 lives, and in 1853 to claim 300 more. In 1864 more than two hundred people died of typhus, including five of the town's doctors and one of its ministers. The last major epidemics in Greenock were outbreaks of cholera and smallpox in 1873.

Whenever the death rate rose meetings were held, resolutions were passed and reports were prepared. The overcrowding, the inadequate water supply and the lack of sewage disposal were repeatedly deplored. The Greenock authorities responded to every outbreak of public concern by instructing the people to keep themselves clean and to whitewash their houses inside and out. Disinfection with chloride of lime, fumigation with burning pitch and positive thinking were also recommended:

> Cholera is a disease which receives visitations to, and is more apt to fasten on, communities in which any panic or dread has arisen of its visitation; and, therefore, it is that everyone should force himself to contemplate with calmness the ravages made by the scourge in places less favoured than our own.[19]

These measures failed to halt any epidemics, but at least they gave the poor something to do during their near-endless wait for sanitary and housing reform.

In addition to issuing advice, the city fathers engaged in a tireless search for an explanation of the high mortality rate in Greenock which absolved them of all responsibility.

In 1852 John Adam, the Chamberlain of Greenock, suggested that the air from the hills and the fresh sea breezes enjoyed by Greenock '... might be expected to impart health and vigour to the inhabitants',[20] but once Greenock's shameful health statistics became known the weather fell into disrepute. In 1865 one of the town's worthies blamed the area's almost constant drizzle for the typhus epidemic that year, and went on to opine that 'the epidemic had been sent by God and would gradually go away'.

But far more popular than God and the weather as scapegoats for Greenock's abysmal health statistics were the poor themselves. The authorities took shocked satisfaction in finding evidence of indolence, immorality, intemperance and disregard for the sabbath throughout the more crowded parts of town. They concluded self-righteously that if the poor were stunted, smelly and dirty, if they lacked fresh water, sewage disposal and decent housing, if their spindly legs were bent with rickets and they coughed black blood — well then — they had only themselves to blame.

Trapped alongside the poor and destitute in old Greenock — confined to one or two tenement rooms by the national housing shortage and their own low wages — were many steady reliable workers. Their families queued with the poor at street wells in all weathers for water, and carried the heavy pails home over muddy, uneven lanes. They used the same overflowing communal privies or emptied their chamber pots into the street. They breathed the same dank, smoke-laden air. They smelled the same nauseous stomach-churning stenches. They saw, all around them, the same filth and degradation. But against the odds some Greenock working-class families clung to a fragile dignity. They paid their bills, educated their children and went to church on Sunday. Their menfolk wore clean collars, avoided bad language and did not smell of drink. Their women wore white aprons and kept their stairs well scrubbed. They were, in the parlance of the times, 'respectable'.

On 1 September 1844, into one such respectable working-class family, Williamina McCulloch was born.

Chapter VII

———— ~ ————

A GREENOCK CHILDHOOD

I am deeply engrossed in Scottish history when the Australian novelist comes to visit. When I tell her about Sir Edward Pine Coffin, co-ordinator of poor relief for the Scottish Highlands during the potato famine of the late 1840s,[1] she says, 'I could never get away with a name like that! People just wouldn't believe it!'

She talks of fledgling fiction writers who defend unconvincing stories with, 'But it's true! That's exactly how it happened!' She points out that factual truth is irrelevant in fiction. Fiction writers may start with true stories, but then they play fast and loose with the facts — changing some, discarding others and inventing more than a few — in order to create stories that, above all, *sound* true.

Non-fiction writers have no such freedom. Non-fiction writers must take factual events and real people, no matter how bizarre and unbelievable, and without distortion, suppression or invention weave them into stories that both *sound* and *are* true.

Long after the Australian novelist's visit I find myself wondering what she would make of the stranger-than-fiction Greenock Free Gardeners' Society, an organisation formed to protect the Inverkip Cemetery from body snatchers.[2] I puzzle over the extraordinary name with my family. Why 'Free'? Why 'Gardeners'? We conjure up visions of furtive-looking men with shovels stalking other furtive-looking men with shovels through the tombstones. Which ones are the Free Gardeners? Which ones are the Resurrectionists?

'Maybe the Free Gardeners had a secret handshake,' suggests my younger son. 'And a rhododendron bush tattooed onto the right forearm.'

Driven by curiosity I write to the Greenock librarian, knowing, even as I write, that any details she uncovers will probably join the ninety per cent of my research that floats unseen, just below the surface of the printed page. (For example, here are some choice bits that didn't make it into the previous chapter: ♦ In 1867 a quarter of Scotland's total income went to 5,000 very rich men. Each earned on average 200 times more than any of the half million workers at the bottom of the socio-economic heap. ♦ The Scottish land-tenure system encouraged landowners to throw up tenements as quickly as possible, and the unregulated Scottish economy, unlike that of the English, inflicted no legal penalties on landlords who allowed their properties to deteriorate into slums. ♦ In 1860 the Greenock Master of Works modified the official statistics to ensure that deaths among Highland and Irish immigrants were not held against the town. ♦ The poor people who made matches for a living absorbed so much phosphorus that they glowed in the dark. ♦ See what I mean?)

My elder son wonders whether my preoccupation with the Greenock Free Gardeners' Society and other such items of unusable research is a displacement activity, an excuse for not facing up to some more pressing problem with my book. He's right of course.

The urgent question is this: to what extent, within the limits of non-fiction, may I recreate Williamina McCulloch's childhood from my extensive knowledge of Greenock, and my limited knowledge of her past? May I say that when she walked to school — pale face freshly wiped, clean white apron over dark woollen dress, long hair brushed and shining — she kept to the crown of the road to avoid the accumulated filth? May I say that when men in top hats and claw-hammer coats rode horseback through the narrow lanes she was forced to step aside into muck? I want to believe that these things happened. I want to write them. I want to breathe into this story the warmth of a life being lived. But *I don't know*, and I can't pretend that I do.

Here are the facts: Williamina McCulloch was born on 1 September 1844 and baptised into the Church of Scotland one month later. Her father was John McCulloch, a railway engine driver. Her mother's maiden name was Elizabeth Swan.[3]

John McCulloch was born at Killearn, thirty kilometres north-east of Greenock in the rolling Stirlingshire hills. His father was a sawyer. Elizabeth Swan was the daughter of a farmer from Cardross, a rowboat ride away across the Clyde.

On census night 1851 forty-year-old John McCulloch, thirty-three-year-old Elizabeth and their daughters Elizabeth (twelve), Williamina (six) and Christina (four) lived at 65 Ann Street, Greenock.

The smoke-blackened stone tenements that lined Ann Street ran in two unbroken rows from the centre of town to the Greenock Cotton Spinning Company on the hill. The inhabitants of Number 65 were mostly poor. (Well they must have been. Of the eight households in the building four were headed by widows and, under the rampant capitalism that prevailed in Scotland at the time, widows were always poor. It was a fact of life.*)

---

* Nearly all the 69 women in the Greenock Poorhouse on census night 1861 were widows.

As in all Victorian towns, the working class district of Greenock was full of shops and pubs. In the McCulloch's tenement there was a grocer and a spirit retailer. Spirit dealing was big business. During the 1830s every Scot over the age of fifteen drank an average of almost a pint of duty-charged whisky a day and consumption fell only slowly over the following decades. In Glasgow there was one liquor outlet to every 130 people.[4] In some parts of Greenock every third or fourth door carried the sign 'Licensed to deal in British and Foreign Spirits.'[5] All over old Greenock the streets, the tenement walls, the doorways and the stairs must have been splattered with the slimy, acrid vomit of drunks.

Apart from the grocer, all the residents of 65 Ann Street were home on census night 1851 . . .

Reader, it's no use. These census returns, these birth, death and marriage registers — their facts lie grey and flat on the page. I am trying to understand what it meant and how it felt to be Williamina McCulloch growing up in Greenock in the 1840s and '50s. I have to toss the facts in the air. I have to hold them to the light. I have to spin them in the mirrored wheels of imagination and marvel at the patterns. In short, I have to speculate.

I don't know how many rooms Widow Carsell the spirit retailer occupied and I don't know where in the tenement she lived but I do know she lived alone and paid six pounds ten a year in rent maybe for a large ground floor room while John McCulloch engine driver plus wife and three daughters John Calder tidewaiter which is another name for a customs officer plus wife and baby and Widow Todd mother of five and spinster which is another name for a person who spins paid five pounds each probably for one room per household upstairs somewhere upstairs but I don't know where one room per household imagine that Widow Todd poor soul living in one room with five kids George seventeen unemployed John sixteen blacksmith Archie twelve ropespinner Catherine nine and Mary seven both scholars well you've got to give her credit for sending the two youngest to school you didn't have to in those days she could have sent them to press cloth for twelve hours a day she must have believed in education God bless her and what about Widow McIndoe the polisher and her widowed brother-in-law who paid the least of all which was four pounds I suppose for a dark poky little room you would think because most Scots spent more on drink than on any single item of food the spirit dealer could afford more than one room but maybe she was a drunk herself a toothless drunk with matted hair and rheumy eyes and stains all down the front of her tattered apron unlike the probably quite respectable Widow Neuman and her grown-up daughter who paid eleven pounds for I suppose two rooms and Mr Black the widowed cabinet maker and his teenage son who paid the same but I'm not sure about Mr Drummond the grocer who paid nine pounds now would that be for two poor quality rooms or one relatively good one as well as eight pounds for his shop his probable prime-site street-front ground-floor shop. Maybe.

Reader, I shall spare you any more meandering musings. From now on I shall try to write concise factual-sounding sentences. Sixty-six-year-old widow Carsell the spirit retailer had a room on the ground floor. Though from time to time I'll probably throw in a 'probably'. The important thing to remember is this: behind most factual-sounding sentences there is some informed speculation — but only speculation. No invention. Promise.

If all the McCulloch offspring had survived there would have been six children and two adults living in their one-roomed apartment on census night 1851, but during the previous decade three of the McCulloch's daughters had died. The births of Janet (in 1840) and Isabella (in 1842) were recorded in the West Greenock Parish baptism register, but like most Scots who died before 1855 their deaths went unreported.

For most of their short lives Janet and Isabella were probably busy, giggling, little girls; bright-eyed chatterboxes who slept head to tail with big sister Lizzie while mother and father tucked down with wee Minnie and the bairn in the hole-in-the-wall.[*] After school, when mother sent the girls out to play in the narrow cobbled street, it was probably Janet and Bella who minded wee Minnie, while Lizzie carried the bairn in a shawl on her back.

It was the epidemic of 1847 that killed them, I think. Isabella succumbed first, then Janet became listless, aching and hot. Then before Minnie's frightened eyes the tell-tale typhus rash appeared and the terrible, helpless vomiting began. Within a week the two girls were delirious. Within a fortnight they were dead.

I'd better rein in this speculation. The truth is I don't know what killed Janet and Isabella. They probably died at different times and from different ailments, but I'm pretty sure Minnie was old enough to have loved them and felt the loss. They almost certainly lived until she was two; maybe even until she was six. The McCullochs did not reuse the names Janet and Isabella until their fourth surviving daughter (Janet) was born in 1853, and their fifth surviving daughter (Isabella) was born in 1855.

The third death, of an unbaptised baby girl,[**] probably occurred between 1847 and 1851 — where the pattern of two-year intervals between McCulloch births was broken by an unusually long gap.

The unnamed baby may have been weak from birth, surviving only a few short hours in the dank, smoke-laden air of a Greenock winter — such deaths were commonplace in the tenements. Minnie and her sisters probably learnt young to temper their grief with the fatalism of the age.

---

[*]   A large cupboard-like bed set into the wall – a standard feature of nineteenth-century Scottish tenement housing.

[**] When John McCulloch registered the birth of the second Isabella in 1855 (the first year of state registration) he reported a total of eight births (all girls – five living, three dead) but only seven were baptised.

§ *A note concerning infant mortality in Victorian Britain*

> Grandmother, Grandmother
> Tell me the Truth
> How many years am I
> Going to live?
> One, Two, Three, Four . . .

> — *Victorian street game*

After 1870 the shockingly high death rate of Scottish adults began to fall as improvements in sanitation checked the great epidemics of cholera and typhoid, but throughout Britain the death rate of infants continued to climb for another thirty years.[6] The high infant mortality rate among the lower classes, coupled with the tendency of comfortably-off Victorians to think the worst of the masses, led to a widespread belief that infanticide, usually by suffocation or starvation at the hands of baby farmers, was common among the poor.

Baby farmers (a pejorative term that came into vogue in the 1860s) were the professional child-care workers of the nineteenth century. Unlike their amateur sisters, who made casual, short-term arrangements to care for the children of friends and relatives in exchange for a modest fee, baby farmers ran large-scale, long-term operations. Strangers paid them by lump sum or monthly fee to care for motherless infants and children whose mothers were unable or unwilling to raise their own offspring. The system was unregulated, and baby farmers were suspected of ill-treating and neglecting their charges. As doctors and social reformers were quick to point out, the system provided a financial incentive for baby farmers to take more babies than could be adequately cared for and to hasten the deaths of sickly infants. Baby farmers were also suspect because their existence mocked the sentimental Victorian ideal of motherhood, and their practice of insuring babies and collecting a lump sum when an infant died was seen as an invitation to murder. (Though when conventional families insured their offspring the practice was considered plain commonsense.)

Infanticide certainly occurred: between 1855 and 1860 London coroners found verdicts of murder on 1120 infants;[7] during 1870 London police found bodies of 276 newborn babies[8] — in the Thames, in canals and ponds, under railway arches, on doorsteps, in cellars, under hedges, in the street. Court reports suggest that many, perhaps most, were abandoned or murdered by their parents, grandparents or midwives, but the Victorian authorities had too much respect for the sanctity of the family to acknowledge the implications of such evidence, so it was baby farmers who got the blame.

With baby farmers serving as scapegoats for the high infant mortality rate, 'the scandal of baby farming' was much discussed in the British press. From the 1870s many baby farmers were charged with infanticide and their trials were reported in lurid detail.

The accumulated evidence suggests that enough criminal baby farming occurred to contribute in a small, steady way to the British infant mortality rate throughout the nineteenth century (for example, in the 1860s Charlotte Winsor of Exeter smothered infants while their mothers waited in the next room, and in the 1890s Mrs Dyer of Reading strangled babies and threw their bodies in the Thames), but in most cases, though there was some evidence of drugging and neglect, there was little evidence of criminal intent and convictions were few.[9]

A far more significant, but less recognised, cause of the ongoing high infant mortality rate was the medical reality that the overwork, malnutrition[10] and disease suffered by girls and women during most of the nineteenth century damaged not only their own health, but the health of the next generation.

The survival chances of weak babies born of malnourished mothers in dirty, overcrowded homes were put further at risk by bottle feeding. Cow's milk was the most adulterated food in Victorian Britain and even pure milk quickly became contaminated when domestic hygiene was poor. During the late nineteenth century the death rate of bottle-fed infants was around forty per cent higher than that of their breastfed peers.[11]

Another major cause of infant deaths was the use of patent medicines containing opium. Dr James Wallace, in his 1860 report *Observations on the causes of the great mortality in Greenock* complained of:

> the practice of *blind and ignorant* drugging which prevails here to a most inordinate extent . . . there is too much reason to believe that, among the children of the middle and lower classes, the mortality from this cause is something frightful . . . A lazy mother fretting at the demands made on her time and attention by an ill-nourished and sickly, because neglected child, begins to dose it with laudanum, or the syrup of poppies, in order to keep it quiet. And certainly she does effect her purpose, but, unfortunately, only at the expense of the life of the child.[12]

The use of opiates was widespread. A Manchester chemist told a Committee of the House of Lords in 1857 that chemists in the town sold between twelve and fifteen gallons of laudanum (alcoholic tincture of opium) per week and that between 100 and 150 customers called each day to buy opium. In Nottingham one member of the Town Council, a druggist, sold 400 gallons of laudanum annually.[13] Opiates were in such common use that Mrs Beeton offered advice on the treatment of overdoses in her *Book of Household Management*.[14]

The most popular 'quietening mixture' for babies was 'Godfrey's Cordial', a patent medicine containing opium, treacle, water and spices. In a typical case in 1841 a Somerset mother gave her twelve-day-old baby 'a pennyworth' of Godfrey's Cordial because it 'was disordered in its bowels'. The coroner attributed its death to a 'visitation of God'. In 1876 a Nottinghamshire child of four months was dosed with ten drops of Godfrey's Cordial every evening, according to the father, 'to send it to sleep'. On the night of the baby's death this proved ineffectual, so it was given 'four or five drops of laudanum and some castor oil'. Inquests on babies dying of opium overdoses were reported in Britain at the rate of about one per week throughout the nineteenth century.[15] According to the 1859 edition of *Taylor on Poisons*, three-quarters of all opium deaths were in children under the age of five.[16] Many more babies, after periods of drugged indifference to food, died of starvation.

> The boy was healthy, and at first expressed
> His feelings loudly, when he failed to rest;
> When cramm'd with food, and tightened every limb,
> To cry aloud, was what pertain'd to him;
> Then the good nurse (who, had she borne a brain,
> Had sought the cause that made her babe complain)
> Has all her efforts, loving soul! applied
> To set the cry, and not the cause, aside:
> She gave the powerful sweet without remorse,
> *The sleeping cordial* — she had tried its force,
> Repenting oft: the infant freed from pain,
> Rejected food, but took the dose again.
> Sinking to sleep; while she her joy express'd,
> That her dear charge could sweetly take its rest.
> Soon may she spare her cordial; not a doubt
> Remains, but quickly he will rest without.
>
> This moves our grief and pity, and we sigh
> To think what numbers from these causes die.
>
> — *George Crabbe, 1810*

Ironically, mass opium poisoning in Victorian Britain was averted only by an equally scandalous and widespread practice: the wholesale adulteration of foods and medicines. The list of additives found in most foods and drinks reads like the stock list of a mad and malevolent chemist (strychnine in beer, copper sulphate in bottled fruit, lead and mercury in confectionery) but for opiates the main additive was water. In 1838 a sample of opium from a 'first rate' Edinburgh chemist, which was claimed to contain 130 grains per ounce of fluid, was found to contain only seventeen grains per ounce. In the same year five samples purchased from a London druggist were found to be diluted by up to sixty-three per cent with added water. In 1897 a Nottingham druggist was fined for selling laudanum containing only ten per cent of its claimed opium content.[17]

§ *The Minnie Dean story resumes*

Despite the early deaths of three of John McCulloch's daughters, life for the engine driver and his family was relatively secure; unlike the heads of many Greenock working-class households, John McCulloch was a steady, reliable breadwinner.

As a young man he followed in his father's footsteps and become a sawyer. He would have begun literally at the bottom, the junior in a two-man team with sawdust cascading over his sweaty face as he hauled the long saw to and fro from the bottom of a muddy pit.

But when iron began replacing wood as an industrial building material, and coal began replacing wood as a fuel, John moved with the times. In 1841, at the dawn of the golden age of steam, Minnie's father became a fireman* with the Glasgow, Paisley and Greenock Railway. Two years later he became a driver. When he died in 1888 John McCulloch had been a railway engine driver for a remarkable forty-five years.[18]

§ *A note concerning the Glasgow, Paisley and Greenock Railway*

The railway system was the growth industry of the age and the people of Greenock were more interested than most in its possibilities — after all, the massive and diverse contributions made by the steam engine to the industrial revolution were thanks in no small part to Greenock's favourite son, James Watt.**

In the late 1830s the merchants and industrialists of Greenock, who could never find the money to address the town's desperate housing, water and sewerage needs, wasted no time in raising money for a railway to link the port of Greenock with the industrial metropolis of Glasgow.

Work on the Glasgow, Paisley and Greenock Railway began in 1837. Over most of the distance a straight, level track was quickly laid, but at Bishopton three thousand miners, masons, blacksmiths and navvies, two hundred horses, one locomotive engine and three fixed engines sweated night and day for four years, accompanied by a cacophony of iron bores, warning bugles and deafening explosions, on the construction of two tunnels. When they were finished, the line was complete.

---

* A man who stoked the fire on a steam locomotive.
** Watt did not actually invent the steam engine, but his innovative condenser, which according to folklore was inspired by childhood observations of tea kettles, improved its efficiency by 75 per cent.

LINES WRITTEN ON THE OPENING OF THE GLASGOW, PAISLEY AND GREENOCK RAILWAY

What is it we hear on the distant plain
Careering its thunder along?
'Tis that fleet, fleet horse with his railway train,
Unerring, gigantic and strong.

Untired he approaches, unspurred he moves on,
Though he sweats, pants and puffs all the way;
No storm can o'erpower him, his strength is unknown,
And he needs no repose night or day.

On, on to the goal, over valley and mound,
How wondrous and rapid his race,
Afar as he speed rock and river resound,
'Neath the tread of his fire-brightened pace.

His rival the ship, with stern, rudder and sail,
Now lashing along in her pride,
He leaves far behind to the sport of the gale,
And the surge of the billows and tide.

Today is his triumph, on summit and tower,
To welcome him wait the gay crowd;
He comes in the pride of his beauty and power,
Saluted with cheers long and loud.

Encircle his brow with a branch of Green-oak,
Let a statue of Watt him bestride;
To the bright car of commerce the gallant steed yoke,
And with him round the world we'll ride.

— *W. M'O.*
Paisley, 30 March 1841[19]

The journey that had taken two-and-a-half hours by river boat and more than three hours by stage coach was cut to a little over an hour by rail. The coal that had trickled into Greenock by cart and barge began arriving in a steady, generous stream. The ravenous industrial fires of the town were satisfied, and there was plenty left for export. Even the common folk could afford coal heating.

The demand for passenger traffic exceeded all expectations. An 1835 prospectus predicted that 425 people per day would use the train (half the number then travelling daily between Greenock and Glasgow by road and river). As the years passed expectations rose. When the line opened in 1841 provision was made for two thousand passengers per day, but even that proved inadequate. Within months the service expanded to cater for an astonishing six thousand people per day. As the Duke of Wellington had gloomily predicted, the advent of passenger railways did indeed 'encourage the lower classes to move about'.

Many travellers were drawn by Greenock's role as a terminus for migrants entering Britain from Ireland and the Scottish Highlands, or leaving for North America, Australia or New Zealand. In summer the huddled masses were joined by Highland-bound holiday-makers and crowds of high-spirited day-trippers from Paisley and Glasgow seizing to the full the wonderful opportunities offered by steam travel.

§ *The story of Minnie Dean resumes*

Amid the colour and clamour of Greenock railway station Minnie's father would have been a familiar figure. According to Frank McKenna,[20] the driver of a steam locomotive was: 'a large, beefy, weather-beaten and heavy-booted figure exuding bluffness and geniality, a trusted coal-stained representative of solidity and service'. Whether John McCulloch was large, beefy and bluff we shall never know, but he would have worn heavy boots and he must have been strong — driving a railway engine for fifteen hours a day, six days a week, was heavy physical work. He must also have been weather-beaten — early railway engines had no cabs; drivers and firemen needed thick skins and heavy beards to protect their faces from wind and weather. And John McCulloch must have been reasonably genial; despite his family's cramped domestic circumstances, and despite the death of his first wife in 1857 and his remarriage in 1859, all his daughters except Minnie lived at home until they married. It is also safe to conclude that any man who could give forty-five years' service to the railways at a time when drivers faced instant dismissal for speeding, lateness or drunkenness must have been 'a trusted coal-stained representative of solidity and service'.

The men who drove steam locomotives needed other qualities that McKenna doesn't mention: they had to be skilled and resourceful (to keep their complex and temperamental engines running on time), they had to be highly safety-conscious (between 1840 and 1860 as many as one in thirty-seven railway employees were killed or injured at work each year) and they had to be literate (a full knowledge of timetables, rule books, regulations, amendments and posted notices was essential for their work).

Train drivers of John McCulloch's era were relatively well paid and highly visible (even when they had cabs, drivers spent most of their time leaning out for a better view of the line ahead). And, if they were good sober workers, they enjoyed a privilege rare among members of the Victorian working class — job security for life. So — despite their exhausting, exacting and dangerous work, and their sooty faces, red eyes and black, oily hands — to the railway-besotted Victorians the men who rode locomotive footplates were the aristocracy of the working class. No wonder train travel was one of the lasting passions of Williamina's life.

As her last statement indicates ('I came of respectable parents and in comfortable circumstance none more so'), nothing was more important to members of the Victorian upper working class than respectability. They were thrifty, God-fearing, sober, genteel, snobbish, self-satisfied, patriotic and hard-working. And despite the back-breaking drudgery of carrying and heating water to wash their bodies, clothes and homes, they were obsessively clean. Their values were those of the middle class and they disdained 'The Great Unwashed', among whose ranks — in the absence of unemployment benefits, old age pensions and state intervention in education, housing and health — it was all too easy for the unlucky and less diligent among their ranks to fall.

As befitted a man of his station John McCulloch probably belonged to a friendly society, attended church regularly and paid his debts on time. And if he did not belong to a temperance organisation he would at least have ensured that he never went out smelling of drink. As a respectable housewife, Elizabeth would have laboured to keep the linen washed, the grate polished and the stair scrubbed for as long as her health allowed; and as a respectable mother she would have kept the children tidy, sent them to school and instilled in them the virtues of thrift, sobriety and restraint.

Like most Scottish children of her era Williamina McCulloch received a sound basic education. The Scots education system of her formative years was the best in Europe and her last statement shows her to be a fluent writer and an avid reader.* She probably attended her local parish school up to the age of eleven or twelve. There is even a tantalising possibility that for some of her schooling she attended the prestigious and expensive Greenock Academy. In August 1895 the *Bruce Herald* (a small bi-weekly newspaper in the southern New Zealand township of Milton) reported, 'It is said that she [Minnie Dean] attended college at the same time as Justice Denniston.' Justice Denniston was John Edward Denniston, son of a Greenock sugar merchant who later became a New Zealand Supreme Court judge. He was born near Greenock a few months after Williamina McCulloch. In 1855 he was a foundation pupil at the co-educational Greenock Academy, an institution that 'promised to secure to children of the upper and middle classes a course and style of instruction hitherto unenjoyed in Greenock'.[21] To a respectable engine driver with no sons,

---

* For the train trip that led to her arrest Minnie carried a copy of 'The Family Reader', indicating that she intended to read rather than engage in handiwork during the journey.

modest savings and aspirations of upward mobility, the Greenock Academy may have seemed just the thing for his middle daughters, Minnie and Christina. (His eldest daughter, Elizabeth, had finished school and the younger two — Janet and Isabella — were still babies at the time the Academy opened.)

The Academy accepted girls and boys from the age of six. The curriculum included 'English Composition Grammar &c, Mathematics, Arithmetic, Writing, Drawing, Geography, Bookkeeping, Latin, Greek, French and German'. The cost of around £3 per child per term (depending on the subjects studied) would have put a considerable strain on the engine driver's budget.[22] Williamina McCulloch may not have attended the Greenock Academy for long, but her experiences there could have laid the foundations for her later ability to pass herself off as the respectable middle-class daughter of a Scottish clergyman.

Given the choice, Williamina would have probably preferred to be a clergyman's daughter. In her last statement she barely mentions her engine driver father, though since he worked fifteen hours a day, six days a week, and probably slept away from home on long runs, that is not really surprising. Inevitably, Minnie would have been closer to her mother. It's also possible that Williamina did not get on with her father. He had already fathered three girls, with his wife's fourth pregnancy he was probably hoping for a boy. He may even have chosen the name William. So it's not beyond the realms of possibility that Williamina's arrival may have been a great disappointment to her father.

During the 1850s Minnie's mother developed cancer. By the end of 1855 she was bedridden. Eighteen months later, on 27 May 1857, she died. For twelve-year-old Minnie the loss must have been devastating.

Two years later, on 7 June 1859, Minnie's twenty-year-old sister Elizabeth married Thomas McNeill, a watchmaker. This was the pay-off for the McCulloch's dedication to respectability: it gave their eldest daughter a modest degree of upward mobility.[23]

Four months after his daughter's wedding John McCulloch married Elizabeth Ferguson of Paisley. According to the 1861 census he and his second wife lived with his daughters Christina (fourteen), Janet (eight) and Isabella (five) in a three-roomed apartment at 27 Lynedoch St, Greenock. A search of later marriage records and census returns reveals that Christina lived at home until she married a railway clerk at the age of twenty-four and Isabella lived at home until she married a railway engine driver at the age of twenty-five. By 1881 twenty-eight-year-old Janet was the only daughter of John McCulloch still unmarried. In the census returns of that year she was living with her father and stepmother in a three-roomed apartment at 101 Belleville St, Greenock. All this suggests that their father's second wife made John McCulloch's daughters welcome in the family home. It also suggests that John himself was not disposed to turn his daughters out into the world as soon as they were old enough to fend for themselves.

But what happened to Minnie? At the time of the 1861 census, when she would have been sixteen years old, she appears to have vanished. A search through volume after volume of Scottish census returns reveals that not only was Minnie absent from her father's home, she was not in the home of her married sister or anywhere else in Greenock on census night 1861. Nor was she living in her fathers' home village of Killearn, or in her late mother's home village of Cardross, or in her stepmother's home city of Paisley. So where was she?

New Zealanders have a folk story to explain what happened to sixteen-year-old Minnie. They say that she married a doctor named McCulloch and went to Australia — that was where at least one of her daughters was born and her husband died. The young widow then went to live with her aunt in Invercargill. Part of this story is true — the bit about going to live with her aunt in Invercargill. That happened around the end of 1863. But the part about the doctor is sheer fabrication. There is no evidence in the records of Scotland, Australia or New Zealand to suggest that Williamina McCulloch ever married anyone prior to her marriage to Charles Dean in New Zealand in 1872. And although there is later evidence that her daughters were born in the early 1860s (one in Australia, the other in New Zealand), their births were not registered anywhere in Scotland, Australia or New Zealand.

So what happened to Minnie during that three-year gap between her disappearance from Greenock and her reappearance in Invercargill? Where did she go? And why? And how do those two little girls of hers fit into the picture?

Chapter VIII

~

THE PARISH MINISTER

*T*his chapter is not about Williamina McCulloch but it does contain some important information, so sit up straight and pay attention. I shall reveal the significance of the information in due course.

Oh very well, I'll tell you now. Remember how Williamina McCulloch arrived in New Zealand claiming to be *Mrs* McCulloch, the widow of a doctor and the daughter of a clergyman (when she was really the unmarried daughter of a railway engine driver)? And reader, doesn't this suggest that the doctor part of the story was invented to explain away her illegitimate daughters, and the clergyman part was invented to set the seal on her respectability? (The daughter of a clergyman and the widow of a doctor — you can't get more respectable than that!) Well, this is where the plot thickens — that clergyman and that doctor were not total inventions. This chapter is about the two men on whom Minnie Dean's fantasies of her past were based.

Before he was ordained into the Church of Scotland, James Melville McCulloch was a schoolmaster. In 1821, as a twenty-year-old with an MA from the University of St Andrews, he became rector of the Grammar School of Dunkeld. During his five years there he married Arabella Cargill, the daughter of a prominent local banker. From Dunkeld the McCullochs moved to Edinburgh where James spent three years as headmaster of Circus Place School. The greatest achievement of his term in Edinburgh, and arguably the greatest achievement of his life, was the system he devised for teaching children to read. His *Course of Reading* became the most widely used school book throughout the entire British Empire for more than one hundred years.[1]*

James McCulloch was ordained at a time when the kirk was torn by schisms, but that was nothing new. From 1690, when God-fearing Scots replaced what they saw as the idolatry and corruption of the Catholic and

---

* At a remote New Zealand country school, in 1914, Sylvia Ashton-Warner was taught to read using the system devised by James Melville McCulloch.

[55]

Anglican churches with the Calvinistic theology of Presbyterianism, the Church of Scotland was plagued by evangelicals within and dissenters and secessionists without. After a series of schisms (and an occasional recombination) the upheavals came to a head in 1843 with a schism so great that its title needs no explanatory modifiers. In Scotland to this day the event is known simply as 'the Disruption'.

The Disruption, like most of the upheavals that preceded it, had its origins in the Patronage Act of 1712 which allowed lairds, rather than congregations, to appoint parish ministers. Under this system, laird-appointed ministers tended to be drawn from a wealthy and well-educated élite. They were men who through their university educations had been exposed to liberal and rational ideas from the continent. Their views on heaven and hell were less rigid, and their interpretations of the Bible less literal, than those of their parishioners, and they were confident that the Lord was as moderate in His religious opinions as they were in theirs. They had no time for Puritanism.

By contrast, their parishioners were mainly hard-working artisans and labourers who found relevance in the social teachings of the kirk which emphasised thrift, restraint and self-improvement. They held puritanical views on matters of Sabbath-breaking and dancing, and gave ready support to the growing numbers of evangelical ministers from humble backgrounds who regarded the lairds' uncalvinistic appointees as backsliders.

At the General Assembly of 1843 centuries of simmering dissatisfaction boiled over. The charismatic Church of Scotland leader, Thomas Chalmers, together with one-third of his fellow clergy, walked out and set up the Free Church of Scotland. They took with them almost as many elders, most of the Church's overseas missions and nearly forty per cent of the Church's communicants.[2] Four years later, when the Lay Association of the Free Church was close to turning its dream of establishing a theocratic community in the New World into a reality, Thomas Chalmers' death prompted the Association to name the port of its proposed colony in Otago, New Zealand, 'Port Chalmers'.

The ministers who remained in the Established Church were predominantly wealthy and politically conservative men who were not interested in changing the world. Among their number was the Reverend Dr James Melville McCulloch.

James McCulloch had been a minister for fourteen years at the time of the Disruption. He took up his first parish of Arbroath in 1829. Three years later he was presented by the Duke of Roxburghe to the important border parish of Kelso. During his term in Kelso he was awarded the degree of Doctor of Divinity by the University of St Andrews, but apart from that his eleven years in Kelso, like the rest of his life, were unremarkable. In a volume of biographical sketches published in 1849 under the title *Our Scottish Clergy*,[3] he was described as 'devoid of all claims of eccentricity' and 'not an eloquent speaker', though in an unconvincing attempt to sound more positive the author added 'the great charm of his discourses lies in their intrinsic excellence'.

When the Established Church in Greenock was decimated by the defection of six of its eight ministers at the time of the Disruption, Sir Michael Shaw Stewart, Baronet and heir to the original John Schaw of Grenok, offered James McCulloch charge of the West Parish, and that was where the Reverend Doctor spent the rest of his long and uneventful life.

James McCulloch's predecessor at the West kirk, the Reverend Dr Patrick McFarlan, was one of the ablest of the seceding ministers. When he left he took with him all but a few dozen parishioners. Among the loyal minority was the family of a respectable railway engine driver named John McCulloch. When John McCulloch's daughter Williamina was born in the year following the Disruption it was the Reverend Dr James McCulloch who baptised her.

James and Arabella McCulloch, together with their seven surviving children and two servants, lived in a ten-roomed manse in the gracious West End of Greenock.[4] James proved himself to be a judicious minister; before long the more respectable folk of Greenock who wanted nothing more than the calm continuation of the existing order began to fill his pews, and the merchant princes of the town welcomed him into their social orbit. The rewards were many: in 1860 James and Arabella's eldest daughter Louisa married John Paterson, merchant son of the Provost and Chief Magistrate of Greenock; in 1861 their youngest daughter Janet married another merchant, James How; and during his years in Greenock James McCulloch was the beneficiary of six testimonials. At the last and most generous of these (held in 1879 to mark the jubilee of the Reverend Doctor's ordination) Sir Michael Shaw Stewart presided over the presentation of twelve hundred guineas and a silver salver to the West kirk's loyal minister.

Like most of Scotland's privileged citizens, James McCulloch regarded himself as the innocent beneficiary of his own natural superiority, but he was not devoid of concern for the less fortunate. As a good churchman he honoured the tradition of philanthropy established by Thomas Chalmers during the three decades preceding the Disruption. Chalmers believed that the existing political, social and economic order was divinely decreed. His message to the disadvantaged was that no virtues were more praiseworthy than submission to one's superiors, patient endurance and gratitude for mercies received, but his message to the advantaged carried the warning that the possession of wealth and power was ignoble without a corresponding degree of philanthropy. Through the propagation of this message Chalmers was almost single-handedly responsible for making nineteenth century Scotland as famous for its philanthropists as it was for its drunkenness and bad housing.[5]

The Reverend Dr McCulloch's philanthropic interests included The Ladies

Sanitary Association, which was formed in October 1865 in response to Dr Buchanan's forthright report on the typhus epidemic of the preceding twelve months:

> The cause of the great epidemic prevalence of fever in Greenock is essentially the one condition of overcrowding, and together with it the dirty habits of the people . . .
>
> The habits of the population among whom fever has prevailed are particularly dirty. Of course, in a dark room, all corners and recesses, with flooring of earth, or of boards rotten or uneven, tenanted promiscuously and leading off a common stair it is everyone's business to attend to, cleanliness is not to be expected; and when it is added that out of the 50,000 residents in Greenock 35,000 are estimated to be unprovided with any water but such as they carry up from the public streets, and that the great bulk of the poor houses have no privy or ash-pit accommodation whatever, no condition appears to be wanting to ensure the extreme of filth.[6]

Along with most members of his social class the Reverend Dr McCulloch believed that each individual had prime responsibility for his or her own material well-being and spiritual health. He was therefore opposed to large-scale expenditure by the rich on the provision of adequate housing, effective sewage disposal and an ample supply of clean water for the poor. His speech to the inaugural meeting of the Ladies Sanitary Association advocated a more patronising and less expensive form of philanthropy:

> But, even supposing that all were done which can be encompassed by Acts of Parliament and Magistratic exertions — even supposing that our streets were widened and our water supply increased, and all those squalid dens demolished which depress the vital powers of their occupants, and drive them for relief to narcotic drugs and intoxicating liquors, nay, even supposing that commercial enterprise should come to the help of legislative enactments, and cover the town with houses for the poor and working-classes in entire harmony with the conditions of health and the laws of life; still the work of sanitary reform among us would not be complete and comparatively fruitless . . . if effectual steps were not also taken to redeem the humbler classes of our townsmen from low tastes and squalid habits . . . the humbler classes must be . . . taught to value air, and light, and water, instructed in the conditions and laws of health, and formed to a taste for cleanliness in their persons and tidiness in their dwellings . . . and it is just because the Association which we have met today has this desirable object in view, and bids fair, by means of its tracts, and lectures and domiciliary visitations, to accomplish it, that it deserves a place among our benevolent institutions . . .[7]

While the crusading ladies of his parish sought to save the poor by means of tracts, lectures and domiciliary visitations, the Reverend Dr McCulloch concentrated on the souls of his more affluent parishioners.

The Church of Scotland recognised many sins: greed, pride, untruthfulness, self-righteousness, hypocrisy, blasphemy, idolatry, drunkenness, Sabbath-breaking, adultery and fornication; and the greatest of these were adultery and fornication. There may have been an element of convenience in this unscriptural emphasis on sexual offences: while irrefutable evidence of most forms of sinning was difficult to obtain, the birth of an illegitimate child was proof positive that an offence had occurred.

To avoid the wrath of the kirk many Scottish women attempted to hide their ex-nuptial pregnancies, but in the eyes of the Calvinistic authorities this was the greatest sin of all. In 1690 a law was passed that made it a capital offence for a woman to conceal her pregnancy, should the baby be subsequently found dead or missing. The last hanging under that Act was carried out in 1776; thereafter, under a peculiar Scottish procedure, an accused woman could avoid trial by electing to be 'banished' instead.[8]

When the bastard was neither dead nor missing the mother could not be charged with infanticide, so the kirk authorities satisfied their misanthropy by charging her with fornication instead. Until the end of the eighteenth century any woman found guilty of fornication was required to sit before her congregation on a 'stool of repentance',[9] but by the time James McCulloch moved to Greenock kirk punishment for the offence had become less harsh.

During his term at the West Parish the Reverend Doctor met with his elders in formal session three or four times a year. At each session they elected new elders, listed new communicants and tried up to four cases of fornication. The minutes always told the same story: the names of the guilty parties and their home parishes were noted, and it was stated that the Reverend Dr McCulloch had interrogated the couple and was satisfied with their profession of repentance. The kirk session then resolved that the guilty parties should be rebuked for their sin and absolved from further scandal. Married couples whose first child was born less than nine months from their wedding date were not exempt from this humiliation; in such cases their sin was 'antenuptial fornication'.[10]

Both the established and dissenting Scottish Presbyterian churches poured more than 350 years of impassioned energy into the suppression of fornication, but studies of Scottish baptism records over that period show that the incidence of babies conceived out of wedlock remained unchanged. According to historian T. C. Smout, the only lasting effect of the crusade was that it transformed the outward attitude of Scottish society towards sex from one of great permissiveness before 1560, to one of rigorous and inquisitorial disapproval by the seventeenth century.[11] Fornication still occurred, but after

Calvinism came to Scotland those who fornicated, especially in urban areas,* did so a great deal more furtively and guiltily than before. And when the private act brought forth public issue some young women were driven by terror and shame to kill their babies. Several commentators believed that infanticide increased as a result of kirk discipline.

Of course the five children of the Reverend Dr James Melville McCulloch who survived into adulthood were pure — or if they weren't they managed to avoid having their sins recorded in the kirk session minutes. They were also impressively well-connected and extremely well-travelled. In the early 1860s at least three, and possibly all five, young McCullochs made the long sea voyage to Sydney, New South Wales.

John Paterson, husband of James and Arabella's eldest daughter Louisa, was a merchant in the Sydney firm of Caird, Paterson and Company. His partner, George Caird, was the fourth of six sons of a wealthy Greenock shipbuilder. George's eldest brother John achieved later fame as Principal of Glasgow University, his youngest brother Edward became Master of Balliol College, Oxford, and yet another brother, Colin, made his mark as a major Scottish shipowner.[12]

John Paterson married Louisa McCulloch in Greenock in 1860 and immediately took her off to Sydney. The following year he and his wife were joined by Louisa's newly married sister Janet and her husband James How, a merchant in the Sydney firm of How, Thompson and Company. The minister's youngest son James, a bank clerk, also took a trip to Sydney sometime between 1861 (when he was recorded as living at home with his parents in the census of that year) and 1866 (when he died aboard ship en route from Sydney to London). The two remaining McCulloch offspring, Mary (twenty-five) and John (twenty-six), were not home for the census of 1861. Maybe they went to Sydney too? All we know about Mary is that she was back in Greenock in time for the census of 1871, and that she stayed there, a spinster in the manse, until the end of her parents' long lives.[13]

That leaves the minister's son John. What happened to him? Reader, brace yourself for this: in 1860 he graduated Doctor of Medicine from Glasgow University (Yes! A doctor!) According to the university graduation roll John McCulloch became a ship's surgeon, and in the Medical Directory of 1865 he is listed as a ship's surgeon with the 'British and North American Royal Mail Steam Packet Company'.** As the name suggests, the British and North American Company confined its activities to the Atlantic Ocean, but that doesn't rule out the possibility that sometime in the early 1860s John

---

* In some rural areas where determining a woman's fertility before marriage was a matter of commonsense agricultural economics, community attitudes were more relaxed.
** Otherwise known as the Cunard Line.

McCulloch visited his siblings in Australia as a surgeon or passenger on some other line. Of that period one thing is certain: for the privileged children of James Melville McCulloch sailing to far-off Sydney was the thing to do.

There seems little doubt that the minister and his family moved in the best of circles, but the extent of the Reverend Dr McCulloch's contact with his more humble parishioners is open to question. Presumably he was aware of engine driver John McCulloch and his wife and family; they were respectable, they shared his name, they went to his church, he baptised four of their babies and (though burial records have not survived) he probably officiated at the funerals of John's first wife and two of their daughters (the first Janet and the first Isabella).

For their part, the engine driver and his family would have observed the comings and goings of the minister and his family from their place in the pews. They must have been impressed by the minister's soft, clean hands and high social standing. When they lived in one room, or even when they lived in two or three, they must have been impressed by his ten-roomed mansion. They must have been impressed by his servants and his well-educated, well-connected, well-travelled children. In fact there was probably nothing about the minister and his family that did not impress the engine driver and his offspring. And out of all this did the motherless adolescent, Minnie McCulloch, trapped in the congested squalor of old Greenock and at odds with her father, create a fantasy life in which she was a daughter of the manse? And, when she fell in love with the distant, unattainable minister's son, did fantasy build on fantasy? In her dream-world did she transform herself from the daughter of the manse, to the daughter-in-law — the romantic heroine, the star of a story in which love triumphed over differences in rank and fortune?[*] In her dream-world where anything was possible, did she become the young doctor's wife?

Of course there is no way of knowing whether Minnie McCulloch wove that minister and that doctor into her adolescent fantasies. But there can be little doubt that her memories and dreams of that minister and that doctor formed the foundation on which she built her later claim that she was the daughter of a clergyman and the widow of a doctor, for these things are certain: that minister was the only Reverend McCulloch, and that doctor was the only Doctor McCulloch, with whom Minnie had any long-term contact. So it all fits, doesn't it?

Of course the question then arises, how much truth was there in Minnie's desperate fantasy? We know that Dr John McCulloch was not her husband, but was the privileged young son of her parish minister — twenty-five years old and fresh out of medical school — the father of one or both of her illegitimate daughters?

---

[*]   A popular theme of romantic novels of the day, which were often serialised in newspapers.

Chapter IX

―――――― ❦ ――――――

TERRA AUSTRALIS / TERRA INCOGNITO

There is a three-year gap between Williamina McCulloch's disappearance from Greenock and her reappearance in New Zealand. What little evidence there is suggests that she went to Australia.

The adult certificates of Minnie's daughters indicate that they were born during the gap, so if Minnie registered their births her movements could be easily traced; but she didn't. The first official record of either child is the marriage certificate of Minnie's elder daughter, but it doesn't help; at the time of Ellen's wedding, marriage documents recorded only the names and marital status of the betrothed couple.

The following year, when Ellen's first child was born, the demands of officialdom had increased. Her infant's birth certificate states that the nineteen-year-old mother was born in 'Hobart Town, Tasmania'. Seventeen months later came another birth, and a certificate that recorded Ellen's birthplace as 'Launceston, Tasmania'. Less than a year later, when Ellen and her two children were tragically drowned, her husband reported that Ellen was born in 'Tasmania', but no town was named.

Ellen's birth date is also a mystery, since certificates of that era record only a person's age — but by subtracting the stated age on each certificate from the date of that certificate we can estimate that she was born in late 1860 or early 1861.

The answers to the question 'Number of years in New Zealand' on Minnie's death certificate and on Ellen's later certificates all suggest that Minnie and Ellen landed in the colony near the end of 1863. They must have arrived just in time for the birth of Minnie's second daughter. Isabella's adult certificates say that she was born in Invercargill, and calculations of her birth date locate the event in late 1863 or early 1864.

Forty-six years later, Southland historian F. G. Hall-Jones provided further evidence of Isabella's Invercargill birth. His handwritten notes of 20 September 1941[1] read:

Minnie Dean

Her second child was born at Mrs Kelly's house . . . . They left school to go out to the country to Mrs Dean's about 1870 or early in the 1870s . . .*

 Mrs Kelly was in a neighbour's crying after they went away saying she didn't mind parting with the elder but not with the younger as she was born in her house & very attached to her . . .

This evidence suggests (but does not prove) that Isabella was Minnie's natural daughter; in Ellen's case there is no hard evidence either way. Previous historians have assumed that Minnie gave birth to both girls, but the question must be asked: could one or both of Minnie's daughters represent her first excursion into baby farming? (This is what research is about: asking questions. Important questions, trivial questions, silly questions, unlikely questions, questions for which the answer is obvious, questions for which there is no answer at all. This injunction should be engraved into every researcher's consciousness: *question everything.*) But without facts we have to fall back on common sense: Minnie would have been sixteen when Ellen was born. Would any mother in Australia or anywhere else, however desperate, entrust her infant to an unmarried, working-class, sixteen-year-old girl who lacked both family support and financial security? Would any sixteen-year-old who lacked these things want to care for (or be in a position to care for) a baby that was not her own? On the grounds of common sense alone we must assume that Ellen and Isabella were Minnie's natural daughters.

 Minnie probably claimed to be a widow from the time she arrived in New Zealand, though that claim does not appear in the official record until her marriage to Charles Dean in 1872.[2] The story that her first husband died in Tasmania presumably also dated from her arrival, but it did not appear in print until 1895.[3]

 But did Minnie really spend her three missing years in Australia? In pursuit of more convincing evidence I searched Australian immigrant lists, convict lists, prison inmate lists and lists of residents of benevolent institutions, but found not a shred of proof that Minnie ever set foot in any Australian colony.[4] Again we must turn to common sense. Why would Minnie spread the story that her daughter was born and her husband died in Tasmania if she had never been near the place? How else, than by living in or near Tasmania, could this Scottish working-class girl have acquired the knowledge and confidence to carry off that story — a story that remained unquestioned throughout her life and for nearly a hundred years after her death?

 The identity of the girls' father (or fathers) is another mystery. Ellen's marriage certificate is silent on the subject. Isabella's states that her father was

---

*   Minnie married Charles Dean and moved with her daughters into his home at Etal Creek, Western Southland, in 1872.

Dr John Henry Proctor (a name unknown to any British, Australian or New Zealand medical register of the time); Ellen's death certificate names Charles Dean as her father. Minnie's marriage and death certificates do not name her first husband. It wasn't until Isabella died that a doctor named McCulloch was officially recorded as the father of one of Minnie's daughters.

There is something very odd about those three blank years in the life of Minnie Dean. Some gaps in the story of any nineteenth-century working-class woman are inevitable, but this story is nearly all gaps — gaps and fabrications. The gaps suggest that Minnie deliberately covered her tracks; the fabrications suggest that she laid a false trail. So what really happened during those missing years, and why didn't Minnie want anyone to know? Reader, we must ask more questions, we must speculate.

Why did Williamina McCulloch leave Scotland for Australia when she was no more than sixteen years old?

Scenario 1: *She joined one of the immigration schemes recruiting servants for the colonies. Many such schemes operated from Glasgow during the 1850s and 1860s.* This is unlikely for at least three reasons. Firstly, it would have been out of character for John McCulloch, who kept his other daughters at home until they married in their twenties, to allow Williamina to go to the other side of the world at such a tender age. Secondly, Williamina (or Minnie) McCulloch (or Proctor) does not appear on any lists of assisted immigrants into Tasmania, Victoria or New South Wales for the late 1850s and early 1860s. And thirdly, if Minnie did somehow get to Australia as an assisted immigrant — without her father's consent, without being recorded on any shipping list — well, there's still that first-born daughter to explain. Surely no servant girl in such circumstances would be in a position to keep a baby born out of wedlock?

Scenario 2: *She travelled to Australia as an unassisted immigrant.*
The only way a young woman without means could travel to Australia independent of any government scheme was as the servant of wealthy migrants. I haven't found Williamina (or Minnie) McCulloch (or Proctor) on any lists of unassisted passengers entering the colonies of New South Wales, Victoria or Tasmania — but that proves nothing; many such migrants entered Australia unrecorded. However the arguments that make Scenario 1 unlikely also apply to Scenario 2: Minnie's father wasn't the type to let her go so far away with strangers and, once there, she would have been in no position to keep her baby.

Scenario 3: *She was transported to Australia as a convict.*
No such luck. Australian convict records are the most complete of all and Williamina (or Minnie) McCulloch (or Proctor)'s name does not appear anywhere, which is not surprising — transportation to New South Wales ended

in 1840 (four years before Minnie was born) and to Van Diemen's Land[*] in 1853 (four years before her mother's death).[**5]

Scenario 4: *She arrived in Australia unrecorded (assisted or unassisted) and established a de facto relationship with a man named John Henry Proctor. His support enabled her to keep her first child, but he abandoned her during her second pregnancy. Minnie was then rescued by Mrs Kelly, her aunt in Invercargill, who sent over the fare for her to bring her daughter to New Zealand.*

I haven't found any John Henry Proctors in Australia during this period, but there were quite a few John Proctors. Most of them seemed too busy having children within the bounds of matrimony to have time for de facto relationships. But Minnie may have formed a de facto relationship with someone else (some other Mr Proctor perhaps, who was too inconsequential to rate a mention in the official records of the colony), and that man may have abandoned Minnie during her second pregnancy, and so on. The only reason I'm not seizing on this scenario with delighted cries is that there are better ones to follow.

Scenario 5: *She went to Australia unrecorded and formed a de facto relationship with a man (who may or may not have been named Proctor) who supported her after the birth of her first child. Then in December 1861, under the name of Mrs Proctor, Minnie took her baby and ran off with a pirate. After two years of sailing the South Seas with this buccaneer, Minnie and Ellen ended up on Stewart Island. By that time her second child was due and her relationship with the pirate was coming apart, so Minnie changed her name back to McCulloch and threw herself at the mercy of her aunt in Invercargill.*

Oddly enough, there *is* some evidence for this scenario. In December 1861 the whaling brig *Grecian* left Hobart Town under the command of Thomas James McGrath. Nothing was heard from the vessel for over two years, then early in 1864, after a voyage of unconscionable lawbreaking, McGrath brazenly took the owner of the *Grecian* to court at Bluff, New Zealand, 'for the balance of wages due to him', but instead of being awarded his claimed arrears he was fined £100 for breaches of New Zealand customs regulations and his whole ugly story was exposed.

According to reports of the trial in Southland newspapers, about a week after leaving Hobart Town the brig put into Botany Bay[***] and took on board,

---

[*]   Van Diemen's Land was renamed Tasmania when it ceased to be a penal colony in 1853.
[**]   Transportation of Irish convicts to Western Australia continued until 1868, but there is no evidence to connect Minnie with either Ireland or Western Australia, and she does not appear in any West Australian lists.
[***] Sydney.

apparently by prior arrangement, a Mrs Proctor and her child. The woman was described by McGrath as a 'passenger', and by the crew as McGrath's 'lady friend'. Under cross-examination McGrath admitted that Mrs Proctor did not pay any passage money.

After a few months of whaling, the *Grecian* called at Wellington where the brig was refitted in what was later described as 'a suspicious manner'. After the vessel had left its next port of call, the Chatham Islands, McGrath mustered the crew and 'proposed to them to take the ship for themselves and go on a slaving expedition to the South Seas'.

At Tonga, McGrath gave presents to the natives and induced 130 men, women and children aboard for a feast. Then the natives were enticed below, the hatches clamped shut and the *Grecian* sailed for Peru where the living cargo was sold. The rest of the *Grecian*'s voyage is unclear, but it seems that McGrath had no intention of returning to Hobart Town. At the end of 1863 he built a house for himself and Mrs Proctor on Stewart Island and provided many of its essentials — a stove, some tools, three hundredweight of soap, casks of beef, suet, sugar and vinegar, kegs of butter and pickles and 10,000 coconuts — from equipment and supplies carried on the *Grecian*.

Apart from the information about Mrs Proctor recorded during McGrath's court case at Bluff,[6] no mention of her can be found in the official records of Australia or New Zealand. Could this woman have been our Minnie? The dates fit. And the story would explain how Minnie and Ellen got to New Zealand, and the source of the 'Proctor' on Isabella's marriage certificate.

But our Minnie led an outwardly respectable life before and after these three mysterious years. Surely it would have been out of character for her to run off with a pirate? Was she really that foolhardy at sixteen? Alas, dear reader, there is no way of knowing.

Scenario 6: *Minnie became pregnant by Dr McCulloch, the minister's son, and was sent off to Australia with one of the minister's married daughters to avoid a parish scandal. The minister's family supported Minnie and her baby in Australia until she became pregnant yet again (perhaps by a Mr Proctor, who knows?), whereupon she and Ellen were packed off in disgrace to Minnie's aunt in Invercargill.*

Of course there is no evidence for this scenario either, but if true it would explain a lot. And it could have happened, human nature being what it is — with a young man of twenty-five and a young woman of fifteen in the same parish; a young woman whose mother had died and whose father had remarried, a young woman who was perhaps unhappy, perhaps unruly, who was perhaps reading romantic fiction about true love transcending social barriers and daydreaming of life in the manse. It's possible reader, it's possible. Minnie may have even convinced herself that the dashing young Dr McCulloch would marry her if she bore his child. That was another theme of popular romantic fiction: pregnancy — the star-crossed lovers' way of forcing parents to accept a forbidden marriage; and as the kirk session minutes show, marriages under such circumstances were not unknown in the West Parish of Greenock. But if this was Minnie's fantasy, she was doomed to disappointment. In the real world the everyday rules of parish life did not apply to the minister's family. In the real world it would have been unthinkable for the minister's son to be branded as a fornicator in his own father's church; it would have been unthinkable for the minister's son to marry the engine driver's daughter.

So what is a respectable Church of Scotland minister to do when his son gets the engine driver's daughter pregnant? Of course! Send the young woman as far away as possible. And send the young man away too, dammit. Give him a few years as a ship's surgeon on the British and North American Royal Mail Steam Packet Company. That'll teach him a lesson. (Being a ship's surgeon was a low-status occupation; under normal circumstances it would not have been suitable work for a medical graduate from such a highly placed family.)

The minister's eldest daughter Louisa married Sydney merchant James Paterson in Greenock on 1 June 1860. It would be nice to be able to say that when James returned to Sydney with Louisa, the pregnant Minnie went along too. It would be nice to be able to say that they landed in Tasmania where Minnie's baby was born and then Minnie and Ellen lived with Louisa and James Paterson (or perhaps with the minister's other daughter Janet and her husband James How) in Sydney until Minnie became pregnant again and they packed her off to her aunt in Invercargill.

It would be nice to be able to say these things. It would explain everything: it would explain how and why Minnie went to Australia, how and why she was able to keep her baby and how and why she moved on to New Zealand, and a lot more besides. Living for two to three years in the household of one of the minister's married daughters would explain how and where Minnie, despite being poor, single and working class, with perhaps a brief taste of a privileged education at the Greenock Academy, acquired the experiences that enabled her to pass herself off in New Zealand as the daughter of a clergyman and the widow of a doctor. By living in the Paterson or How household — perhaps as a 'widowed servant', perhaps as a 'widowed family friend' — she would have learnt the speech patterns, deportment and ways of relating appropriate to her future role. She may even have furthered her education by working her way through the Paterson and How bookshelves.

It would have been quite an adjustment, moving from two bare, people-crammed rooms in Greenock to the home of the Hows or Patersons on the other side of the world. As the inventory taken when James How went bankrupt in 1865 shows, the Hows (and no doubt the Patersons too) lived in a large, furniture-crammed house:[7]

Dining Room

Dining table
Tray & stand
Davenport
8 chairs
1 arm chair
Bookcase
Books, about 200 vols
Sofa
Sideboard
Sewing machine
Mirror
Marble stand
8 photographs
Time piece
Sundry ornaments on mantel
Carpet & rug
Cornice poles, curtains etc
Fender & irons
2 kerosene lamps
Microscope

Drawing Room

Piano & stool
Music stand
Chiffonier
— ditto — cabinet
2 card tables
Work table
Oval table
2 tables
Sofa & 2 foot ottomans
2 large chairs
6 chairs
2 folding chairs
Whatnot
Flower stand
Mirror
Time piece
Sundry ornaments
Carpet & rug

Cornice pole, curtain etc
Fender & irons
2 marble vases
Sundry marble ornaments
2 pair lustres
1 kerosene lamps

Bedroom No 1

Wardrobe
Washstand & furniture
Chest of drawers
Folding table
Round table
Dressing table & toilette glass
Spittoon & commode
6 chairs
Iron bedstead, cornice pole
Coal scuttle, fender & irons
Clock & ornaments
Oil paintings

Dressing Room

Chest of drawers
Washstand & furniture
Pedestal table & glass
Photographs & paintings

Bedroom No 2

Iron bedstead & bedding
Washstand & furniture
Table & glass
Chest of drawers
Telescope & stand

Bedroom No 3

Brass bedstead & bedding
Washstand & etc
Table & glass

Bedroom No 4

Iron bedstead & bedding

Child's cot & bedding
Chest of drawers
Books
Chairs
Towelhorse & sundries

Hall & Landing

Hatstand
Oil cloth
Stair carpet etc
Hall lamp
2 photographs

Pantry

Filters etc

Kitchen & Laundry

Dresser
2 tables
Chairs
Kitchen utensils
Clock
Knife cleaners
Sundries

Out House

Tubs, buckets & sundries

Servants' Rooms

2 iron bedsteads & bedding
Washstand & etc
Chest of drawers
Table & glass
Chairs

Dinner service china
Dessert service china
Tea service
Glassware
2 chests containing silver &
    electroplate

Jewellery belong to Mrs How
2 gold watches & chains belong
    to self

After living in that sort of household for a while, and especially after living with the sort of people who lived in that sort of household for a while, Minnie would have had no trouble playing the lady as if she was born to the role.

But once again the problem is lack of proof. Ordinary nineteenth-century women who were not born in Australia and who kept on the right side of the law, ordinary women who did not marry or die in Australia and who failed to register their children, were unlikely to appear in the public record. James How and James Paterson, as merchants of distinction, left their marks, but I have found no trace of Minnie, or of any unnamed woman who could have been Minnie, in any of the archives relating to the Patersons and the Hows.

So, I have no proof that this scenario happened. It could have happened, but I have no proof.

Scenario 7: *You don't like any of my scenarios? Very well, reader, write your own* . . .

Chapter X

———— ❧ ————

NEW ZEALAND, THE EARLY YEARS

*I*n 1861, when gold was discovered at Gabriel's Gully, Otago prospered. In 1862, as word of rich strikes in the Wakatipu basin began to spread, Southland joined the boom. The Wakatipu diggings were really in Otago, but their nearest ports were in Southland. Within weeks, miners, entrepreneurs, rogues and policemen began to pour into Bluff from the worked-out Victorian goldfields. Other new arrivals came by immigrant ship direct from Britain or by steamer from other parts of New Zealand. In less than two years the population of Invercargill swelled from 600 to over 5,000. By the end of 1863, almost 10,000 colonists had taken up residence in the far south.[1]

Somewhere in the midst of all this activity Williamina McCulloch, presumably accompanied by one small daughter and pregnant with another, slipped into Invercargill unrecorded. As fortune hunters poured into Southland, two routes to the hinterland, both of which would later feature in the life of Minnie Dean, became major wagon trails to the goldfields. One trail took the direct route from Invercargill: a backbreaking haul through bush and swamp to Kingston via Winton Bush, where in 1863 Minnie's future home town was laid out to the east of the Oreti River. The other trail, from the old whaling settlement of Riverton, passed along the flax and matagouri-flanked west bank of the Aparima River before joining the Invercargill-Kingston route near the embryonic township of Lumsden (then known as the Elbow). In 1872 one of the regular stopping places on that trail, the Etal Creek Hotel, became home to an unremarkable newly wed couple by the name of Charles and Minnie Dean.

Little is known of Minnie's eight years in New Zealand prior to her marriage to Charles Dean, though most commentators agree that she and her girls initially lived in Invercargill with her aunt, 'Granny' Kelly. F. G. Hall-Jones suggests in *Historical Southland*[2] that she worked as a teacher and, though she had left school by the time she was sixteen, this is entirely possible. During the nineteenth century teaching was the only acceptable employment open to respectable women who could read and write (and who were therefore considered well educated). Before 1877, when free, compulsory, primary education was introduced into New Zealand, such women were much in demand as colonial governesses.

According to handwritten notes made by F. G. Hall-Jones in the 1940s[3] Minnie taught for a time at the Invercargill home of Granny Kelly's married daughter Christina, and this too is entirely possible. Christina married William Newsham West in 1857 and their first child was born the following year. Five more children arrived during the 1860s. The Wests would have been glad of a tutor to occupy and instruct their growing brood. Hall-Jones notes that Minnie's former pupils remembered her with 'great affection as a teacher, kindly, refined and lovable . . . '.[4]

Next, according to Hall-Jones, Minnie boarded her daughters with Mrs Kelly while she taught at various Southland schools,[5] but this statement is a little misleading; state schooling was still a decade away — if Minnie did teach, she would have done so as a private governess, rather than as a public school teacher.

Another version of Minnie's early years in New Zealand appeared in the *Otago Witness* at the time of her arrest:

> After her arrival here she was at the Half-way Bush Hotel in the employ of Mrs Howells, now a hotel keeper in Invercargill.

Electoral rolls confirm that between 1868 and 1873 a hotel keeper named Henry Howells lived at Half-way Bush.* By 1870 he had at least one small daughter.[6] Presumably Minnie, in the guise of a respectable, well-educated, doctor's widow, went to that muddy coach stop twenty miles from Invercargill in the expectation of working as nursemaid or governess to the Howells' children. It can't have been pleasant, discovering the raw colonial truth — that at the frontiers of civilisations, role distinctions were largely irrelevant. Governess, nursemaid, cook, chambermaid, barmaid, domestic servant; Minnie probably had to do the lot.

Hall-Jones states that Minnie later taught at Nightcaps, a settlement not far from Dunrobin Station, the home of her future husband Charles Dean.

Charles Dean was born at Macquarie Plains, Van Diemen's Land, on 22 August 1836. His parents were settlers.[7] By 1867 he had moved to New Zealand where he was recorded as superintendent of stock at Dunrobin Station in the Aparima Valley.[8] White settlement along the Aparima began in 1856 when the Otago Provincial Council[9] advertised the availability of Southland grazing land

---

* Not the Halfway Bush near Dunedin, but a now-vanished spot of the same name near Dacre, on the road from Invercargill to Gore.

for settlement. In 1857 Christopher Basstian, a London-born Tasmanian, landed at Riverton with a large consignment of Merino sheep and Hereford and Ayrshire cattle. With the help of his brothers he took up the Dunrobin Run.

Christopher Basstian did not lack ambition. After replacing his family's wattle and daub hut at Dunrobin with a much grander dwelling and building another fine home in Invercargill he launched into a long and active political career which encompassed membership of the House of Representatives, chairmanship of the Wallace County Council and membership of the Provincial Councils of both Southland and Otago.

During the summer, against a backdrop of honest toil as the station's 25,000 sheep were mustered and shorn and the less productive of their number were boiled down for tallow, the hospitable Basstians entertained their city friends and country neighbours. Visitors could fish and shoot in the surrounding rivers and hills, play cricket on the lawn and partake of dainties set out on tables in the garden — and guests never left without having basketfuls of produce from the Basstian's abundant orchard and garden pressed upon them.[10]

Christopher Basstian was prominent in the Invercargill Club, the Southland Acclimatisation Society, the Riverton Racing Club and the Birchwood Hunt. He liberated rabbits, possums and wallabies at Dunrobin, and was reported to be so concerned for the welfare of the rabbits that he fed them titbits from his garden.[11]

No doubt Williamina McCulloch, the respectable governess from Nightcaps, was included on the Basstian's invitation list. In a photograph of Minnie that dates from this time[12] a round-cheeked woman wearing a pannier skirt, a close-fitting velvet jacket and a small, lightly trimmed hat regards the camera with solemn composure. She has the dress and demeanour of a nineteenth-century governess; she is, the photograph suggests, a model of restrained Victorian respectability. Minnie may have developed her love of gardening from observing Christopher Basstian's fine grounds, and she probably met Christopher Basstian's superintendent of stock, Charles Dean, during her visits to Dunrobin Station.

Earlier commentators have expressed bewilderment that the seemingly well-educated, seemingly well-bred, Williamina McCulloch chose to marry an ordinary workman like Charles Dean. Of course, as we now know, she wasn't as well-bred and well-educated as all that, but more importantly, she was a dreamer. Her youthful fantasy of becoming Dr McCulloch's wife had come to nothing but her adult fantasy of becoming his widow was proving a raging success. No one questioned her widowhood, no one questioned her respectability. The life that was once confined to her dreams had become her everyday reality; Williamina McCulloch was being treated as a woman of status. That heady experience must have validated and encouraged her fantasies — and in the wilderness of western Southland who better to fantasise about than the distinguished Christopher Basstian. Of course, as was the case with Dr McCulloch, she could not marry Christopher Basstian — but she could do the next best thing. When she married the man who had been Christopher Basstian's superintendent of stock, and who by 1872 was the proprietor of nearby Etal Creek Hotel,[13] Minnie may have been marrying Charles Dean in her outer life, but in her dreams . . . could she have been marrying Christopher Basstian once removed?

By a strange quirk of fate, just seven weeks before Williamina McCulloch was married in New Zealand, the man who seems to have been the model for her first husband was married in England. Did news of Dr John McCulloch's betrothal precipitate Minnie's marriage to Charles Dean? She was still in touch with her family in Greenock during the 1870s,[14] so she could have received word of the wedding plans.

After their wedding Dr John McCulloch and his wife Louisa lived comfortably in the better part of Greenock, but they were not immune from the health problems of that dismal town. In 1881 John developed tuberculosis. Early in 1883, as a passenger on the *Rossdhu*, he took the long sea voyage to the antipodes. On 10 May 1883 he died aboard ship at Port Chalmers, in the Otago Harbour.

By the time Williamina McCulloch and Charles Dean exchanged their vows at the Etal Creek Hotel on 19 June 1872 the gold fever of the previous decade had cooled and a new mania was gripping the nation: land frenzy. During the 1870s the New Zealand government borrowed heavily overseas and great networks of road, rail and telegraph links were laid. Lured by the prospect of overnight fortunes as remote tracts of land were opened to farming, speculators scrambled to buy everything from inaccessible swamps to distant mountain tops. Throughout the country land values escalated.

These developments did not favour the Deans of Etal Creek. The march of progress brought with it the growth of Invercargill and the decline of Riverton. By the early 1870s the Invercargill to Kingston wagon trail had become a busy main road and work was under way on a railway along the same route. But with every improvement to the Invercargill to Kingston route the trail from Riverton to the goldfields fell further into disuse. Before long Etal Creek had become a backwater. Around 1875 the Deans abandoned hotel keeping and turned to the latest get-rich-quick scheme sweeping the nation: land speculation.

The story of Charles Dean's economic downfall is a story of badly timed decisions. Going hotel keeping in an area that was about to become a backwater was the first. Buying land in the late 1870s was the second. In the

1875-76 Electoral Roll Charles Dean is listed as the owner of a 'house and farm, freehold', but the purchase must have been informal at first. According to the Certificate of Title for the property, his ownership of 100 acres at Etal Creek (with the help of a mortgage from the Scottish and New Zealand Investment Company) was not formalised until May 1878.

May 1878 was not a good time to buy land: property values were wildly overinflated, the colony's economy was saturated with debt and the inevitable bust was only months away. In October 1878 the City of Glasgow Bank (a key player in the New Zealand land boom) collapsed. The resulting credit squeeze burst the land speculation boil and the country was left to fester in the crater of a fifteen-year depression. Wages and export prices plummeted. Unemployment rose. Poverty spread across the land.

The New Zealand government's initial response was to increase overseas borrowing, and as a result the economy rallied briefly. Exhibiting his unfailing flair for bad timing, Charles Dean took advantage of the rally to arrange another mortgage (this time with the reckless New Zealand Loan and Mercantile Agency)[15] with which, in 1882, he bought a further 200 acres at Etal Creek. According to one estimate, New Zealand farmers of the 1880s needed to graze between 3,000 and 4,000 sheep on 1,000 acres to be economically viable,[16] so with only 150 sheep on his 300 acres Charles Dean didn't stand a chance.[17]

The depression, the remoteness, the miserable rock- and tussock-covered land would have been more than enough to break the Deans, but on top of that was the rabbit plague. The rabbits Christopher Basstian had tenderly nurtured two decades earlier lacked natural predators in their new home. Once established they had proceeded to breed — well — like rabbits. A visitor to Dunrobin Station in the 1870s reported: 'The rabbits were in such numbers that they ate every green thing and even dug up or pulled out the tussocks to get the little moisture at the roots, which they then devoured.'[18]

According to the 1882 'Return of Freeholders in New Zealand' Charles Dean's 300 acres at Etal Creek were valued (or, more likely, overvalued — since the average value of New Zealand land in the 1880s was £2/acre) at £1,200. After a decade of declining fortunes the Deans were stuck at the back of beyond with land they could neither farm at a profit nor sell at a profit, and a mortgage they could not repay. Things could only get worse.

Popular Victorian culture depicted matrimony as a bed of roses — love, security and the patter of tiny feet. But if that was Minnie's expectation she must have been bitterly disappointed. How much love there was we shall never know, but there was certainly no financial security and worse still, in a society that saw motherhood as every woman's true calling, there was no patter of tiny feet.

For a while Minnie had her own daughters with her, but in 1879 Ellen married and moved away. Two years later Isabella followed suit. There were grandchildren of course. Ellen had two, Isabella had nine. Minnie must have gained some comfort from watching Isabella's children grow; they lived several day's journey away but by the 1880s travel had become much easier. If Minnie had had the chance she would have also enjoyed watching Ellen's children grow, but in 1882 a devastating family tragedy denied her that grandmotherly pleasure; in 1882 Ellen and her two children, a two-year-old boy and a nine-month-old girl, were found drowned.

If I am to keep digressions in this book to a minimum I should summarise in one paragraph those aspects of Ellen's death that impinged on the life of Minnie Dean. But Ellen's death, as revealed in newspaper reports and inquest records of the event, is a story in its own right. It demands to be told. In fact it demands to be told so insistently that I keep recounting it compulsively to friends, and they listen transfixed. Ruth said, 'Write it down. You must write it down. Write it as a short story.' And being a writer herself she added, 'We have a duty to tell these stories that would never otherwise be told.' So here, retold as a short story, is the tale the *Southland Times* called:

A MELANCHOLY AFFAIR

Early one Tuesday in the winter of 1882 James left his Woodlands home to work on a ploughing contract at Wyndham, some 25 miles away. He didn't want to go, but the depression was biting and jobs were hard to find. He had no choice.

He was worried about leaving his wife. She hadn't been well of late and their two small children gave her little rest. At least the Alexanders had promised to keep an eye on things. That thought gave him comfort.

'Cheer up,' Ellen chided. 'It won't be for long.' And as he rode off she called, 'May God protect and keep you from all danger, Jamie.'

The Alexanders were also worried about Ellen. She complained of headaches, of not being able to sleep. Nothing they did or said seemed to help. She needed to see a doctor.

'Why don't we go to town on Friday?' Mrs Alexander suggested brightly. 'An outing would do you good — put some colour in your cheeks. And you could see the doctor while we're there. What do you say?'

So that Friday Mrs Trotter took care of the little boy while Mrs Alexander, Ellen and the baby went to Invercargill on the morning train. The doctor wasn't home, so Ellen went to the chemist.

Eighteen-eighties New Zealand had its share of pill pushers, but Mr Bailey was not among them. Mr Bailey's specialty was dispensing advice; dispensing medicine was only a sideline. Ellen explained that she had no appetite, she couldn't sleep. Yes, she admitted, my husband is away. Yes Mr Bailey as it happens you're quite right, I'm not really cooking myself proper meals. And yes, I am still nursing this big, beautiful baby.

Mr Bailey launched into his favourite Lecture for Young Mothers. He told her to look after herself properly. He said she didn't need medicine, what she needed was good nourishing food. He gave her a bottle of tonic and told her to go home and cook herself a decent meal.

The lecture didn't do any good. On Saturday afternoon Ellen complained to Mrs Trotter of pains in the head. On Sunday morning she complained to Mr Alexander of being unable to sleep; he suggested she get someone to stay with her at night.

Throughout the day the Alexanders kept an eye out for Ellen and the children. At about one Mrs Alexander saw them walking in the garden, at about three she popped over for a chat. There was no one around. Perhaps they've gone for a walk, she thought.

Over the next hour the weather closed in and rain began to fall. The Alexanders watched anxiously for Ellen's return. What had become of her? Why hadn't she come home? Soon it would be dark. At five Mr Alexander checked the house. The fire was out. There was no one there. Then he noticed the lid was off the well.

The following Wednesday twelve good and lawful men of the neighbourhood, duly chosen and duly sworn, assembled with the coroner at the Woodlands Hotel. Their task was to inquire for our Lady the Queen, when, how, and by what means Ellen Anne and her children Ellen Anne and John Henry came to their deaths.

In the opinion of the *Southland Times* there were three possible explanations. The first was that both children had fallen into the well and Ellen, in a frantic effort to rescue them, had fallen in too. The second version suggested that the toddler had fallen in and Ellen had placed the baby on the ground while she tried to save him. Then she too had fallen in, and the baby, attracted by the cries, had crawled to the well and tumbled in after her. The third possibility was that Ellen had thrown the children and herself into the well while temporarily deprived of reason by a paroxysm of pain in the head.

The inquest jury took a less detached view of the tragedy. James and Ellen and their children had lived in Woodlands only three months, but James had been raised in the district and two of his brothers still lived there. Also, most of the jurymen had some personal connection with the sorry events into which they now had to enquire. The wife of Mr Trotter, the foreman, had visited Ellen the day before the tragedy; juryman Dawson, a relative of James's parents, had emigrated from Scotland with them sixteen years earlier; juryman McKenzie, a blacksmith, had provided the hook used to retrieve the bodies from the well; juryman Neil had been on hand to wipe away the wet hair clinging to Ellen's cold white face when she was dragged from the water. Those twelve good men were in no doubt where their responsibility lay; whatever the facts of the case their first duty was to make the ordeal as gentle as possible for poor bereft James.

They were even willing to excuse James from giving evidence but, red-eyed and trembling, he insisted on making a statement. He told of his happy marriage and his sad parting, and of Ellen's last words. Then he wept and shook his head. He had nothing more to say.

Next Mr Alexander told of visiting Ellen on Sunday morning and looking for her later that day. He told of peering down the well by candlelight and seeing, far below, tiny feet on the surface of the water. He described the well: four feet by six feet wide, sixteen feet deep, containing ten feet of water. In the platform across the top was a hole sixteen and a half inches square through which water was drawn. When not in use the hole was covered with a heavy lid. On the day of the tragedy the lid, which was too heavy for a toddler to move, was found some distance from the well, and the rope was still wound around the windlass.

James rose unsteadily to his feet. 'The lid was always kept on,' he sobbed. 'That was the rule. It was only taken off to draw water. It was always put straight back on again.'

One by one other witnesses took the stand. Mrs Alexander told of her trip to town with Ellen on Friday. Mrs Trotter told of visiting Ellen on Saturday. Mrs Atwool told of washing the bodies and finding no marks of violence. Mr Bailey told of the advice he gave. And out of all this evidence one very curious fact emerged. All the witnesses were unanimously of the opinion that Ellen was normally of cheerful disposition, and they had noticed nothing unusual in her demeanour in the days leading up to the tragedy. They mentioned her headaches, her sleeplessness, her loss of appetite, but every one of those witnesses — her husband, Mr and Mrs Alexander, Mrs Trotter, Mr Bailey, Mrs Atwool — insisted that right up to her tragic death Ellen was unquestionably her usual cheerful self.

After hearing the evidence the coroner did not point out that if Ellen had been trying to rescue the children the rope would have been hanging down the well; nor did he comment on the impossibility of an adult falling by accident down such a tight squeeze of a hole; nor did he question witnesses' claims that Ellen's cheerful demeanour gave them no cause for concern — claims that lose all credibility when held alongside their responses to her headaches, sleeplessness and loss of appetite: they took her to town to see a doctor, they visited her at home several times a day, they offered her advice — they *must* have been worried about her.

Instead of addressing these points the coroner stated that there was nothing to show how the event had occurred. The jury duly concluded that while the three had undoubtedly drowned, by what means 'no evidence doth appear to the jurors'. That they managed to reach such a verdict in the face of compelling evidence that Ellen had thrown herself and her children down the well while suffering from severe depression is testimony to the affection with which the tragedy-struck family was regarded by their community. At that time suicide was a crime and a sin — but as far as James's friends were concerned he had suffered enough. They were decent compassionate men and they did what they had to — they ignored the evidence of suicide. And by ignoring the evidence of suicide they gave James the gift of divine consolation; they enabled him to give his precious wife and children a Christian burial. The end.

§ *The story of Minnie Dean resumes*

Back at Etal Creek with Ellen and her children dead and Isabella and her family living far away, poor bereft Minnie would have had no children to care for had she not, in 1880, adopted a motherless five-year-old named Margaret Cameron. Margaret's mother, a Scots-born shepherd's wife, died in childbirth at Winton in June 1880, leaving behind her widowed husband and three small children.[19] The eldest girl was brought up by relatives at Waikaia station. The middle child, a boy, stayed with his father. Margaret, the youngest, was adopted by Minnie Dean.

I'm not sure why John Cameron placed his youngest daughter in the care of Minnie Dean. The affectionate comments made about Minnie by her former Invercargill pupils indicate that she was fond of children, but she was not actively soliciting unwanted infants at the time of Catherine Cameron's death. Minnie and Catherine were probably friends: the arrangements John Cameron made for his two older children suggest that he would not give his youngest to a total stranger, and Minnie indicated in her last statement that she knew Margaret's mother. Perhaps they were related by blood or marriage. Perhaps they had friends in common. The only, admittedly tenuous, link I have found is this: the owner of Waikaia station, where Maggie's older sister was raised, came to New Zealand on the same ship as John Edward Denniston, the future New Zealand Supreme Court judge who was reported to have attended school with Minnie Dean.

Margaret Cameron lived with the Deans from late 1880 until early 1895 when, at the age of eighteen, she went to Mataura to learn dressmaking. Later she worked at Riversdale. Then in 1908 she married a Dipton farmer and became the mother of three sons. After her husband's death in 1918 she remarried and went to live in Timaru where she died in 1937.[20] These are the bald facts of her life, but the important question is this: after spending fourteen formative years in the care of the infamous Minnie Dean, how did Margaret Cameron turn out?

Margaret had every reason to grow up embittered. After the death of her mother and the breakup of her family she had been sent to live with people she barely knew. Over the years she saw her new mother battered by crisis after crisis. In 1882 there was Ellen's triple tragedy. In 1883 Minnie may have read in the newspaper, or heard from relatives in Scotland, the shocking news that John McCulloch, the young doctor himself, had sailed to this distant country and had died alone no more than a train journey away. And through all these crises Margaret was trapped with the Deans in a frightening plunge into poverty; a plunge that culminated in Minnie's last desperate enterprise: baby farming. So after all that, how did Margaret Cameron turn out? The answer to this question provides an important clue to the understanding of Minnie Dean.

According to folklore Minnie was an evil monster; according to the children she taught in Invercargill she was 'kindly, refined and lovable'. But what was she really like? Consider this: if Minnie was a monster Margaret Cameron would have grown into a bitter, unhappy woman; if Minnie was fond of children, but unable to adequately mother her adopted daughter, Margaret would have carried some pain of the spirit into adulthood; but if, against the odds, Minnie was able to give Margaret the love she needed, Margaret would have grown up little the worse for the traumas of her early life.

According to *Moonlight Ranges — the story of Dipton 1877–1977* Margaret Cameron was 'a bright, happy girl full of mischief and good clean fun'.[21] For their part, Margaret's descendants remember her as a gracious lady whose early life was never discussed — it wasn't until Minnie's biographer and Margaret's granddaughter compared notes that the connection was made.

'You don't need to pretend any more, Auntie,' the granddaughter told her father's aged cousin. 'I know that Grandma was raised by Minnie Dean.'

The old lady seemed relieved, even eager, to cast off the lifelong burden of secrecy.

'Dear,' she said. 'There's something you should know. Your grandmother was very happy with Minnie Dean. Her sister had a miserable childhood at Waikaia, but Margaret was happy. Margaret was well looked after and happy with Mrs Dean.'

Another witness to the upbringing of Margaret Cameron was Minnie herself. While in prison awaiting execution she wrote:

> Maggie Cameron the first child I brought to my heart and home without reward or thought of reward but the child's love. And that I have loved and cherished her with a mother's love she cannot deny. I had no thought of self where she was concerned. It did not matter whether I had a dress to wear or a pair of boots to put on I was satisfied so long as Maggie looked nice. How often has she said when I have been getting something new for her, Mother think of yourself. But I never did think of myself and this is my reward . . . If no one else will give me a welcome at the last day Maggie's mother will for she knows I have been a mother to her child and tried in every way to fill the place of the mother she lost. Would that I

was as well prepared to meet my maker I would be sure of a full acquittal. But a more loving obedient or dutiful daughter than Maggie has been to me — since the day she came to me a child of a little over five years of age until the day when I parted with her to go on a visit to Mataura little thinking it was our last — a mother never had.[22]

Margaret Cameron had been with the Deans four years when the financial disaster that had been stalking them finally struck. In December 1884 Charles Dean was declared bankrupt.[23] He was one of many small farmers forced into bankruptcy when the overextended New Zealand Loan and Mercantile Agency began foreclosing on mortgages. As bankruptcies go it wasn't very big or very serious. The £755 Charles owed on the mortgage, combined with various smaller arrears, brought his total debt to £910. At a creditors' meeting he explained that his land had been put up for auction but no offers had been received, and everything else he owned (apart from £25 worth of furniture and some bags of oats and wheat) had been sold by the loan agency. He said that he and his wife had no other property, and though they were still on the farm they had nothing to live on.

Within six months the land was sold, the mortgage paid off and the bankruptcy discharged, but by then Charles, Minnie and Margaret were destitute.

The largest of Charles Dean's unsecured debts was the £37 he owed a ploughman named Dunlea, and because of the depression Dunlea too was under stress. One night during the winter of 1885 he vented his desperation in a drunken rampage. According to a report in the Riverton *Western Star*,[24] in late July of that year Dunlea entered the Deans' bedroom at about one in the morning and attacked the sleeping couple with a carpenter's hammer before proceeding to demolish almost everything in the room. Margaret Cameron, disturbed by the fracas and fearing for her parents' lives, slipped from her bedroom window and ran in her nightgown to a survey camp half a mile away. When she returned with a surveyor the Deans were standing outside covered in blood, and Dunlea had possession of the house.* A member of the survey party rode off to alert Constable Buchanan of Otautau, who left for Etal Creek without delay. After travelling all day through a snowstorm he arrived, almost 24 hours after the assault, to find that tempers had cooled; Dunlea and his victims were sitting around the fire, and no one was willing to lodge a complaint.

Though peace had been temporarily restored, the Deans must have realised it was time to move on; time to try yet again, somehow, somewhere, to eke out a living. Some time between July 1885 and August 1887 Charles and Minnie Dean and Margaret Cameron moved to Winton. There Charles became a casual farm labourer and Minnie began taking unwanted babies for money.

---

* The teeth in Minnie's upper jaw may have been damaged and subsequently extracted as a result of this episode.

Chapter XI

————— ～ —————

PRIVATE TRAGEDY AND PUBLIC SCANDAL

The following excerpts from letters, advertisements, editorials and news items published in southern New Zealand newspapers during Minnie Dean's years as a child-care worker provide eloquent testimony to the misery and desperation of the Victorian age.

ADOPTION — Lady is willing to take Child as her own. Send particulars to 'Confidence', G.P.O., Dunedin.

Advertisement, Southland Daily News,
2 January 1889

. . . charge of child murder against . . . the father of a child which was illegitimate. He went to the mother's home . . . to remove it to his sister's house. He did not go straight to his sister's house, four miles distant, but went by a road which made it thirteen miles, stating that his purpose was to collect money owing him. While carrying the child he said it fell out of his arms, rolled down the bank of the river, and was carried away. This occurred at night. The jury, after about two hours deliberation, acquitted the accused.

News item, Southland Times,
10 January 1889

An inquest was held . . . touching the death of a female infant found at North East Harbour . . . They were wading on the beach when, looking round, she saw the body floating in the water . . .

News item, Otago Daily Times,
18 January 1889

An old miner named Philip Bevan, about 70 years of age, deliberately blew himself to pieces with dynamite at Waiomo, near the Thames . . . The scene of the tragedy presented a sickening spectacle, fragments of brain and neck being scattered about on shrubs and trees in the vicinity.

News item, Otago Daily Times,
23 January 1889

. . . the body of a man named George Ward was found hanging by a rope suspended from a beam in a stable at the rear of Mr Reay's Globe Hotel.

News item, Southland Times,
23 January 1889

Thomas Richard Dodd Fitzgerald was charged with being a neglected child . . . . it being illegitimate and its mother being in indigent circumstances and unable to support it. — His Worship committed it to the Industrial School . . .

News item, Otago Daily Times,
8 February 1889

Alexander (10), George (8), Henry (6), William (3), and Alfred Leonard Blue (2 years) were brought before the court as destitute children ... the father and eldest son of the family were in gaol, and the mother had left Dunedin, being unable to obtain work here owing to the father's misconduct, and there was no one to support the children, who were running about the streets ... His worship remarked that if he sent these children to the institution they would cost the country £104 a year.

News item, Otago Daily Times,
8 February 1889

The bungling job made of the hanging of Louisa Collins at Sydney recently recalls a more exciting experience, when three failing attempts to execute a man in Sydney resulted in his being reprieved.

News Item, Southland Times,
14 February 1889

Wanted: Someone to adopt a female child. Address — Maternal, News Office.

Advertisement, Southland Daily News,
22 February–4 March 1889

A woman has been committed for trial in New South Wales for systematic baby farming. Her method seems to have been to abandon the unfortunate infants in the streets, and it is supposed that twenty such cases will be sheeted home to her.

News item, Southland Times,
26 February 1889

Yesterday forenoon a boy ... was searching for birds' nests along the bank of the old Puni creek ... when he observed a bundle floating in the water. Natural curiosity prompted him to drag it out, then untie a string, and unwind a towel and piece of calico which formed the covering when there was disclosed the body of a male child. ﹐

News item, Southland Times,
4 March 1889

One night in June last an infant was found in the garden attached to the residence of Mr B. Hallenstein in Dunedin ... Emma Brookland was charged with having unlawfully abandoned a female child ... The child was well clothed and quite warm when found. It had been left in a sheltered place, and a feeding-bottle was left with it. It had been well nourished and cared for ... The child was ultimately sent to the Industrial School ... it died of pleurisy and inflammation of the membranes of the brain the following month ... Margaret Fish, labour agent, stated that accused called at her office several times last year in want of a situation as housekeeper where she could take a child with her. Witness said that would be very difficult to get .... Witness advertised for a person willing to adopt the child, but did not get anyone ...

News item, Southland Times,
11 March 1889

At an inquest on the body of Martha Astridge, a suspected case of malpractice, a verdict was returned that the deceased died of blood poisoning, brought on by abortion.

News item, Southland Daily News,
12 March 1889

Sergeant Devine ... arrested a young unmarried woman named Margaret Fitzgerald and her sister, a Mrs May Curtis, on a charge of wilful murder of an infant. A second charge of concealment of birth was also laid against them.

News item, Otago Daily Times,
15 March 1889

Wanted — someone to adopt a male child. Reply — Mother, News Office.

Advertisement, Southland Daily News, 22–30 March 1889

At the Magistrate's Court this morning Julia Maria Thorpe was charged with unlawfully using an instrument on Flora Brown (now Mrs Nash) in December 1887, for the purpose of causing a miscarriage.

News item, Southland Daily News, 29 March 1889

MRS LOUISA HAWKINS FEMALE PILLS are invaluable No irregularity or obstruction can resist them.

Advertisement (for abortifacient), Southland Times, *throughout 1889*

Wanted — Kind person to adopt baby girl, month old. Apply Times office.

Advertisement, Southland Times, 6-17 August 1889

A servant girl named Eliza Crimmin died yesterday . . . the woman was *enciente* . . . the probable cause of death was metallic poisoning . . . The police found a white powder, probably chalk, a packet of sulphate of quinine, a box of female pills, and a bottle containing medicine.

News item, Southland Times, 10 August 1889

A boy named Clarke met with a horrible death today, being crushed to a shapeless mass by a ponderous steam road roller.

News item, Southland Times, 24 September 1889

The body of a newly born infant was found in a garden in Nairn St, today. Medical examination proves that the child was born alive . . .

News item, Southland Times, 19 October 1889

Informations have been laid by the police against Annie and Charlotte McDowell, of

Lyell, for manslaughter. The case arises out of the death of the infant child of the former.

News item, Southland Times, 23 October 1889

On the verger of St Paul's Cathedral opening the doors early in the morning he found Mr Ashcroft lying near the chancel, with a six-barrelled revolver (one chamber of which was discharged) near him. He moaned, 'Money, money,' but was fast dying . . . Deceased . . . leaves a wife and three children.

News item, Southland Times, 21 December 1889

John Eliason and his wife, Mary Louisa Eliason, appeared on summons, under the Destitute Persons Act, 1877, to answer a charge of having deserted their child . . . Miss Stewart, a domestic servant, having an infant for whom she could not very well provide, came to an arrangement last year with the defendants by which they agreed on consideration of payments of £5 from the child's putative father and £5 from herself to adopt it.

News item, Press, 5 March 1890

. . . inquest into the circumstances attending the finding of the body of a male child . . . . inquiries had been made, which had resulted in Lily Ella Patten being arrested on a charge of concealment of birth.

News item, Press, 27 September 1890

Wanted to adopt a baby — good home — no premium required. Must have comfortable outfit or £5 to purchase one. Further particulars, apply, M. T. B. Post Office Christchurch.

Advertisement, Press, 4 October 1890

BABY FARMING (?)
Sir — A few days ago I saw an advertisement

in your columns asking to adopt a baby. Now, far be it for me to say that the basis of that effort is not true benevolence, or the natural craving of some poor woman to whom the joys of maternity have been denied. But the case looks suspicious . . .

Letter, Press, *9 October 1890*

. . . in the house were found five children, the oldest apparently about the age of four years. The accused besides these had five children of her own and when Constable Walker examined the place he found them all in a very pitiable state . . . He had previously been informed that Mrs Smith had a baby farm, and that she illtreated and neglected the children in the house . . . . the lower portions of the child's body bore signs as if it were scalded, the skin being red and the flesh inflamed and swollen. The whole of the body of the child was covered with a mass of filth . . . when Mrs Smith was undressing the child it gave forth no sound, and did not cry in any way. He had a very strong suspicion that it was drugged.

News item, Otago Daily Times, *7 November 1890*

At the Supreme Court this morning Sarah Jane Flanagan and Anna Flanagan (her mother) were charged with the wilful murder of a male child . . . The daughter was delivered of a child, which was put out to nurse . . . On the 5th of January the prisoner went to the nurse's house and took the baby away. Next day the head of a child was found, terribly mutilated . . . The body was not found, but a quantity of clothing which was discovered was proved to have been taken away with the baby from the nurse's . . . When they were sentenced to death there was a terrible scene.

News item, Otago Witness, *26 February 1891*

The two women, Flanagan . . . are not to be executed . . . The murder was in every one of its features brutal and unnatural . . . the decision of the Executive was weak and indefensible.

Editorial, Southland Times, *17 March 1891*

THE FLANAGANS
Sir — The public, for whose safety the criminal law is supposed to exist, must be indeed shocked at the escape of these atrocious criminals. It is notorious that this is due to Roman Catholic influence . . . Yours, &c., A PROTESTANT

Letter, Press, *17 March 1891*

THE FLANAGANS
. . . nothing can be said in defence of mothers who, utterly destitute of maternal love, do turn and rend their offspring . . . Mothers of such a degraded type should certainly suffer the full penalty of the law . . . Yours, &c., CITIZEN

Letter, Press, *20 March 1891*

An inquest was held concerning the death of an infant, Bella Watson, who died in a sort of private Children's House at Mount Eden, managed by a Mrs Stickley . . . At present, she had twelve children, mostly illegitimate, under her care, aged from three months up to fifteen years.

News item, Press, *11 July 1891*

An inquest was held at the Police Library yesterday afternoon touching the death of a female infant child, found in the estuary, near the Heathcote Bridge, on the 4th inst.

News item, Press, *13 September 1892*

The eldest, a girl of ten years, handed him a note from her stepmother addressed to the Charitable Aid Board, and stating 'I now give these children up to you, you are responsible for their safety' . . . The eldest girl gave evidence to the effect that their stepmother had locked up the house and the gate, left them to find their way to the Board, and then went away in a cab . . .

News item, Press, *25 September 1892*

A man named Makin and his wife have been arrested on suspicion of having caused the deaths of seven infants whose bodies were found buried in the backyard of their [Sydney] premises.

News item, Southland Times,
4 November 1892

A sensation was caused today by the discovery of four bodies of children in the yard of a house formerly occupied by the Makins.

News item, Southland Times,
10 November 1892

Two more bodies of infants have been found in the yard of a third residence occupied by the Makin family.

News item, Southland Times,
12 November 1892

The bodies of two more children, suspected of being murdered by the Makins, have been discovered. When the occupants moved into the premises after the Makins had vacated them a piece of cloth bearing blood stains was found, along with a number of bonnet pins. This discovery goes in the direction of confirming the theory advanced that the unfortunate infants were deprived of life by puncturing the heart with a thin sharp instrument or driving some instrument into the spinal cord. One of the bodies previously found bore an indication of puncture on the breast, though the remains were too decomposed to enable it to be definitely ascertained whether the wound was inflicted before or after death. The floor of another residence formerly occupied by the prisoners is being taken up by the police. The present tenants, who succeeded Makins, detected a great stench, and it is known that the flooring was removed and replaced while the premises were in occupation of the late tenants. The digging operations of the police create intense interest.

The strong chain of evidence obtained by the police proves without the slightest possibility of doubt that the children were cruelly murdered.

News item, Southland Times,
14 November 1892

Almost every day now some new development of a horrifying character is brought to light by the police in connection with the Makin baby farming case. Hundreds of people gathered in the street, lined the fences, and crowded even the housetops to watch the police at work. The two bodies found bring the total up to fifteen unearthed so far.

News item, Press, *22 November 1892*

Mrs Ingam deposed to the girl Ledger coming to the Oamaru boarding-house, and obtaining a bed on the 9th November. Next morning witness knocked at the door, but the girl did not get up, and subsequently she said she was ill. In the afternoon witness threatened to beat open the door, and the girl got up and opened it. When witness went in she saw the body of an infant lying on the floor . . .

News item, Press, *13 December 1892*

Further charges of infanticide against the Makins are being investigated before the coroner. Again a distressing scene occurred through the daughter Blanche accusing her father of not looking after her mother, adding 'We have told enough lies to screen you and through telling lies we are here.' Makin met the remarks with defiant jeers.

News item, Southland Times,
15 December 1892

SIR — I am requested by the Victorian Suffrage Society to give an emphatic denial to the statements made in your issue of 31 March over the signature 'Holdfast'. He affirms that we who advocate the extension of the franchise to women affirm the equality of the sexes. We do not so affirm and never did. We do not affirm that the Scriptures teaches such doctrine. We do not deny that the husband is head of the wife . . . I am, &c. , CHAS. E. HUTCHINSON

Letter, Southland Times, *20 June 1893*

At the Benevolent Institute today a woman stated that by dint of hard working from dawn to dark she was only able to earn 2s 6d per week at shirt making.

News item, Southland Times, *21 June 1893*

The Benevolent Institute has discovered that the alleged sweating in connection with the shirt making trade is unfounded . . . The woman who made the charge has been discovered to be a very slow worker who could not stitch more than a dozen shirts in a week.

News item, Southland Times, *28 June 1893*

At the Christchurch Resident Magistrate's Court yesterday morning, before Mr Beetham, R. M., Mr Burgess made an application under the Adoption of Children Act, 1881, on behalf of Alice Maria Weller, who prayed to be allowed to adopt an illegitimate child, aged about eighteen months. . . He was glad this one had been made in open court, as it enabled him to make public what he thought about them. In the present case an order had been made by the Court against the putative father, directing him to pay 6s per week for the support of the child until it reaches the age of fourteen years. The applicant described herself as the wife of a labourer, and the consideration she was to receive for taking the child was a payment of £5 and clothes for it to the value of £10. If the application were granted the father's money liability would cease, and the mother's responsibility would also be wiped out. The total sum the man might be called on to pay was something like £220, so that the

transaction if it came off would be a great relief to him. If anything happened to the adopting parents, and the child lived, it would be thrown on the State. He had been frequently asked to make such orders, and had as frequently refused, as it would have been distinctly encouraging immorality, and it was neither more nor less than baby farming under its worst possible aspects.

News item, Press, *5 September 1893*

The bodies of three infants, much decomposed, have been unearthed at Brunswick, a suburb of Melbourne. The police believe that they are on the track of an extensive system of baby farming which will probably exceed that carried out by the Makins in Sydney.

News item, Southland Times, *6 September 1893*

In the Supreme Court today the second trial of Caroline McGovern charged with performing an illegal operation on Isabella Guinan began.

News item, Southland Times, *7 September 1893*

The woman Thwaites or Knorr [of Melbourne] . . . affirmed her innocence, and accused the man Thompson of strangling a baby girl and burying it. She admitted she had buried two children in back yards, but declared that they had died naturally. The statement created a great sensation.

News item, Southland Times, *2 December 1893*

A terribly impressive scene took place in the [Melbourne] Supreme Court while the judge was sentencing the woman Knorr to death for child murder. She had to be supported in the dock, and at the conclusion she fainted.

News item, Southland Times, *16 December 1893*

When the agent called at the house this morning Mrs Brown was absent, but a woman, named Sarah Smith, was lying drunk on a bed in one of the front rooms. One of the infants was also in this room, and the other was in the next room. The infants were in a dirty, neglected state, and were covered with house flies.

News item, Press, 16 January 1894

Referring to the prevalence of juvenile suicides the London Evening News says: 'We qualify our boys for suicide by the excessive humanitarianism of our educational methods. The boy who had learned to clench his teeth and hold his tongue as he took a flogging, and to bear a bold front to his little school world as he wrestled through the pain and shame of his punishment, did not in later years run to blow his brains out because he lost a situation or a sweetheart. Young men were made of sterner stuff when the birch survived in schools.'

Editorial, Southland Times, 11 July 1894

Sarah Gregory who had pleaded guilty . . . to a charge of concealment of birth . . . was brought up for sentence. His Honour said . . . everyone would pity her in her position . . . he would take her good character into consideration, and the sentence would not be a severe one. She would be sentenced to three months imprisonment with hard labour.

News item, Southland Times, 27 September 1894

The household of Mr J. P. Jameson, Cashel Street East, was surprised about 7. 30 am yesterday, to find a baby girl lying on the front doormat . . . accompanying it was a note, written in pencil, 'The finder of this will please give it a home for charity's sake, as I am too poor to keep it, and God will reward you.'

News item, Press, 22 November 1894

Maggie, a daughter of Mrs Mason of Kaiwaiwai, was spending a holiday at Martinborough, and left a letter saying she had committed suicide, and indicating where her body was to be found. An investigation showed that she had tied a rope to a flax bush and round her neck and then jumped into the Ruamahunga river under the Waihunga bridge, thereby both drowning and hanging herself. When found this morning she was dead and showed signs of having struggled furiously and of having suffered terrible agony.

News item, Otago Daily Times, 17 January 1895

Death has carried off, after a fortnight's illness, the second daughter of Mr David Gilbert, a bright girl of about twelve years. The deceased suffered from brain fever, which it is thought was brought about by over-study — another victim to our education Juggernaut.

Gore notes, Southern Cross, 25 May 1895

. . . proceedings were taken by the police against Bessie Davy, a resident of Jervois Road, Ponsonby, on a charge of having, in consideration of the payment of 7s per week, retained in her care and in her house one John Moore or M'Cracken, an infant, without having registered the child and such house under the Infant Life Protection Act . . . police are endeavouring to trace the child registered last year and stated to have been adopted by a lady up north.

News item, Otago Daily Times, 7 June 1895

ADVICE TO MOTHERS! Are you broken in your rest by a sick child suffering with the pain of cutting teeth? Go at once to a chemist and get a bottle of MRS WINSLOW'S SOOTHING SYRUP. It will relieve the poor sufferer immediately. It is perfectly harmless, and pleasant to taste; it produces natural quiet sleep . . .

Advertisement (for opiate), Otago Witness,
throughout 1895

'That's what I call hush-money,' remarked
the father when he put down the cash for a
bottle of paregoric to take home for use in
the infantile portion of the house.

Humour column, Southern Cross,
27 April 1895

At the Magistrate's Court this morning,
Arthur Newman, a remittance man, was
charged with attempted suicide at the
Provincial Hotel and ordered to pay costs
and bound over to keep the peace.

News item, Southland Daily News,
13 May 1895

MRS DEAN, THE MURDERESS.
Just issued, a splendid lithographed sheet
24in x 18in, CONTAINING Mrs Dean and
Husband, Judge Williams, four Solicitors,
two Detectives, Witnesses, Magistrate, and a
host of others.
Will be highly appreciated all over the
colonies and abroad.
Everyone should have a likeness of the first
woman hung in New Zealand . . .

Advertisement, New Zealand Mail,
September 1895

Chapter XII

———— ～ ————

A NEW START AT WINTON

*Reader, be warned. Hanging from the chain of events that led Minnie Dean to
the scaffold are jangling clusters of names. Some names hold the keys to long-
hidden family scandals. As we turn rusted locks the skeletons of your ancestors
may be among the bones that tumble from musty closets and clatter out over
the floor.*

Between her marriage in 1872 and her husband's bankruptcy in 1884,
Minnie Dean's life was indistinguishable from that of thousands of
respectable, law-abiding, married women of her times. She was a
mother, a grandmother and a Christian. She led a home-centred life: she took
no part in the women's suffrage movement, wrote nothing for publication, had
no independent career, made no impact on the wider society. The limits of her
narrow world were circumscribed by the Victorian imperatives of status, duty,
domestic order, proper appearances, acceptance of the status quo and
resignation in the face of adversity. But after the bankruptcy everything
changed.

The year of Charles Dean's bankruptcy was also the year of the Married
Woman's Property Act. After 1884 married women could own property and
incur debts in their own names, and in the coming years Minnie made much
use of the new law. Charles Dean, as a discharged bankrupt, was also free to
make his own financial arrangements but he rarely if ever did so. He has been
described in published accounts of the Dean case as 'feckless and dull',[1] 'mild
and weak'[2] and 'decent and harmless'.[3] Ken Catran is the only commentator to
indicate in print that Dean's financial problems were exacerbated by a fondness
for alcohol,[4] but the suggestion seems to have been in circulation for a long
time. At the inquest following Dean's death in a house fire in 1908, the first
person on the scene indignantly rebutted the rumour that Charles Dean had
died with one leg through the window and a bottle of whisky in his hand. He
said that Dean died in bed, and there were no bottles of any description in the
remains of the fire. Other witnesses confirmed that Dean was 'always a

temperate man' and was sober on the night of the fire.[5] This may be true, or it may be a cover-up. There was certainly a cover-up concerning his nearest living relative — the local Constable named a niece in Tasmania, though it was probably common knowledge that Dean had a brother in New Zealand. And there was certainly a cover-up when the name of his wife was recorded on his death certificate as 'Not Known'.[6] All we really know about Charles Dean following his bankruptcy is that he was a shadowy figure in Minnie's life, a low-paid farm labourer, away from home a lot. After 1884 all the couple's financial transactions that I have been able to trace were made in the name of Minnie Dean.

Sometime between July 1885 (when the Deans were attacked in their beds at Etal Creek) and August 1887 (when a loan to Minnie Dean of East Winton was registered under the Chattels Securities Act) Minnie, Charles and nine-year-old Margaret Cameron moved to The Larches — a two-storeyed house on 22 acres of land, half a mile from the nearest neighbours and a mile and a half from Winton. The property was ideally suited to two of the great passions of Minnie's life: gardening and train travel. There was a neglected half-acre flower garden in front and an overgrown orchard and vegetable garden behind, and the Invercargill to Kingston railway ran past 200 yards away.

In the seven-roomed house there was plenty of room for children. Minnie may have considered the commercial possibilities of child care early on, but it wasn't her first priority. With thirteen cows and 115 fruit trees the Deans probably expected their primary income to come from dairying and fruit growing. And with a loan of £200 from Minnie's aunt, Granny Kelly,[7] the future must have looked bright.

Within two months the Dean's financial arrangements had begun to unravel. On 27 October 1887 two civil claims, one for £5 5s, the other for £1 18s, were brought against Minnie Dean in the Invercargill Magistrate's Court.[8] Before the year was out it must have been obvious to Granny Kelly that as a financial manager Minnie Dean was no better than her luckless husband; by the following year she must have realised that her loan would never be repaid.

Most of Granny Kelly's money, and along with it Minnie's only remaining source of security, respectability and hope, went up in smoke at three in the afternoon of 29 April 1888, when Charles, Minnie and Margaret were away from home. They returned to find The Larches burnt to the ground.[9] While Charles salvaged timber and roofing iron from the wreckage and built a rough, two-roomed cottage with a lean-to on the site, the Deans lived in a rented seven-roomed house in Winton.

With the loss of her home and possessions, and with rent to pay in Winton, Minnie's financial problems multiplied and her relationship with The Larches' owner, Alexander Nicholson, deteriorated. Nicholson too had financial difficulties. He met his June mortgage payment, but that was his last and he was not prepared to walk away from his property empty-handed. In July 1888, unobserved by Minnie, Charles or Margaret, Nicholson removed all 115 fruit trees from The Larches and replanted them on the land of a friend, James Thomson. Minnie located the trees and, believing that Thomson had stolen them, sued him for their estimated value of £82. On 9 October 1888, in the Invercargill Magistrate's Court, it was established that the trees had in fact been removed by Nicholson. The case was heard on the same day that the Southland County Council sued Minnie Dean for 18s 9d in unpaid rates. She lost both cases.[10]

The Deans presumably continued to farm The Larches, but later reports indicate that their thirteen cows were reduced to one or two over the following six years. Were the missing cows sold, stolen or slaughtered, or did they fall ill and die? Alas, we shall never know. At all events the farm was a failure and by the end of 1888 the Deans were again facing financial ruin. Minnie's choices were limited; she could work as a servant, she could take in laundry or needlework or she could care for unwanted babies for money. In view of her fondness for children her decision to take the latter course is understandable. As the *Southland Times* reported after her arrest:

> All who know Mrs Dean, including her adopted daughter and the children in her house, appear to be united in the opinion that she was naturally very kind-hearted and did many kindnesses in times of affliction to both grown up people and children.[11]

Over the years Minnie's reputation for kindness has been buried by her reputation for evil, but nearly a century later one fond memory surfaced: 'Mother liked Minnie Dean,' confided the daughter of a woman who grew up near the Deans. 'There was always warmth in her voice when she spoke of Mrs Dean.'[12]

The financial viability of Minnie's enterprise was enhanced by the considerable demand for discreet child-minding in colonial New Zealand. During the 1880s the establishment of labour-intensive industries in large cities, together with a high level of male unemployment, drew increasing numbers of unmarried women into the paid workforce. Their wages were low and their hours were long, but for many young women freedom from parental supervision and a pay packet of one's own were luxuries to be enjoyed. To the alarm of social commentators, the illegitimacy rate rose,[13] but on the surface at least traditional Victorian values prevailed. Respectability ruled, and for unmarried women the price of respectability was chastity. Newspaper reports of dead newborn babies — murdered or abandoned — attested to the anxiety of transgressors to hide their sins.[14] Reports of dead women — single, pregnant victims of suicide or abortion — confirmed that many transgressors would rather die than bear the shame of a bastard child.

Unmarried mothers who lacked the desperation to kill themselves or their infants turned to their parents or the child's father for support. Many Victorian couples, anxious to keep a daughter's scandal within the family, raised an illegitimate grandchild as their own. Others paid, or persuaded the child's father to pay, a full-time, long-term child minder to take the infant off their hands.

Unmarried mothers who lacked family support were faced with the humiliation of giving birth in a Home for Fallen Women or the danger of giving birth alone, followed by the financial necessity of going straight back to work. These women were caught in a vicious cycle: they couldn't afford child care until they found work, and they couldn't find work unless they put their babies in care first. Some children of mothers rendered destitute by low wages, ill health or unemployment were cared for at no charge by kind-hearted baby minders, others ended up in orphanages or industrial schools, others died of neglect. In the 1890s illegitimacy was seen as a major threat to public morality — it would have been unthinkable for Charitable Aid Boards to assist unmarried mothers to keep their own babies.

When Minnie went into business, about 300 people lived in Winton; it was little more than a village carved from the Southland bush. The local men were primarily farmers, sawmillers, blacksmiths, boot makers, carpenters, storekeepers and hotel keepers.[15] The women were primarily wives and mothers. Winton was hundreds of miles from the main population centres where the demand for child care was greatest, but the railway system gave city folk a chance to hide their illegitimate offspring as far away as possible.

Though the plan had economic appeal, Minnie must have known that her chosen occupation would put her fading respectability further at risk. 'The scandal of baby farming' had been an issue in the British press since the 1860s, and court cases concerning the ill-treatment of children in paid care were often reported in colonial newspapers.

In 1884 New Zealand interest in the issue quickened when the Dunedin coroner reported that 'something very much akin to baby farming' existed in the city.[16] In November 1887 a headline in the Christchurch *Press* screamed 'BABY FARMING IN DUNEDIN. HORRIBLE REVELATIONS' and in March 1889 a Dunedin police inspector reported that 'Some few cases of Baby-farming have cropped up; one notably, recently'.[17]

Later that month, around the time that New Zealand newspapers were reporting the trial and execution of Edinburgh baby farmer Jessie King, the Police Commissioner ordered a survey of the incidence of baby farming in the colony.

All police districts, with the exception of Dunedin, reported that the evil did not exist in their areas (though some noted evidence of baby farming in adjacent districts), and all assured the Commissioner of their continuing vigilance. The Wellington police inspector took a benign view of the child care cottage industry in his area:

> There are married women here who take charge of a baby for a barmaid or servant girl, but in nearly every case the person having charge of it is a friend or acquaintance of the mother of the child and keeps it for the sake of a weekly sum paid by its mother, who is unable to take care of it and at the same time follow her business.[18]

Like the baby minders of Wellington, Minnie probably had every intention of providing an honest child care service. Besides, she wasn't doing anything illegal. There were no laws to stop her taking as many children as she wanted for whatever fee she desired and keeping them in whatever manner she chose. She was not allowed to neglect or mistreat them, but that was all.

Her first advertisement appeared in the *Southland Times* on 17 April 1989 and ran for a month:

> WANTED, by a respectable married woman with no young children — a baby to nurse, or one or two young children to bring up, or a baby to adopt. Thoroughly comfortable home in the country. Terms very moderate. Apply by letter addressed 'B. D.' office of this paper.

Minnie took up child care for economic reasons, and though it quickly became apparent that the enterprise was eroding what remained of her respectability and would never be a financial success, she persisted. Like the present-day eccentrics who take in large numbers of stray cats and dogs without any clear idea of how they are going to look after them all, there can be little doubt that Minnie loved her charges (though she may have loved some more than others) and she had every intention of caring for them all to the best of her ability. Her determination to continue, year after year, despite every obstacle life threw in her path, suggests that her career choice was underpinned by a stubborn irrationality. Perhaps it was the pain of a childless marriage that drove her, or the emptiness left by the deaths of so many loved ones (her three sisters, her mother, her daughter, her two grandchildren and the doctor who was probably the first husband of her dreams). Whatever the reason, the records show that Minnie's need for babies often took precedence over her need for respectability, and frequently transcended her need for money:

> It is six years past on the 28 of April since I first took children for pay. The boy Arthur [Wilson] was the first . . . He was eight weeks old when I brought him home. His mother was a young girl little more than a child and on whose shoulders all the burden of the boy's keep rested. I agreed to keep and clothe the child at the rate of 20/- per month for two years. This I did. At the expiration of the two years she called on me again and I agreed to keep him for other two years at 40/- a quarter. At the end of

this term I told her if she gave me £10 I would give her a receipt in full. She paid me the £10 in three instalments. I intended from the first to keep the boy whether I received payment from her or not.[19]

It hasn't been easy to chart the course of Minnie Dean's career. The available records, of which her last statement is by far the most detailed, are often contradictory, confusing and incomplete. However it is reassuring to note that whenever background details provided by Minnie about her charges were checked by police, they were found to be correct. Since Minnie's version must of necessity be my primary source, I shall proceed on the tentative assumption that when writing about the babies she received — how many she took, when, from whom and for how much — Minnie usually told the truth. Whether she always told the truth about the fates of these children is another matter.

Minnie wrote in her last statement, 'since April 1889 I have had in all twenty-four children', and added that the total did not include the two whose deaths were the subject of her trial. Her figure probably also excluded a baby she looked after for two days in Christchurch in 1893. By adding those three the total reaches twenty-seven. Of those twenty-seven I have identified nineteen and traced the origins of eighteen. Not unexpectedly, sixteen of the eighteen were born out of wedlock. The other two were born shortly after their mothers married men who disclaimed paternity of the child. The babies came to Minnie from around Southland and from cities, towns and villages near the Invercargill to Christchurch railway line. Of the sixteen babies for whom the source of payment is known, four were paid for by their mothers, five by their fathers and seven by their grandparents.[20]

As for the fates of the babies — well, some of them died. This should come as no surprise. In the late nineteenth century, when most New Zealand babies were breastfed and raised by their own mothers, the mortality rate for European infants was around eight per cent.[21] No separate statistics for bottle-fed babies are available for New Zealand, but in Britain when registered illegitimate infants were artificially fed in foundling hospitals or private homes the death rate sometimes exceeded ninety per cent.[22]

Here are the bald statistics of Minnie Dean's enterprise: of the twenty-seven small children who passed through her hands, six are known to have died (this is not an unusually high number — many family plots in the old Winton cemetery contain the bodies of six or more children), ten are known to have survived (a number that any Victorian family would have been proud of) and three were unaccounted for despite police efforts to trace them. The fates of the remaining eight are unknown.[23]

From these figures we can calculate that the infant mortality rate at Mrs Dean's home during her six years in business was at best twenty-two per cent and at worst sixty-three per cent. The deaths may have distressed Minnie, but they would not have surprised her. During her youth more than twenty per cent of babies born in the tenements of Greenock died before they reached one year of age. In her own family three of her seven sisters died young. Minnie probably felt that childhood deaths were to be expected — they were a fact of life.

In 1889, as she bustled about caring for little Arthur and preparing to take more babies, infant deaths would have been the last thing on Minnie's mind. She was probably looking forward to providing a grateful stream of abandoned children with a stable, happy home. She was no doubt expecting to enjoy emotional fulfilment and financial security for the rest of her life. And she was likely to have been particularly excited by an offer that came in response to her advertisement: a baby girl to raise from birth. A doctor warned Minnie that the infant was unlikely to survive, but in a burst of parental optimism she and Charles adopted her in May 1889, and named her May Irene Dean. Perhaps it was Minnie's determination to cherish the child as her own that kept her alive. After the doctor's pessimism, every day of her daughter's life must have felt like a triumph.

By September 1889 Minnie was caring for three small children on a long-term basis and had taken two other babies 'from time to time for weekly payments'. She charged what were in effect standard market rates:[24] from five to eight shillings per week for long-term care, and a lump sum of twenty to fifty pounds for what were loosely termed adoptions. A down-payment of four week's fee (for long-term care) or ten pounds (for an adoption) was usually handed over with the child. Regular monthly payments or the balance of the lump sum were to follow. Such agreements were sometimes verbal and sometimes written, sometimes drawn up by lawyers, sometimes not.

Weekly payments were the preferred option for single or abandoned women who wanted to set themselves up financially before reclaiming their babies. So-called adoptions — which were usually arrangements of dubious legality whereby the adopting parents accepted legal and financial responsibility for the child — were the preferred option for respectable Victorians who wanted to expunge the stain of bastardy from their lives and family trees. Adoptions were also favoured by baby farmers because they came with lump-sum payments and a clear message that the natural parents never wanted to see the child again. Prior to 1895 the rules governing legal adoptions were highly restrictive and few officially sanctioned adoptions actually took place.[25]

By September 1889 Minnie had earned around £23 for the care of five babies for various lengths of time.[26] It was more than she would have earned as a servant or dressmaker,[27] but even with the occasional six shillings a day Charles earned for casual farm work it was barely enough to live on.[28] Also, Minnie was discovering to her cost, at times of crisis men and women desperate to retain their respectability would agree to anything, but getting them to honour their financial agreements later was another matter. By September 1889 she had fallen so far behind with the rent that the Deans and their babies had to move out of their Winton home. Minnie must have been devastated to realise that there was nowhere to go but back to the rough two-roomed shack with a lean-to that Charles had built on the site of the original Larches.

In the coming years the size of the rebuilt Larches was much discussed by the press, and the more it was discussed the smaller it became. In March 1891 it was '24 feet by 16 feet'. By May 1895 it had shrunk to '22 by 12 ft'. Two weeks later it was down to '18ft 10in by 11ft 3in'. The *Otago Witness* described it as:

> . . . an unpainted weatherboard structure. The walls are unpapered and the floor uncarpeted, and in the room at the back . . . the ground can be seen between the rough boards of the flooring. There is very little furniture in the house, and the beds are of a very rough description, the bedding portion of which consists of old bags . . .[29]

The Deans were no sooner back at The Larches when another tragedy befell them. A framed memorial card on the mantlepiece marked the loss: *In loving memory of May Irene Dean, died October 10, 1889, aged six months. To those who mourn her here below this consolation's given: she's from a world of woe relieved, and blooms a rose in heaven.*[30]

The blow of May Irene's death did not deter Minnie from child care. In December 1889 she brought home another long-term child, eight-week-old Ethel Maud Hay:

> I got her from her paternal grandmother. I was to have received a premium of £20 with the child but have only received £10. The balance was to be paid when adoption was completed. My husband refused to sign the papers and the adoption fell through. I afterwards learnt that her father was married. I made enquiries but could gain no information as to whom he had married but went purposely to Oamaru to find out. I learnt that he had not married the child's mother and did not hear a very favourable account of the woman. But I obtained the mother's address and wrote to her. In reply she said she was only a servant — not strong and unable in any way to give anything towards the child's support but advised me to take the child and leave it with its father as she was sure he would be pleased to have her. Now I know that there are not many good stepmothers, and I knew that not one woman in a hundred would be good to her husband's illegitimate child, so I decided to trouble the parents no more but if they tried to take the girl from me that I would appeal to the court.[31]

For about three months the Deans had the use of The Larches free of charge,[32] but it was too good to last. On 1 February 1890, presumably to avoid eviction,

Minnie agreed to purchase the property for £125 on time payment. The following month, perhaps because she knew that The Larches was no place to raise babies, Minnie also took out a purchase option on a seven-roomed house opposite the Winton railway station.

To meet the payments required for both properties she set about lifting her income by taking more children, and in April 1990, with Charles' consent, she adopted ten-year-old Esther Wallis[33] to help with the anticipated influx of babies. Because of Esther's testimony at her trial, Minnie felt no warmth when she wrote of the girl in her last statement:

> As for Esther Wallis. She came to me a girl a little over nine years of age. The day before her arrival a friend told me I would rue it. I little thought how bitterly. She was too old, her nature already formed. She was sullen, deceitful and cunning. She came to me from Christchurch. Her mother brought her to me. She had been living with her grandparents at the north Opawa, although she was in ignorance of the relationship. Her mother paid them for her keep. They were paid by the month and Miss Wallis told me that when the month was due they were there for the money frequently before she herself had got it. They looked upon the child as an outcast and treated her as one. She would be sent into the garden during the fruit season to keep the birds from injuring the fruit and to prevent her picking it her hands were tied behind her back. That treatment she never received from me.[34]

After adopting Esther, Minnie threw herself into taking more babies. In August 1890 she received £30 for one-month-old Cyril Scoular. In October she received the same amount for seventeen-month-old Cecil Guilford and took a long-term baby from Invercargill for £1 6s a month. That brought the total number of people living in the cottage to ten, six of them under three years of age.

Large families in small homes were common in colonial New Zealand. Where natural families were concerned no one gave the matter a thought, but in natural families the children arrived at two-yearly intervals, not all at once.

According to later reports Charles Dean was never happy with his wife's plan to fill the cramped and squalid Larches with babies. Minnie, having spent her childhood in the overcrowded slums of Greenock, probably found his objections unreasonable. She must have realised that coping with her expanding enterprise would not be easy, but her childhood experiences would have taught her that it could be done.

In that miserable cottage, with the clamour of little children ringing in her ears, Minnie's work must have been never-ending. Each day she would have battled with sullen, wet wood and rogue billows of ash, her hands cracked and blistered from cold axe handles and hot iron pots as she struggled to clean and nourish her demanding household. Through the long Southland winter her laundry probably either froze on the line or steamed wetly before the smoky fire. The harsh realities of her life were such that, despite her best intentions, Minnie would have had no time or energy to save money or move house.

The living conditions in The Larches must have put the children at risk from infections, and the stresses in Minnie's life must have put them at risk from physical abuse. But despite the risks it wasn't a bad life for the children; you could even say it was a good life. There is plenty of evidence that they were well cared for, well nourished and well loved. According to Minnie the babies were fed fresh milk and the toddlers had cream twice a day plus meat, bread, soup, rice and maizena. In May 1895 the *Otago Witness* reported:

> The children seemed quite happy and contented. They do not appear to be very well provided with clothing but were strong and healthy looking, and seem to have been well fed . . . Those who have come a good deal in contact with Mrs Dean say that she always appeared to have an affectionate regard for the children in her care . . . All the children who were in her care at the time of her arrest are said to be well mannered, and show signs of having had some religious training.[35]

At night some children slept with Charles in the lean-to. The rest crowded into the bedroom with Minnie — three in her bed, the others in boxes around the floor. Maggie and Esther shared a bed in the kitchen.[36]

By day the world was theirs. A couple of cows, a dog, a horse, some pigs, a few sheep, a clutch of hens — what riches for children; imagine the babies snuggled into the arms of Maggie and Esther, the toddlers holding their hands or trailing along behind. When the cows were milked, the laundry washed and the animals fed, they could search for hen's eggs where thistledown spiralled to the sky or collect dry twigs in the bush. Minnie wrote:

> If they were poorly clad I could not help it. I would have clad them in gold if I had had it. But if poorly clad they were well fed and as happy as children could be. Of the four children in the house they never went to bed a night without putting their little arms about my neck and saying — Good-night, God bless you Mother. Would that I could hear them but once more.[37]

Children were even more important to Minnie than the other great passions in her life, gardening and trains. Children were her greatest constant and her greatest joy. Everything else — the endless backbreaking chores, the lashing ignominy of living in a rough shack and the risk of a police investigation — must have weighed heavily on her spirit.

In theory Minnie was living within the law, but because respectability was so important in Victorian society, and because — with all those children that were not her own in that shabby cottage — Minnie's respectability was fast draining away, she had good reason to fear the police. To save her reputation she needed to transform herself into a respectable lady running a respectable business in a respectable home before the constabulary started asking questions. She arranged to take possession of the big house in Winton on 1 May 1891. Then she embarked on another burst of fund-raising.

One response to her advertisement in Dunedin's *Evening Star* in December 1890 came from the mother of two-year-old Willie Phelan. And Minnie, financial crisis and all, agreed to take him with only the promise of payment. She may have persuaded herself that this was a special case in her otherwise professional business dealings, but Charles was probably less easily convinced. He may have accused her of using poverty as an excuse to indulge her compulsion to collect babies. He may have complained that she was so addicted to collecting babies she just couldn't stop and the whole thing was getting out of hand. And he may have been right. Not that he could do anything about it. All he could do was escape to labouring jobs that took him away a lot, sometimes for weeks at a time.

At least eleven-month-old Florence Smith, whom Minnie received in January 1991, brought with her a regular payment of £1 16s a month:

> I refused to adopt this child as she was deformed and a cripple. Her parents lived in Southland. The woman — a Mrs Jacobs — who had the nursing of her, said that when she had taken the child to the hospital for the Drs to prescribe for her, when they saw the little one they cried shame and told what the child was suffering from, and that she would have to go through an operation before she could walk. I had arranged to take her so there was no help for it but to bring her home with me. The mother met me at the Invercargill Railway station. I showed her the child's legs and repeated what Mrs Jacobs had said. I brought this child home on the 10th January 1891 and since then the mother has seen her twice, once by appointment and once by accident. And the father only saw her once and that by accident. The mother wrote to me urging me to get the operation performed. I appealed to the father but he refused in any way to allow anything toward expenses and further told me that if I got the operation performed that it would be at my own risk. I then got my husband to make splints. I covered the splints with cotton wool and encased them in flannel and strapped them on to her legs, tightening the straps occasionally. She was three years old before she walked but her legs are all but straight now, and [she] is now strong and well.[38]

In early February 1891 five-month-old John Clark added £27 to Minnie's income and a ninth baby to the overcrowded Larches. At that point her total income from caring for thirteen children for varying lengths of time over the previous two years was around £125, which was considerably short of the £240 she would have received if all her adoptions had been finalised and all her regular payments had been made.[39] And not only was Minnie's income smaller than it should have been, instead of managing it prudently she often treated herself to first-class train travel and plants from commercial nurseries. These extravagances were Minnie's escape hatches into a make-believe world of status and affluence. The *Southland Times* of 16 May 1895 reported that Minnie Dean boasted that her roses, chrysanthemum, penstemons and dahlias exceeded in beauty and number the varieties to be found in local nurseries. Only one receipt remains: *7/8/93, T. Abbott, Exeter Nurseries, Papanui Rd, Christchurch — Received from Mrs Dean the sum of £9-4-6 in full payment of a/c rend'd.*[40]

The seeds of Minnie's love of gardening were probably sown by Christopher Basstian at Dunrobin Station, but her love of trains would have taken root at a much younger age. Most Victorians were train-mad, and as the daughter of an engine driver Minnie was probably more so than most. For the price of a second-class ticket she could buy the rhythm, hiss and shriek of the engine, the odour of hot oil and the exhilaration of speed in the sealed security of the carriage, but Minnie needed more. She needed the illusion of a life safely on the rails that came with the soft cushions, deep-buttoned seats and shining brass in first class. A first class ticket from Invercargill to Dunedin cost £1 9s, a second class ticket cost 19s 4d, but Minnie nearly always travelled first class.

By changing trains at Invercargill Minnie could leave Winton at eight-forty in the morning and arrive in Dunedin soon after seven the same evening,[41] but in practice she usually broke long journeys with at least one overnight stop, and stayed for two or three days at her destination. The cost of accommodation added a further burden to Minnie's overstretched budget and ensured that her dream of moving to a bigger house would never become a reality.

Back home, with nine children under the age of four, Minnie must have felt like the old woman who lived in a shoe. Sometimes she escaped to her garden, and sometimes she left Maggie and Esther in charge for a week or more while she clattered up and down the main trunk line, but all too often her trips ended with yet another baby being added to the overcrowded Larches.

Perhaps in her travels Minnie was searching for a special child, one she could truly call her own. Perhaps, in late February 1891, when she was offered another baby girl from birth, she thought she had found her. Charles agreed to an adoption and they named the infant, like her unfortunate predecessor, May Irene Dean.

Chapter XIII

———— ∼ ————

RUNNING DOWNHILL AND GATHERING STEAM

Mr D. Nicol, newsagent on the South Express, couldn't help noticing Mrs Dean's comings and goings. He observed that she usually travelled to Dunedin alone, but returned a few days later with a baby and (as he claimed) 'a much better filled purse than on her northward journey'.[1] There was no doubt she was collecting babies, and he knew what that meant: she was a baby farmer. Baby farmers were heartless women who murdered babies for money. He told the police and they were seized with a mission; they had to rid the colony of this evil. Taking babies for money wasn't a crime, they couldn't arrest Mrs Dean for that, but they were determined to catch her for something.

About twenty policemen were involved in the pursuit of Minnie Dean. With the exception of the Winton Constable — a thirty-eight-year-old Swede by the name of Hans Peter Rasmussen — they were all Irish Catholics from labouring backgrounds.[2]

From the end of February 1891 the police had Mrs Dean firmly in their sights. On 2 March Constable Rasmussen, accompanied by Acting Detective Maddern of Invercargill, paid a preliminary visit to The Larches. 'They were civil to me and I to them . . .' Minnie recalled.[3]

Apparently unconcerned by the police attention, Minnie was off again next day, riding the rails and collecting babies. But this time the police were in hot pursuit:

Police telegrams 3 March 1891:[4]

(1) Mrs Dean . . . . left here by express train today supposed for Dunedin. Constable Green goes as far as Milton & will keep watch on her so far. Should she proceed beyond Milton he will request the guard to watch where she leaves the train.
(2) Mrs Dean left the Express at One Tree Point.
(3) The woman who left Express Train at One Tree Point is not Mrs Dean.

Minnie Dean . . . is about forty-five to fifty years, slender build, medium height, sharp features, pointed nose, prominent chin, one tooth on right front of lower jaw projects very much, has a slight lisp. She wore this morning dark dress, black ulster, dark bonnet and veil. Wears spectacles.

Minnie arrived home a week later with yet another baby (Bertha Currie, aged three weeks). That brought her total of young children to eleven. She kept nine at The Larches and placed two (John Clark and the unnamed infant from Invercargill) with Mrs Dunovan of Winton because, Minnie felt, they needed more care than she herself could provide. Her latest addition also needed extra attention; Bertha Currie had a heavy cold and waist-to-heels nappy rash when Minnie received her, and now she had diarrhoea as well. To make matters worse the second May Irene Dean was also ill. So there was Minnie, just home from a week away and nursing a houseful of sick children when Constable Rasmussen and Acting Detective Maddern again came to call:

> . . . to ask if I would tell the names of the children's parents, the children's names and on what terms I had taken them. This I refused to do. I said that while the children were with me they were mine, they were known by my name and that I had never divulged to anyone who their parents were and that I would not do it. They said that they had not come out of idle curiosity nor on their own account but that the Inspector had sent them, that if I gave them the information it would be confined to them three selves, placed in the safe in the strong room and only used if occasion required for the children's protection as in the event of my death. I again refused to give the information. The police said — you have refused to give us the information but we will find it out for ourselves. It will take time, it may take time, but it will be all the worse for you. I then told them all about the children . . .[5]

Using the information provided, the police checked whether Minnie had insured any children's lives in Invercargill, Dunedin or Oamaru. She never learnt about the insurance investigation, but when a woman demanded the return of her granddaughter and a man wrote upbraiding her for breach of trust, Minnie made some enquiries and discovered:

> . . . that the parents or relatives of the eleven children whose names I had given to the two, Detective Maddren and Constable Rasmussen, had been interviewed by some member of the police to learn if my statement was true. And then I declared that as they had obtained this information from me by fraud they would treasure the next I gave them. It was not the loss of money that I regretted but the proof that I was not to be trusted injured me.[6]

That episode marked the end of Minnie's cooperation with the police. 'They never received truthful information from me again,' she wrote. 'If they had kept faith with me I would have kept faith with them.'[7]

From that day on, whenever the police sought information from Minnie she responded with lies and evasions. She had developed the arts of prevarication and guile through years of concealing the dubious aspects of her past and proclaiming the respectability of her present. In this regard she was really no different from her peers. The Victorian age was an age of hypocrisy. To conform to the nineteenth century ideal of womanly purity, respectable ladies had to hide their bodies, observe a code of silence on sexual issues and practice deceit in matters large and small on a daily basis. Such skills had served Minnie well in the past; she had no reason to believe they would not continue to serve her well in the future.

In fact Minnie was wrong. Because she worked at the crumbling margins of society — where surging undercurrents of shame, fear and complicity eroded the fortifications of respectable Victorian life — her business revealed, rather than concealed, the ugly secrets of her age. She would eventually discover, too late, that the problems ahead were far greater than anything her well-developed powers of deception could ever hope to hide. She certainly tried. There's no denying she tried. In fact it could be argued that she tried too hard, because for Minnie lying was like collecting babies; once she started she just couldn't stop, and before long it all got out of hand.

By late March 1891 the overcrowding and poor hygiene at The Larches was seriously affecting the children's health. Bertha Currie's diarrhoea and nappy rash were improving, but her cold was worse. May Irene Dean was still sick and now John Clark was too. Then at 5 am on Monday 23 March, while a storm raged outside, the worst that could happen, did. Constable Rasmussen reported next day: 'A child 3 months old* died rather suddenly at Mrs Dean's baby farm last night. No doctor in attendance, Have wired Coroner that I desire to know cause of death.'[8]

At the inquest held two days later before Mr C. E. Rawson, SM, (who served the district as both coroner and magistrate) and a six-man jury, no evidence of wrongdoing on Minnie's part was produced: Bertha Currie's life was not insured, the cough mixture seized from The Larches was harmless[9] and since Minnie had made a special trip to Invercargill for medicine and had later called the doctor, she could hardly be accused of neglecting the infant.

Dr Hunter had ignored Mrs Dean's request for a house call because the night was so stormy, but he did perform a post-mortem next day. He reported that the infant was well nourished and showed no signs of violence or neglect. Her stomach contained a large quantity of proper food. He had no reason to

---

* The child was in fact six weeks old.

believe she had been poisoned. (The poison the police had in mind was an opiate, such as could be found in a range of readily available and widely used infant soothing mixtures.)

Minnie and Maggie Cameron were also questioned: How many children were in the house? Where did they sleep? What did they eat? Why were they allowed to paddle about in the mud barefoot? (That question drew a sharp response from Maggie, 'If they went about without boots and stockings in cold weather it was their own fault. They often took them off.') As Minnie complained in her last statement, 'Most of the questions . . . had nothing to do with the public, or with the case.'

The inquest jury accepted Dr Hunter's finding that Bertha Currie had died of inflammation of the heart valves and congestion of the lungs, and added a rider about the unsuitability of the premises and the need for legislation to control baby farming.[10] On Friday 27 March the *Southland Times* carried the headline: INQUEST AT WINTON — A PECULIAR INSTITUTION.

The inquest was reported in newspapers throughout New Zealand and even made its way into the *Yorkshire Weekly Post*. The publicity left Minnie deeply embittered: 'That inquest made me a social outcast, a pariah. The press painted me in as black colours as it was possible for them to paint me . . . I then vowed that I would have no more inquests.'[11]

As far as Constable Rasmussen was concerned Minnie had slipped through his fingers, but he wasn't going to let her get away. He had found no evidence that she was poisoning or starving or neglecting or beating babies, but he was sure she was up to no good. When he heard that Dr Hunter did not expect May Irene Dean and John Clark to live he seized on a new theory: Minnie was trying to kill her charges by exposure.

At 8.00 pm on 29 April Constable Rasmussen and Acting Detective Maddern crept up to The Larches under cover of darkness. For three hours, with cold mud seeping into their boots, they watched shadows moving against flickering candlelight and listened to the fading tapestry of voices. When all was quiet not one child had been put to sleep outdoors. At 11 pm, just to make sure, they spent half an hour checking the outbuildings.[12]

Without even trying Minnie was making the police look foolish. They never told her about their night visit, or about their fruitless insurance enquiries, but they made no secret of their hostility and suspicion towards her and she returned their feelings in full. When they questioned her she replied with falsehoods and fabrications. To escape their attention, and to hide her now-notorious name from potential clients, she advertised under false names. When travelling she avoided the Winton Station (but used whistle stops each side instead). To the police each deception was further evidence of her guilt.

On 9 May 1891 another of the events that Constable Rasmussen anticipated and Minnie feared occurred: the second May Irene Dean died. Rasmussen's report on the death illustrates the suspicion and loathing that prevailed between the police and their quarry:

I have found nothing which would lead me to suspect any foul play in connection with the death, but I have no faith whatever in the woman and she could administer drugs to any of the children without me being able to detect such. The Dr says he has no suspicion of anything unusual having been given the child, but of course cannot say as he has not seen the child of late or immediately prior to its death, he will not give a certificate of death. Mrs Dean came herself and reported the death to me at 8.30 am this day. The manner in which she reported the death or rather the way she spoke to me at first caused a slight suspicion of something being wrong. She kept up a general conversation for fully 1/4 hour before she said anything about the death of the child. At last when she said, and I have to tell you that Irene is dead she died at 5 o'clock this morning, she asked me if I would see the Dr. I replied why should I see the Dr, and she said well if you would see him I won't. I did not tell her that I would see the Dr but she did not go near to Dr . . . She also said if there would be an inquest on the child she would scarcely think it neccessary as the last inquest did not shut the mouths of the people & she did not think another one would. There may be nothing wrong, the death may be from natural causes, as the last exposure which she got by the inquest has considerably damaged her reputation in the way of getting other people's babies, & that may be the reason why she wanted the death kept quiet, but this woman is not by any means truthful.[13]

The Coroner saw no need for an inquest, which must have disappointed Constable Rasmussen, but it did not deter him. He continued his surveillance and, in a stream of opinionated letters and telegrams, reported on her activities throughout 1891.

He presumably maintained his surveillance throughout 1892, and Minnie presumably continued to struggle on: caring for her existing babies, taking in more, avoiding the police when she could and lying to them when she couldn't, tending her garden, riding the rails. We'll never know what really happened because police files for that year have not survived. All we know for sure about 1892 comes from a court case the following year. According to evidence presented in court, in May 1892 Willie Phelan's mother, unable to pay her son's maintenance costs and weary of Minnie's demands, arrived at The Larches to reclaim her child. Minnie refused to hand him over.[14]

The surviving police files for 1893 are more complete. They reveal that on 12 April Constable Rasmussen ordered Mrs Dean to give him details of the seven children then living at The Larches (who were all, he had to admit 'looking well and fairly well clothed'). Six of the children had appeared on his

1891 list (Cyril Scoular, Ethel Maud Hay, Cecil Guilford, Florence Smith, Arthur Wilson and William Phelan). The seventh, John Brookland, was a two-year-old Minnie had accepted eight months earlier.[15]

About five children came and went from The Larches between 1891 and 1893. Their names do not appear on any police list. One of these children was Sydney McKernan. We will hear more of him later.

Five of the children on the 1891 list were absent from the 1893 list. Two of the five (Bertha Currie and the second May Irene Dean) had died and two (Maud Moffett and 'no name') had been removed by relatives. But where was John Clark? Constable Rasmussen attacked the mystery with a will.

Two years earlier he had reported to his inspector on at least five occasions that John Clark was suffering from a severe cold and Dr Hunter did not expect him to live. The most likely explanation for the child's disappearance is that he died, and Minnie buried him secretly to avoid another inquest, but in 1893 neither Minnie nor Constable Rasmussen was prepared to acknowledge that possibility.

As a result of the search for John Clark, Minnie found herself trapped like a hunted animal in the police spotlight.[16] She coped in the only way she knew, with lies and evasions. Constable Rasmussen reported:

> Mrs Dean informed me that this child had been sent home and that she took it part of the way, when she was relieved of it. She promised to adopt this child when the sum of £30 was paid but it appears the money was not paid & the child was sent back. I would respectfully ask that enquiries be made at Strath Taieri with the view to find this Mrs Clark and ascertain if the child reached its destination.

John Clark's mother, Mrs Cockerill, who had not seen her son for more than two years, produced a receipt showing that Minnie had been paid in full. When confronted with this information Minnie became even more evasive: the boy had been adopted ... she would not name the adopting parents ... Mr Macalister had drawn up the deed.

Constable Rasmussen wasted no time in establishing that no adoption application for John Clark had been filed in the Winton court, and the names on the deed drawn up by Mr Macalister had been left blank. Next Sergeant Macdonnell of Invercargill took up the case. 'I shall visit her to see what I can do with her,' he informed his inspector. 'She does not like Constable Rasmussen and will tell him nothing.'

When Minnie ran out of excuses she resorted to defiance. She had consulted lawyers in Invercargill and Dunedin. She knew her rights. She informed the police, with infuriating frequency, that she would tell them nothing until there was a law compelling her to do so.

She also used the legal system to obtain money owing her. In fact Sergeant

Macdonnell's planned visit 'to see what I can do with her' had to wait until Minnie had returned from pursuing two court cases in Invercargill and Dunedin.

In the first case, which was undefended, Michael Phelan, father of Bertha Currie, was ordered to pay burial and cemetery fees of £3 6s 6d for his deceased child. The second, a complicated claim for the maintenance of Willie Phelan (son of Mary Olsen née Phelan and grandson of Michael Phelan), resulted in Minnie being awarded £22 13s. Despite the court decisions no payments were made and Minnie returned to Winton empty-handed.[17]

A few days after her return, Sergeant Macdonnell sought to ingratiate himself. Minnie responded with yet another desperately dishonest explanation for the disappearance of John Clark (who, to complicate the story, was also known as Henry Cockerill). Minnie wrote:

> He was very suave and polished and confined his questions to the business he said he had come on. He began his enquiries by untruthful statements about the boy Henry and I replied in a similar spirit. He said coaxingly, 'You might tell me where he went and who has got him.' I told him the people's name was Thompson and they lived in Christchurch . . .[18]

Sergeant Macdonnell's soothing manner was not entirely wasted on Minnie. Before long she found herself telling him about some of her other children: she did not like John Brookland, his payments had not been kept up and she had no wish to keep him; but she was very fond of Florence Smith, the little girl who used to be a cripple. When he returned to Invercargill the sergeant arranged for John Brookland to be taken into state care, which may have pleased Minnie, but his response to her comments about Florence Smith did not:

> Macdonnell, who called on the lady she had been staying with, wanted to know if she had a child belonging to me staying with her, and asked to see the child. This person was very wroth and although her and I had been friends for years she said that upon no account would she have it known that she had one of my children staying with her, so she sent Flossie home to me at once. I had Sergeant McDonnell to thank for the only unpleasantness that ever existed between this person and myself.[19]

But as long as the whereabouts of John Clark remained a mystery the police were not really concerned about John Brookland or Florence Smith or any of the other children in Minnie's care. In fact they were so preoccupied with the search for John Clark they never noticed that around that time another child, Cyril Scoular, disappeared from The Larches. Cyril was not missed until 1895; we shall deal with the mystery then. After Sergeant Macdonnell's visit the search for John Clark moved to Christchurch where, over a two-week period, all nineteen Mrs John Thompsons residing in the city were interviewed.* None had adopted a child.

'Christchurch' as the supposed destination for John Clark may have popped into Minnie's head because she was about to collect a baby from that city. She left Winton in early August and, having still not received payment for Willie Phelan, took the child as far as Dunedin and left him with his mother before going on to Christchurch.

At ten past nine on the morning of Wednesday 9 August, John Barrett, a boarding house keeper of Christchurch, advised the police that a woman had come to his establishment the previous Saturday and had acquired a baby two days later. According to Mr Barrett the baby had not been washed since it was brought to the house, and had cried all night.

Chief Detective O'Connor, fresh from the search for Mrs John Thomson, rushed to investigate. If this was a baby farming case, he was the man for the job. Minnie fought off his enquiries with more lies, and more evasions:

> She gave me her name as Mrs A. Presnell, & said that she was going to Dunedin, but intended to break the journey at Oamaru, where she would stop one night at the Northern Hotel. She several times refused to answer my questions, & I had to threaten that I would take her & the baby to the Police Station. She then told me that she was the wife of Frederick Presnell, who was formerly a farmer at Clinton, Southland, but now residing with a Mrs King, who kept a boarding house in Albany St Dunedin, & that her husband would meet her at the express, & they would then go to their lodgings, & that she would call on the Inspector of Police at Dunedin, on arrival, & show him the baby, if that would please me. I said, 'No, you will have to satisfy me before you go.' She stated that she had got £25 cash, in gold, to adopt the baby from a Mrs Brown, & did not know who she was, or where she lived. Met her in the street by appointment and took the baby from her. I then told her that I was convinced that she was telling me a lie. That I had reason to believe that she came from near Invercargill, where she kept a baby farm, & that I had a lot of correspondence from Invercargill lately, about a child, which she was supposed to have given to a Mrs John Thompson of Christchurch & that I had reason to believe that her name was Mrs Dean. She then admitted that her name was Dean.[20]

According to the detective the baby was very dirty, 'the clothes evidently not having been changed for some time', and her feeding bottle contained sour, curdled milk.

---

* Sergeant Macdonnell reported that, according to Mrs Dean, a 'Mrs *John* Thomson of Christchurch' had adopted the child.

Chief Detective O'Connor could hardly believe his luck when the cab he called to take Minnie to the police station turned out to be the same one that had taken her to Dr Ovenden's to collect the baby two days earlier. He interviewed the doctor and learnt:

> . . . that a Miss Cameron who had got into trouble, came from the North Island with her mother . . . On the 18th of July last, he confined this girl, at the house of a Mrs Pope, Papanui Rd. It appears that some little time before the confinement, Miss Cameron noticed an advertisement in the Christchurch Press 'Wanted to adopt a baby &c'. She replied & in that way got into communication with a Mrs Milne, who got the baby from Mrs Cameron at Dr Ovenden's house on Monday last & £25. It appears that this Mrs Milne represented that she had no children of her own, & was anxious to get a baby to adopt and when she got the baby, she kissed & cuddled it & appeared to be overjoyed. Mrs Cameron & Mrs Pope called at the Police Station & saw the baby, & declared that they would scarcely know it, there was such a marked difference for the worse in its appearance in two days. They also took possession of the child's clothing & what money the woman had on her, only £7 8s 8d so that Mrs Cameron is still £17 11s 4d out of pocket by the transactions. Mrs Milne, or Dean wanted them to give her sufficient money to pay her fare to Dunedin, but they would not . . . I believe this woman would have killed, or abandoned this child before she got to Dunedin, if it had not been taken from her.[21]

I don't know about you, reader, but I don't like the way this story is developing. Even bearing in mind that the police account is probably exaggerated — after all, Chief Detective O'Connor already believed the worst of Minnie before he met her — and even bearing in mind that the mother, grandmother, midwife and doctor, having been caught dealing with a baby farmer, probably felt they had to join in the chorus of horror in order to save face — even bearing all these things in mind, I'm worried about Minnie. Deceitful, neglectful, improvident Minnie. She lied. Frantically and transparently. She let a large sum of money run through her hands like water. And no matter how many times I read the denials in her last statement* there's no getting away from it — she did neglect that baby in Christchurch. Our Minnie who loved babies. How could she do such a thing? The police thought she was cold-hearted and devious, but maybe she was just panic-stricken and stressed beyond reason. Maybe, after years of clinging to a fragile reality as she struggled through the mire of her life, by 1893 Minnie was finally losing her grip.

The police thought she was a monster, but of course they always thought that, even before they knew her. And once they did get to know her they

---

* Minnie claimed that the baby appeared to be neglected because it had thrush. All the other evidence suggested that the baby had thrush because it was neglected.

invariably brought out the worst in her. Reader, if you examine the evidence, if you read every report still in existence concerning any child, living or dead, who ever passed through Minnie's hands you will find that, apart from that unfortunate Christchurch infant and another baby who may or may not have been smothered, none of Minnie's charges ever showed any sign of ill-treatment or neglect. It's true that she sometimes chastised the children. Corporal punishment was the norm in Victorian families and Minnie admitted to administering it in both sorrow and anger:

> I had a hot passionate temper and have struck a blow when in a passion, both with my tongue and hands, that I have been sorry for directly afterwards, but if I struck or punished a child no one else was ever allowed to do it.[22]

It's also true that she loved children. Her last statement shows that even at her darkest hour her love for the little ones in her care at the time of her arrest (Florence Smith, Arthur Wilson, Ethel Maud Hay and Cecil Guilford) never faltered:

> Since receiving sentence I have had every care and consideration shown me. My bodily and spiritual welfare have been well cared for, but the one yearning wish of my heart has to remain ungratified, I have been refused to be let see the children. The thought and hope of being able to see them only once has sustained me in all my bitter trouble. And surely I have been punished enough without inflicting this worst of all troubles on me. What is to become of them now? Who is to love them and care for them as I have done?[23]

So what went wrong in Christchurch? Perhaps a cumulation of long-term stresses finally began to take their toll. Florence, Arthur, Cecil and Ethel Maud were lucky. Minnie took them early in her child care career, and she took them as much for themselves as for any money they may have brought. Long after their payments ceased she continued to care for them at her own expense. But as the years passed, with those four little ones meeting her maternal needs and her finances in permanent crisis, Minnie appears to have reached a point where, as least as far as some of her more recent and less attractive charges were concerned, she was no longer interested in looking after them for their own sake. What really mattered was the money they brought.

Between ceasing to care and neglect lies a narrow line. It is difficult to escape the conclusion that during a couple of days in Christchurch in August 1893 Minnie lost her balance and stumbled across that line.

Minnie's financial management is also a worry. She spent £17 11s 4d of the £25 she received with baby Cameron in less than two days. We know that £9 4s 6d went to a Papanui plant nursery and about £1 15s went on boots for the children (which the police later returned to the shop). She must have spent smaller amounts on food and local transport, but how she spent the balance remains a mystery.

If the police had not taken her last £7 8s 8d, Minnie would have had just enough to pay for her Christchurch lodgings and a first-class train journey home with one or two overnight stops on the way. Do you see what this means? It means that if the police had not intervened, and if her trip had taken place as planned, Minnie would have arrived home, new baby and all, as penniless as when she left. So what was the point of it all?

After her failure to raise enough money to buy a big house in Winton, Minnie should have realised that her plans to use babies as fund-raising units would never work. In the long term each new baby, even when fully financed, turned out to be more of a liability than an asset. Maybe she kept going because, in the short term, the money that came with each new arrival temporarily alleviated her ongoing cash-flow problems. Maybe she also kept going because taking babies was her life, and she did not have the energy or inclination to change.

With the funds for her return journey confiscated, Minnie was penniless, 400 miles from home. She pawned her mantle to buy a night's lodging. Next day, having nothing else to pawn,* she walked five miles to beg money for a second-class train ticket to Dunedin from Esther Wallis's mother.

On Friday 11 August, Minnie was back in Dunedin, again penniless — and her troubles were far from over. In an attempt to recover the money awarded her by the courts she trudged around the city, first to the lawyer who acted for Willie Phelan's mother, then to the woman herself, then to Bertha Currie's father (whom she failed to find). At the end of the day, without even a few shillings for a night's lodging, she went to 'Mrs M', who had earlier offered her a bed in Dunedin:

> It was after six o'clock at night when I found her out, but received a very cool reception. It had been pouring in torrents for more than an hour before I found their whereabouts and I was really drenched. I asked if she could let me stay that night as I had lost my purse. She said she had no room as she had a visitor staying with her and no spare blankets. She did not ask me to have anything to eat.[24]

Minnie next walked to the home of another acquaintance and waited for her to return from an evening at the theatre. Again her reception was icy ('Mrs J

---

* Which proves that none of her extravagant spending in Christchurch went on pawnable items.

drew her skirts back as if I was an unclean thing'). On learning that Mrs J's hostility was based on stories told her by the police, Minnie walked back to Mrs M's and sat in her yard for the rest of the night, drenched and frozen, disconsolate and defeated.

Next day Minnie's fortunes improved. She obtained some of the money owed her for Willie Phelan, but Willie came back as part of the deal. By the time she arrived home on 16 August, with Willie in tow, Minnie must have been a nervous wreck.

Then only one month later, what do you think she did? On 19 September 1893, Minnie took another baby. But by then the authorities were hard at work to ensure it would be her last.

Minnie's Christchurch visit did not result in a court case,[25] probably because the young mother's parents were 'very respectable people', but the police were in no doubt as to her guilt. To the forces of law and order Minnie and her fellow child minders were just like the Makins — the baby farmers at the centre of the sensational Sydney trial. The Christchurch inspector wrote to his commissioner:

> I think it is possible that the baby taken from this woman by the Chief Detective would never have reached Winton. The probability is that she would have thrown it into the harbour upon the arrival of the train at Dunedin. The train reaches there late at night. Baby farming is increasing rapidly in this Colony and the adoption of children upon premiums — the system pursued by the Makins in Sydney lately — leads directly to the crime of infanticide. From a return lately prepared by the Detectives I find there are no less than twenty baby farms here; places where there are from two to seven babies . . .[26]

That year the flames of official anxiety were fuelled by the Flanagan infanticide case in Christchurch and by the granting of votes to women. To God-fearing men it must have seemed as if hoards of unruly women were conspiring to destroy the sanctity of the family. In September 1893 New Zealand legislators passed the Infant Life Protection Act. It came into force in January 1894.

The Act required people who cared for one or more children under two years of age for more than three consecutive days to register themselves and their homes annually. They also had to provide full details of the children in their care and allow regular inspections of their homes and charges.

One person for whom the Infant Life Protection Act came too late was Mary McKernan. On 2 October 1893 (the day the Act received royal assent) Mary visited The Larches incognito in search of the 'Mrs McKellar' to whom, eighteen months earlier in Dunedin, she had given her two-week-old son Sydney. Six weeks after her first visit she returned to The Larches, identified herself, and asked to see her child. Minnie responded with a torrent of denial and abuse. She insisted that she had never seen Mary McKernan before and had never cared for her child.

In her last statement Minnie repeated her assertion that she had never seen Mary McKernan before October 1893, but she admitted to collecting Sydney from Dunedin in March 1892 and caring for him for some months. Her convoluted explanation for her hostility to Mary contained several sub-plots involving, among other things, the police. (Goodness knows what Constable Rasmussen made of the episode — his version has not survived.) To explain Sydney's disappearance Minnie claimed that he had been adopted, but she refused to say by whom.[27]

When the Infant Life Protection Act came into force eighty-three women in Otago and Southland successfully sought registration under the Act,* but Minnie Dean was not among them. Constable Rasmussen checked The Larches and found one child under the age of two (baby O'Brian, whom Minnie had taken the previous September, just after her traumatic visit to Christchurch). He ordered Mrs Dean to apply for registration but Minnie, convinced that her application would not succeed,[28] set about trying to return the child to one or the other of his parents.

Whenever Rasmussen called, Minnie claimed to be doing her best to be rid of the child but five months later the boy was still there. In June the constable informed her that the law had to take its course. On 9 July 1894 Mrs Dean was charged with a breach of the Infant Life Protection Act. She had no choice but to plead guilty.[29]

Mr C. E. Rawson, SM, was no stranger to Minnie's activities. As coroner at the inquest on Bertha Currie he had called for the very legislation which he was now required to enforce. He heard the evidence, and fined Minnie one penny.

One penny! Constable Rasmussen's rage inflamed the entire New Zealand police force. The Minister of Justice, the Honourable Alfred Jerome Cadman, demanded an explanation.

'I took a great deal of trouble in going fully into the matter and was much puzzled to know what to do,' Mr Rawson explained. He described the letters produced by Minnie: several from the infant's father telling of his efforts to arrange alternative care and begging Minnie to keep the child a little longer, and one from the maternal grandfather (with whom the mother was living) stating: 'There is no use in you coming here. It shall never enter my house.' The magistrate also noted that Minnie had asked Constable Rasmussen to remove the child but he had refused. Mr Rawson felt it unreasonable to expect a woman with no money to return the baby at her own expense:

---

* The overwhelming majority were raising only one or two children, usually the offspring of relatives.

The mother and the father of the infant live in different directions — each 14 miles from Winton on bad roads. Mrs Dean would have to hire a covered conveyance, with a pair of horses and driver, to take the child out with the risk of a fruitless journey . . . She could not leave the child on the door step, most particularly at this time of the year — moreover the child is delicate and requires careful attention. What was she to do?

After due deliberation Mr Rawson ordered Minnie to hire a suitable vehicle and take the child to its mother, and he ordered the infant's father to pay the transport costs. He was pleased to report that the delivery had taken place two days after the court case. 'I am inclined to think that under the above detailed circumstances Mrs Dean did the best that could be expected of her,' he concluded.

While all the fuss was going on, something else happened at The Larches. Despite his frequent visits, and despite his suspicions, Constable Rasmussen missed it. He didn't find out until much later that in March 1894 Willie Phelan disappeared.

By the middle of 1894 four children had vanished from The Larches: John Clark, Sydney McKernan, Cyril Scoular and Willie Phelan. For a long time the only disappearances known to the police were those of John Clark and Sydney McKernan, then early in 1895 they found out about Cyril Scoular.

Colin McLachlan, father of Cyril (or Colin) Scoular, died, unmarried, on 14 January 1895. He left money to relatives and friends, and a house and section in Oamaru to 'Colin Scoular McLachlan born of Helen Scoular of Oamaru'.

Constable Rasmussen did his best, but his efforts to trace Cyril were fruitless. Minnie claimed that the child had been adopted and 'I had pledged the Lord not to reveal where he was'. She said that if Colin McLachlan's trustees wrote to her she would contact Cyril's adoptive parents. But before that option could be pursued Minnie was off on her last, fateful, baby-collecting expedition.

Chapter XIV

────── ∾ ──────

OFF THE RAILS

Once the Infant Life Protection Act was in force, the only way Minnie could stay in the baby business and remain within the law was to act as an agent for registered child minders — advertising for infants, collecting and delivering them and taking a commission for herself in the process. The extent to which she engaged in this practice during 1894 is unclear. The police claimed that she eluded them by taking circuitous routes. Minnie claimed that she 'had not been for a child since the 19 September 1893 when I brought the baby O'Brian home until I went to the Bluff for the child Carter'. Whatever the truth there can be no doubt that by early 1895 Minnie was again collecting babies, and among those babies was Dorothy Edith Carter.

Minnie may have argued, with some justification, that her new round of infant collecting was driven by financial necessity. After her breach of the Infant Life Protection Act the only small children left in her household were two four-year-olds (Ethel Maud Hay and Florence Smith) and two five-year-olds (Cecil Guilford and Arthur Wilson), and she had received no income for any of them for a very long time.*

Her negotiations for baby Carter were conducted through an intermediary — Mrs Izett, proprietor of a Christchurch servants' registry office. Minnie told Mrs Izett that she wanted her train fare paid, plus a fee of £4 10s per quarter for twelve months. Mrs Izett replied that the child's grandmother 'had 14 children, 15 including the little one. She cannot possibly afford to give more than £10, to be paid on the 1st June.' Minnie's need for money may have been great, but her need to ride trains and collect infants was apparently greater still. She agreed to pick up Dorothy Edith Carter from Bluff on 29 April for the ridiculously small sum of £10, and she agreed to wait a whole month before she received even a penny of it.[1]

I'm not sure what Minnie thought she was going to do with Dorothy Edith

---

* She had received nothing for Ethel Maud or Cecil since 1890, nothing for Arthur since 1893 and nothing for Florence since 1894.

Carter and the other new infants she planned to take long term. I don't think she had much idea herself. If she received only £10 with each baby her options were limited. She had never taken a child into her own care for less than £20, did she seriously believe that other carers would be satisfied with £10 minus Minnie's own commission? Her last statement sheds no light; her plans for Dorothy Edith Carter seem vague, and her plans for the other new babies receive no mention at all. To compound the confusion her comments regarding Dorothy Edith could be interpreted either as the sincere writings of an innocent woman or as the smoke screen of a murderess. Reader, you'll just have to study the evidence and draw your own conclusions.

And here we come to the core event in the story of Minnie Dean; the event that took her to the scaffold and made her a legend. At around 8 pm on Thursday 2 May 1895 Dorothy Edith Carter died in Minnie Dean's care on a train between Dipton and Lumsden. Minnie hid the body in her hat box and carried it with her for two days before burying it in her own garden. The question still being asked is this: did Dorothy Edith Carter die by accident or design?

According to Minnie's last statement her intentions were honourable:

> I was simply putting the child out to nurse for a month and I knew of two places at Gore where I could leave her so long as I had the money to pay for her board, and that I had with me. It was not on account of my not wanting to register the house, but because it was too small. I was having an addition put to it, and had written to Broad Small Timber merchants stating what I wanted and asking them to send an estimate of costs, which they did.

This story could be true. On previous occasions Minnie had passed on children in her care to other child minders,[2] and the risk of another prosecution under the Infant Life Protection Act provided her with an added incentive to keep Dorothy Edith away from The Larches. In the context of the times there was nothing unusual in Minnie's plan. The practice of passing around unwanted children was common within the muddled and underfunded commercial infant care system in the colony, even among registered child minders. The entry of a new baby into the system could set off a chain reaction of small children being handed on for ever decreasing sums. It was like musical chairs. If you passed on the baby before the money ran out you were safe, because whatever happened to it after that wasn't your problem. An Auckland policeman charged with enforcing the Act complained:

> ... the greatest trouble encountered is the continual removing from house to house ... I went to a house in Fitzroy Street last week to measure it and found the child was one for which a Mrs Campbell in Vincent Street was registered for, and this child was in the custody of the present person

(Mrs Bland) for over four weeks without either Mrs Campbell or her saying anything about it ... the same with a Mrs Smith living in Newmarket, and the same with a number of other children who appear to have changed nurses two or three times since first registered.[3]

But all the same, Minnie's explanation raises many questions. Her plan to farm out Dorothy Edith Carter seems vague — had she made any prior arrangement with either of the child minders in Gore? What if neither could take the baby? What if they asked more than she could afford? What then? Her plan to extend The Larches also seems ill-considered. How was she going to pay for it? After failing to save any money as a child minder did she really believe she could raise the money she needed as a child minder's agent? And if she did manage to build the extension, did she really believe she could then become a lawfully registered child care worker? Sergeant Rasmussen had given her a copy of the Act, she must have known that anyone with a conviction entered against them was barred from registration.[4]

The police dismissed Minnie's story as a red herring, a clumsy attempt to divert attention from her real aim: premeditated murder. After all, she was a compulsive liar. But the murder scenario seems as badly thought out as its less sinister alternative. What was the motive? Why would she kill baby Carter before receiving any payment for her? Why did she bother to obtain the money needed for the infant's keep in Gore? If she did want to murder the child why didn't she do it somewhere more private than in a railway carriage? Why did she carry the body around for two days? Why didn't she dispose of it somewhere less obvious than in her own garden?

Whatever Minnie's intentions, her muddle-headedness must be cause for concern. She did not think through the details, or contemplate the consequences, of her actions. She was probably not in a fit state to care for babies at all.

This is how it all started. Between January and April 1895, Minnie placed a series of advertisements in eastern South Island newspapers ('A RESPECT-ABLE married woman wants to adopt a child; comfortable home in the country; address 'Childless' *Times* Office'), which brought at least seven replies. One led to the birth of an illegitimate child at The Larches on 6 April. By arriving at the Dean home *in utero* the baby escaped Constable Rasmussen's attention, and the payments Minnie was offered persuaded her to keep the infant in defiance of the law. The arrangements she made to acquire the other six babies were more conventional; she would collect them by train. She arranged to collect baby Carter from Bluff on 30 April, baby Hornsby from Milburn on 3 May, baby Young from Bluff on 9 May, and so on ...

Minnie's travels involving Dorothy Edith Carter took place in two stages.

Going to Bluff was the first stage. Taking baby Carter with her when she went to collect baby Hornsby was the second stage. Here, in chronological order, are the places at which Minnie Dean climbed on and off trains between Monday 29 April and Saturday 4 May 1895: Winton, Invercargill, Clifton, Bluff, Invercargill, Gap Road, Lady Barkly, Dipton, Lumsden, Gore, Milton, Milburn, Clarendon, Milton, Clinton, Gore, Mataura, Invercargill, Winton. The journey may have been convoluted, but it was not entirely unplanned.

Most of Minnie's planning went into figuring out how to obtain money for Dorothy Edith Carter's care in Gore. She decided to use the payment due to her for the new baby at The Larches. She was expecting the money by mail any day, but when she left to catch the morning train for Bluff on Monday 29 April it had still not arrived. Undeterred, she made contingency plans. She decided to break her journey at Invercargill and collect the money in person. But what if the money had already been posted? In that case she would ask the sender for an advance on next month's fee. What if the man refused? Well then, she'd just have to come home for the money before taking baby Carter to Gore.[5] (You don't have to keep track of all these details. They are not in themselves important. I am recounting them simply to underline this point: Minnie's convoluted journey was not as random and unplanned as it seemed.)

Minnie's travel plans were complicated by her arrangement to collect one-month-old Eva Hornsby from Milburn on 3 May. She had agreed to the same paltry sum of £10 for Eva, but at least the money would be handed over with the child. Minnie never indicated what she planned to do with Eva Hornsby. The most charitable explanation is that she intended to leave the infant with a registered baby minder. The least charitable explanation is that she intended to murder her.

Minnie explained her travel plans to her adopted daughter Esther Wallis and to her husband Charles:[*] if she had to return for the money she would be back next day; if not, she would be back at the end of the week. To cover both eventualities she told Esther to meet the evening train from Invercargill on both Tuesday 30 April (at Gap Road — the last stop before Winton), and Saturday 4 May (at Winton Station).

Why Gap Road? Gap Road was two and a half miles from The Larches. Winton Station was closer. So was Lady Barkly (the first stop past Winton). The answer is that by Tuesday evening Minnie expected to have baby Carter with her. She probably didn't want to be seen alighting at Winton Station, or even passing through Winton Station, because Constable Rasmussen usually met the train and she didn't want him to see her with a baby.

But there was no furtiveness in Minnie's arrangements for her return the

---

[*] Maggie Cameron was no longer in the Dean household, having left the previous month to learn dressmaking in Mataura.

following Saturday. She intended to alight openly at Winton, right under Constable Rasmussen's nose. Her arrival plan sheds no light on what she intended to do with babies Carter and Hornsby, but whatever it was she obviously expected it to be done by Saturday evening.

Minnie spent most of Monday 29 April in Invercargill (where she learnt that she would have to return to Winton for the elusive money). Then she stayed the night with relatives at Clifton* (a village on the outskirts of Invercargill), and set off early on Tuesday for the bustling seaport of Bluff.

At about nine o'clock that same morning Mrs Louisa Cox of Christchurch disembarked from the steamer *Manapouri* at Bluff wharf and made her way to Cameron's Private Hotel with her eleven-month-old granddaughter, Dorothy Edith Carter. The petite, fair-skinned baby girl watched the world through bright, dark eyes. Two days earlier she had been whisked from the familiarity of Granny's home to a life of constant change. In Granny's arms she had been rocked across the ocean, seen wheeling seagulls and bobbing boats, felt the steady throb of the steam engine and sudden gusts of salt spray on her face. This very morning she had heard men shouting as the ship docked, seen horses and carts, railway engines, people everywhere. But Granny was there; even in the dimly lit sitting room where the strange lady held her, admired her hands and eyes, spoke her name, Granny was there. She did not cry. She'd had a busy morning. She went to sleep.

Minnie tucked Dorothy Edith down on the sofa and slipped out for half an hour to buy a bottle of laudanum:

> I have always given laudanum to children to keep them quiet when travelling. I could not do without it, for a crying child is such an annoyance to other passengers and there would be comments made and questions asked that I was not always disposed to answer. The child Willie Phelan had a sleeping draught given to him before leaving Dunedin and I bought laudanum from a chemist in Dunedin before going for the child Cecil Guilford.

Before Minnie returned, Dorothy Edith woke to find Granny gone. The hotel keeper's daughter tried to comfort her, but the little girl wept inconsolably. At lunch Minnie gave her six drops of laudanum, 'thinking it would make her dozy and sleepy but it had no effect on her whatever and from the time I left the Bluff till I reached Gap Road I do not think I sat down not ten minutes'. Back at The Larches, Dorothy Edith was fed, changed and put to bed, but still she cried. Only when Minnie gave her another dose of laudanum did she sleep. Next day, though Minnie cuddled her and the little children tried to make her laugh, she continued to fret.

---

* Probably at the home of Granny Kelly's married son.

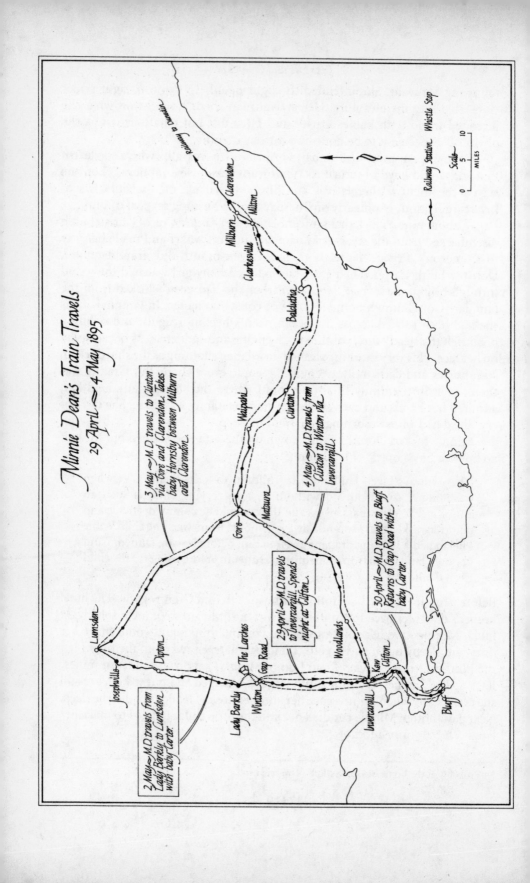

Minnie Dean's Train Travels
29 April — 4 May 1895

3 May — M.D travels to Clinton
via Gore and Clarendon. Takes
baby Hornsby between Milburn
and Clarendon.

4 May — M.D travels from
Clinton to Winton via
Invercargill.

30 April — M.D travels to Bluff
Returns to Gap Road with
baby Carter.

29 April — M.D travels
to Invercargill. Spends
night at Clifton.

2 May — M.D travels from
Lady Barkly to Lumsden
with baby Carter.

⊙—•— Railway Station   •—• Whistle Stop

Scale
0   5   10
MILES

Railway to Dunedin

Clarendon
Milburn
Milton
Clarkesville
Balclutha
Clinton
Waipahi
Matbun
Gore
Lumsden
Josephville
Dipton
The Laches
Lady Barkly
Winton
Gap Road
Woodlands
Clifton
Kew
Invercargill
Bluff

After two nights at The Larches Minnie and Dorothy Edith set off for Gore from Lady Barkly on the morning train. In theory Minnie had a choice of routes. She could travel to Gore via Lumsden (by catching the northbound train) or via Invercargill (by catching the southbound train) — nearly every day trains ran through Winton, both morning and evening, in both directions. She probably chose the less populous Lumsden route in order to avoid being seen with a baby in Winton or Invercargill.

In her purse Minnie carried the long-awaited money, her spectacles, a handkerchief and three pieces of bread and butter for the baby. In an oval tin hat box she carried some larger items: a pair of parcel straps, a piece of oil cloth to protect her dress, clothes and napkins for the baby and the March issue of the *Family Reader*. To ensure a peaceful journey she gave Dorothy Edith a dose of laudanum when she woke and another before they left the house. She did not take the laudanum with her, but with the child well-sedated what could go wrong?

As it happened, things started to go wrong straight away. Minnie learnt to her dismay that the connecting train from Lumsden to Gore did not run on Thursdays. She would have to spend the night in Lumsden and go on to Gore next day. And because of the delay she would miss her Saturday morning appointment to pick up Eva Hornsby at Milburn.

A little over an hour after leaving Winton, Minnie and Dorothy Edith alighted at Dipton. 'When I got off at Dipton I was undecided whether to go on to Lumsden by the [northbound] evening train or return to Winton [by the southbound evening train],' Minnie explained in her last statement. Her final decision was determined by another vagary of the railway timetable. 'If I returned to Winton I would have to go on to Invercargill that night, as there was no down train to Winton [and Invercargill] on Friday morning. I decided to go on to Lumsden.'

Minnie and Dorothy Edith spent the day in a private parlour of the Dipton Railway Hotel. By then the large amount of laudanum fed to the baby would have been taking its toll. The infant probably began to pass in and out of consciousness. Minnie told the hotel keeper that the child was sick. She didn't leave the room all day. She even took her meals in there. When a servant offered to mind the infant while Minnie went to the dining room she said, 'No, thank you, I can't leave the baby'. The child certainly sounded ill. The hotel folk heard her crying on and off all day. Not loudly. More of a whine really. A quiet sort of whine.

At about seven thirty Minnie and Dorothy Edith left to catch the evening train for Lumsden. This is Minnie's account of what happened next:

When I got on the train I laid the child down on the cushions. She was asleep. After giving my ticket to the guard I took off my cloak and put it around the child and it was not until we passed Josephville that I saw that the child was dead. What to do I did not know and think for a time I was bereft of reason. I know that it was not until the train stopped that I put her in the box and I lost no time in getting to the hotel and up stairs to the bedroom, when I at once took the child out of the box and no sleep visited my eyes that night.[6]

Whatever the circumstances of the infant's death, it is hard to imagine anything in Minnie's life up to that point that could have prepared her for the nerve-fraying horror of finding herself alone in a hotel room with a dead baby. Next morning, in what seems like a mindless survival response, she stuffed Dorothy Edith's little body back into the hat box, pulled the lid down tight, padlocked it shut and tied it with string. Then she wrapped the baby clothes in Dorothy Edith's shawl, tied the bundle together with parcel straps and set off for the railway station with her hat box, purse and parcel as if nothing had happened.

Before she left Lumsden, Minnie telegramed Mrs Hornsby (Passenger, South Express, c/- Railway Station, Milburn) explaining that she could not keep her morning appointment. She asked Mrs Hornsby to wait at Milburn for her arrival on the afternoon train. Then, as she rattled across the Waimea Plains, no doubt struggling to think about something other than the contents of her hat box, Minnie realised that her unscheduled stops at Dipton and Lumsden, and her telegram to Mrs Hornsby, had used up almost all her money. To make her funds last until she received the £10 less expenses that she had been promised with Eva Hornsby, Minnie changed to second class from Gore to Milton, and then transferred back to first class for her meeting with Mrs Hornsby.

Minnie's presence on the train from Gore did not go unnoticed by long-time railway newsagent, Mr Nicol. Each morning Mr Nicol caught the south-bound express from Dunedin to Waipahi, and each afternoon he caught the northbound express back again. No one knew the express passengers like Mr Nicol. He knew their names. He knew where they lived. He knew when and where they got on, when and where they got off, and why. And if he didn't know, he made it his business to find out. Four years earlier he had alerted the police to the activities of the notorious Minnie Dean, and when he boarded the train at Waipahi on Friday 3 May there she was, in the second-class carriage bound for Milton. Up to no good he was sure.

On his southbound journey that morning Mr Nicol had helped the Milburn station master deliver a telegram to a passenger named Hornsby. After reading the message Mrs Hornsby had left the train carrying a baby. When he discovered Mrs Dean on the northbound train it occurred to the suspicious Mr Nicol that the journeys of Mesdames Hornsby and Dean may have been somehow connected. He checked at Milton. Ah ha! Mrs Dean bought a first-class ticket to Milburn. (She also left her hat box in the station master's room, but that detail escaped Mr Nicol's vigilance.) He kept a sharp lookout as the train drew into Milburn. Ah ha! There was Mrs Hornsby waiting on the platform with the baby. Next, sure enough, there she was with Mrs Dean in the first-class carriage. He told the guard all about it. Wicked Mrs Dean is at it again, he said (or something to that effect). You mark my words, he said (or some equally emphatic turn of phrase, because he was very sure of himself), she'll get off at Waihola with that baby and wait for the late train to Clinton.

Minnie achieved a minor victory over the inquisitive Mr Nicol by alighting at Clarendon on the side of the train away from the platform. He didn't realise she had gone until the express drew into Waihola. He noted that Mrs Hornsby was still aboard though, and what's more . . . *she no longer had the baby*!

Dusk fell during Minnie's hour-long wait in the cold, lonely, Clarendon railway shed. This is her account of what happened there:

> I went into the shelter shed when the child started crying and cried bitterly for a time. I tried to get her to suck the teat. I then took the teat off the bottle and drew the milk up the tube to find that the milk was ice cold. If Mrs Hornsby had been near me then, she would not have felt at all flattered, as I would have told her my opinion of her. I thought the least she could have done was to have had a warm bottle for the child. She knew how far I had to travel with her that night before I could get a warm drink for her. After the child stopped crying I laid her on the bench in the shed, spread the pink shawl on the ground, placed the two paper parcels [of clothes for babies Carter and Hornsby] in the shawl to make them into one parcel. I was on my knees doing this when I saw the baby reeling over. I made a spring to catch her but was too late. The child fell to the ground and never moved again.[7]

Reader, are you as uneasy as I am about this story? One-month-old babies don't roll. And even if little Eva did roll, falling off a low bench would be unlikely to kill her. So how did Eva Hornsby die? Minnie indicated that the infant cried long and hard, and that Minnie herself became angry when she found that the milk was cold. These admissions are a worry. Experts on child abuse say that when a crying baby dies at the hands of an angry care giver the excuse is nearly always the same: 'My baby had a fall.' This story of Minnie's sounds like some of her other explanations — part wish-fulfilment fantasy, part coded admission of the truth. Later in the month an inquest will be held into the death of Eva Hornsby. We'll look at the evidence again then.

Minnie didn't say what she did with Eva's body, but with her hat box back at Milton there is only one thing she could have done — wrapped the little corpse in the shawl parcel and tied it up with travel straps. It must have been a suspicious-looking parcel. It must have felt suspicious too. When the train arrived and Minnie settled herself into first class she was probably glad to have the carriage to herself.

At Milton she retrieved the hat box containing the body of Dorothy Edith Carter from the station master's room. This is what I think happened next. Between Milton and Clinton, after the guard had passed through, Minnie opened the hat box and packed the body of Eva Hornsby in with the body of Dorothy Edith Carter — there was room for both inside.[8] Then she closed the lid firmly, padlocked it shut and tied it with string. Next she rewrapped the shawl parcel and secured it with travel straps. She would have had plenty of time to do those things during the three-hour journey from Milton to Clinton.

At the boarding house in Clinton where Minnie spent the night, she left a shawl parcel tied with travel straps on the dining room side table while she had her tea. Surely she wouldn't have done that if the parcel contained a dead baby? I don't think even Minnie, confused and exhausted as she undoubtedly was, would have done that.

Next morning, after she had retrieved her hat box from where she'd left it at Clinton station, Minnie continued her journey. She probably wanted to rush straight home, but the railway timetable wouldn't let her. So when she reached Mataura she left her shawl parcel and hat box at the station and went to the Mataura Hotel for breakfast. Despite her troubles she couldn't help admiring the flowers on the dining table and asking for cuttings. Mrs Cameron, wife of the hotelier, instructed the hotel gardener to make up a parcel of marguerites, pansies, Canterbury bells, Muscovy roses and carnations for her guest.

Then Minnie (compulsive baby collector, compulsive train rider, compulsive gardener, compulsive liar, compulsive spender) found herself with a whole morning to fill in and the remains of Mrs Hornsby's £10 burning a hole in her purse — so she went shopping. She bought dress lengths for herself and Esther, a shirt for Charles and two yards of American cloth for a valise. After lunch she caught the express to Invercargill, transferred to the late train to Winton and arrived home as planned just after six o'clock on Saturday evening.

That same Saturday, further up the main trunk line, Mr Nicol the newsmongering newsagent was pursuing the case of the disappearing baby farmer. Not being one to keep his suspicions to himself, he raised the subject with the guard who had been on the early train from Clinton to Invercargill.

'So you had Mrs Dean on the train this morning with a baby?' he said. (His very words, as recorded by his friend Daniel Clark from Waipahi.)

'She had no baby,' said the guard.

'No baby, that's very strange,' said Mr Nichol.

He told the Clinton policeman of his suspicions but (as Daniel Clark put it) that functionary did not appear to be much impressed. The Clinton policeman probably thought that Mr Nicol was a tiresome busybody. So what if Mrs Dean received a baby at Milburn? So what if she no longer had it at Clinton? At least she wasn't keeping it in defiance of the Infant Life Protection Act. Mr Nicol, undeterred by the rebuff, made his point more strongly when the northbound express reached Milton. He urged Constable King to trace Mrs Hornsby and find out what had become of the baby. And Constable King took up the challenge.

That evening Minnie alighted at Winton with a handbag, a shawl parcel containing baby clothes, a brown paper parcel containing fabrics, a newspaper parcel containing plants and a hat box containing two dead babies. On Minnie's instructions Esther took the shawl parcel and the brown paper parcel to the Winton butcher with a message that Mr Dean would call for them later. (Surely Minnie wouldn't have done that if the shawl parcel contained a dead baby. She *must* have put both bodies into the hat box somewhere along her journey.)

Minnie and Esther walked home along the railway line, sharing the weight of the heavy hat box between them. Just past the cemetery they climbed over a fence and headed along a rough track through a paddock to The Larches. They were almost home when Minnie told Esther that the hat box was too heavy to take any further. Leave it in the rushes until morning, she said. It's full of bulbs. Mr Dean won't like the mess.

Back at The Larches, Minnie asked Charles to pick up the parcels from the butcher. Charles asked Minnie where the hat box was. Minnie said it was in the garden. She told Charles, as she had told Esther, that it contained bulbs given her by Mrs Cameron of Mataura.

Next day Minnie sent Esther to retrieve the heavy hat box, and later, when no one was around, she took out the bodies of Dorothy Edith Carter and Eva Hornsby and buried them in her flower garden. Dorothy Edith had the old oil cloth wrapped around her; Eva was totally bare.

Minnie probably tried not to think about what had happened, but she was haunted by the words of an old Scottish ballad, 'The Four Marys'. The title refers to four women, all named Mary, who accompanied Mary Queen of Scots to France. One of the Marys, Mary Hamilton, tried to conceal the birth of her illegitimate child and was hanged for murder. During Minnie's childhood 'The Four Marys' was one of Scotland's most popular folk songs. The kirk fathers would have seen it as a warning to sinners, but women probably valued it for a more subversive reason: in nineteenth-century Scotland respectable women could not speak openly of their secret shames — their banished daughters, their lost sisters, their murdered or abandoned bairns — so they sang about them instead. The great popularity of 'The Four Marys' suggests that in their hearts Scottish women transformed Mary Hamilton into Everywoman, and when they sang her story they sang their own. At The Larches, Minnie wrote down all the words of the troubling ballad that she could remember:[9]

> Little did my mother think,
> The day she cradled me,
> What land I was to travel in,
> Or what death I should die.
>
> Oh that my father had ne'er on me smiled;
> Oh that my mother had ne'er to me sung;
> Oh that my cradle had never been rocked,
> But that I had died when I was young.
>
> Oh that my grave it were my bed;
> My blankets were my winding sheet;
> The clocks* and the worms my bedfellows,
> And oh sae sound as I should sleep.

Constable King spent all Sunday 5 May investigating the newsagent's claims. From the Milburn station master he learnt the contents of Mrs Dean's telegram to Mrs Hornsby. From Mrs Dryden, whom Mrs Hornsby had visited between trains, he learnt Mrs Hornsby's address. From the guard on Friday's late southbound train, he learnt that a woman answering Mrs Dean's description had joined the train at Clarendon, without a baby, and had stayed the night at Clinton before taking the first train to Gore next day. He passed on the news to his colleagues in Dunedin and Invercargill, and ventured the opinion that the notorious Mrs Dean had done away with the missing infant.

By Thursday 9 May the police were ready to confront Mrs Dean. Detective McGrath of Dunedin brought Mrs Hornsby to Winton and then proceeded to The Larches with Detective Herbert of Invercargill and Constable Rasmussen. When three policemen arrived on her doorstep Minnie sent Esther away with the little children and faced them alone.

According to Detective McGrath the interrogation took place in stilted police-speak:

> I said, 'I have come from Dunedin to inquire of you about a baby; we have reason to believe you took possession of a baby at Milburn on the 3rd. inst. Is that so?' She replied, 'No, I took possession of no baby on the 3rd. inst.'

---

* Woodlice or slaters.

Opposite: *The telegram from Constable King (of Milton) that led to Minnie Dean's arrest.*

National Archives, Wellington

Inspr of Police

TO

A Woman named Hornsby
or Hormsly — came to
Milburn by train on
friday last — & returned
by evening train she
brought a baby to
hand over to a
Mrs Dean who returned

TO

by South train same evening
without a baby If Mrs
Hornsby did not bring back
the baby Its probably done
away with which I suspect
Mrs Hornsby said she lives
at Kaikora & her children
goes to school there and
the mother of this child
is in Dunedin Hospital &

TO

She was handing it over
to its grandmother who is
no other than the notorious
Baby farmer from near Invercargill
Mrs Dean is well known
to southland police

Thos King

In the sparring that followed, Minnie denied corresponding with Mrs Hornsby, denied visiting Milburn and denied taking a baby at Milburn. In a devious sort of way her claims were true: she did not correspond with Mrs Hornsby (but with someone who signed herself 'A. B. C.'), she did not visit Milburn township (but only the railway station) and she did not complete her arrangements for taking the baby at Milburn (but on a train between Milburn and Clarendon). Detective Herbert saw through the smokescreen:

'Did you receive any baby this month between Invercargill and Dunedin,' he asked.

'I did,' said Mrs Dean. But when pressed to say where, when and from whom, she refused to answer.

While Detectives McGrath and Herbert were questioning Minnie, Constable Rasmussen returned to Winton and brought Mrs Hornsby back to The Larches.

'That is the woman,' Mrs Hornsby confirmed, which Detective McGrath immediately translated into police-speak: 'Is that the woman to whom you gave the baby on the 3rd inst.?' Mrs Hornsby said 'Yes,' Mrs Dean said, 'No, you gave me no baby,' and though he had no evidence that Eva Hornsby had been murdered by Minnie Dean or anyone else, Detective McGrath decided it was time to act.

'I now arrest you for murdering Eva Hornsby on or about the 3rd May, 1895, at or near Waihola,' he said.

As the police were leaving with Minnie, Charles Dean arrived home.

'I am arrested,' she told him.

'When will you be home?' he asked, bewildered. 'Today or tomorrow?'

Minnie Dean (twenty-eight) at the time of her marriage in 1872.
New Zealand Graphic

Dee Street, Invercargill, early twentieth century.
Muir & Moodie, Hocken Library

Bluff, early twentieth century.
Hocken Library

The Larches (note the white crosses — two near the bottom mark the site of infants' bodies; one about 2 centimetres from the bottom on the left-hand side marks site of skeleton).
Hocken Library

Police search of Minnie Dean's garden.
New Zealand Graphic

Milton Railway Station, 1899.
J. Dangerfield

Lumsden Railway Station, early twentieth century.
Southland Museum

Winton Railway Station, early 1890s.
J. Dangerfield

Milton Railway Station, 1899.
J. Dangerfield

Clinton Railway Station, late nineteenth century.
J. Dangerfield

Invercargill Railway Station (middle left) and gaol (top right),
late nineteenth century.
Southland Museum

Children taken from The Larches after Minnie Dean's arrest.
From left: Ethel Maud Hay, Florence Smith, Esther Wallis with
'Baby Gray', Cecil Guilford, Arthur Wilson.
Invercargill Public Library

Mr A. C. Hanlon.
Otago District Law Society

Mr Justice Joshua Strange Williams.
Hocken Library

Minnie Dean leaving Milton Court House.
New Zealand Graphic

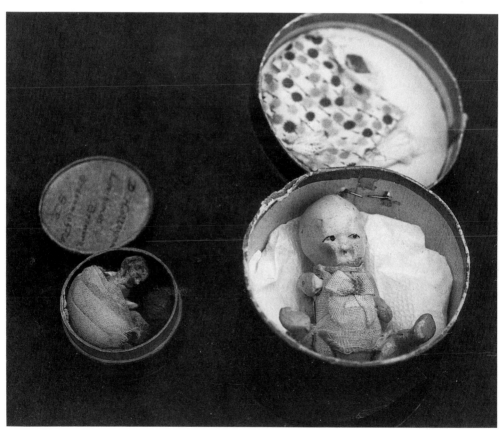

*Dolls in miniature hatboxes said to have been sold as souvenirs
outside the courtroom during Minnie Dean's trial.*
McCleery, Invercargill

Chapter XV

———— ~ ————

LOADING THE SCALES OF JUSTICE

A brief notice appeared in the *Southland Times* on Friday 10 May 1895:

> CHARGE OF INFANTICIDE — Minnie Dean was arrested yesterday at her home, The Larches, East Winton, on a charge of having, on or about the third inst., murdered a female child named Eva Hornsby. She was brought before Messrs Keith and Gilmour, J.P.s, and remanded to the 16th inst., to appear at Milton.

Next day there was more. 'What are they saying about me in the paper?' Minnie asked Detective McGrath on the train to Dunedin. 'That woman is giving me terrible looks.' He refused to tell her about the account of her travels and transactions involving Eva Hornsby (which could only have been supplied to the press by the police) but Minnie continued to worry. 'Are they bringing up old matters or are they making new discoveries?' she asked.[1]

They were indeed making new discoveries. That very morning two groups of policemen had been dispatched to search for the body of Eva Hornsby, one to Clarendon, the other to The Larches.

At the Dean home the police began by digging a few exploratory holes in Charles's vegetable patch, then they turned their attention to the rough swampy bush beyond the shelterbelt of fir trees surrounding the house and garden. It was heavy going; so much mud, so many deep boggy holes, so many tree roots. Shortly before noon they assembled at the front door of The Larches to assess the situation. The bush seemed the most likely place. Unappealing as the idea was, they could see no alternative but to continue searching the bush. Detective Herbert drew a coin from his pocket and promised it to the first man who found a baby.

As they dispersed, Constable Barrett cast his eyes over Minnie's neat flower beds. About sixty feet from the front door he noticed what looked like a bunch of cut flowers (marguerites, pansies, Canterbury bells, Muscovy roses, carnations) pressed into the top of a dark patch of soil. He tested the ground with his spade — the earth seemed unusually free. He pushed his spade deeper

[129]

— he struck something solid. He dug carefully until he came to the foot of a baby. Then, as he and his colleagues cleared away the soil by hand, they were astonished to find not one, but two, freshly buried little corpses. Charles Dean was immediately arrested. 'My God,' he said, staring at the dead babies laid out on the ground before him. 'I suppose I'll be brought into this. I know nothing about it.'

That weekend Alfred Charles Hanlon, the Dunedin barrister engaged by Josiah Hanan, Minnie's Invercargill counsel, visited his client in the Dunedin gaol. He was struck by her self-control, which faltered only briefly when he told her about the police discoveries. 'She was wearing an apron, and I noticed her pluck agitatedly at the hem of it with the thumb and two fingers,' Hanlon recalled. 'The momentary weakness passed almost as quickly as it came, and I do not think it ever recurred.'[2]

Monday's headlines ('STARTLING DISCLOSURES', 'GRUESOME DIS-COVERIES AT WINTON'), and the long columns of salacious details that accompanied them, inflamed the nation. It was as if every family that had ever lost a child — whether through illness, accident or neglect, whether through death or adoption — was convulsed by spasms of recognition and guilt. Angrily they tore at their own gnawing secrets and flung them in a frenzy of rage and relief at the monstrous baby farmer. Then, intoxicated by their new-found purity, they howled for revenge.

Lurid stories about the Deans poured off the colony's presses. It was reported that Charles met Minnie at the station and carried home a large parcel, commenting to a bystander, 'My wife's got a bargain this time.' It was reported that just as the police were arriving to search The Larches, Charles rode off with a sack 'containing something' on the saddle in front of him. And so on. Such stories were always prejudicial and usually factually wrong as well. Concepts like 'confidentiality', 'natural justice' and 'the right to a fair trial' were not unknown in nineteenth-century New Zealand, but they tended to be applied more rigorously when the accused was a person of power and influence. It is instructive to compare the quality of mercy, both strained and restrained, that trickled down through the New Zealand justice system to Minnie Dean, with that showered on a well-bred, well-connected young man by the name of Thomas Hall.[3]

§ *A note concerning Thomas Hall*

English-born Thomas Hall was the handsome, charming nephew of New Zealand's leading nineteenth-century conservative politician, Sir John Hall. As a youth he managed one of his uncle's sheep stations. In the early 1880s, after a period as a bank manager in Timaru, he went into business as a land and stock agent. 'He talked well, dressed well, shot well, danced well, was ready

for any amusing enterprise, always had a good horse and knew how to sit it.'[4]
Like Minnie Dean, Thomas Hall was accused of murder.

Though seemingly prosperous, by the mid-1880s Hall was heavily in debt.
On 19 May 1885 he borrowed Headland's *Action of Medicines* from a Timaru
bookseller. He said he wanted information on antimony. A few weeks later
he bought from the same bookseller the medico-legal textbook, *Taylor on
Poisons*. Between those two events he married Kitty Espie, stepdaughter of the
reputedly wealthy Captain Cain, a former mayor of Timaru. Two months after
the wedding, Hall arranged for his wife to leave everything to him in her will.
The following month he took out two life insurance policies in her name. That
December, Captain Cain, cheered by the news of his stepdaughter's pregnancy,
prepared a deed that left most of his cash and property to her in the event of
his death. Then his final painful illness began.

Until his death in January 1886, Thomas Hall was in almost constant
attendance at his father-in-law's bedside.

Soon after the old man's death the Halls and their live-in companion
Margaret Houston moved into Cain's large home. In June, Kitty gave birth to
a son. A few weeks later she too fell ill. Despite her husband's constant attention
she became steadily worse. Around the same time rumours of Tom Hall's
financial troubles began sweeping the town. Extensive forgeries were
mentioned. Mrs Hall's doctor, suspecting poison, sent specimens of his
patient's urine, vomit and drinking water to Professor Black of Dunedin for
analysis. They all contained toxic levels of antimony. On 16 August 1886
Thomas Hall and Margaret Houston were arrested and charged with the
attempted murder of Mrs Hall. The *Timaru Herald* was aghast:

> Hall has been so long known in South Canterbury, where his family
> have taken so prominent a place for many years, that the report was
> not generally believed, but proved to be only too true ... We may
> state that widespread sympathy is felt for the parents of the male
> prisoner, who have, for so many years now been residents of Timaru and
> district; have always been very highly respected, and have earned the good
> wishes of all classes during a residence in South Canterbury over thirty
> years.[5]

Before long the authorities began to wonder about the death of Hall's father-
in-law. One month after Hall's arrest Captain Cain's body was exhumed. It too
was found to contain high levels of antimony, but, in the interests of justice,
that incriminating finding was not made public until after the October trial of
Hall and Houston for the attempted murder of Mrs Hall. In this and many
other ways Thomas Hall enjoyed a more gentle justice than that dealt to
Minnie Dean. We shall hear more of his experiences anon.

§ *The story of Minnie Dean resumes*

After Minnie's arrest, Maggie Cameron returned to The Larches. After Charles's arrest she and Esther looked after the little children while the nation worked itself into a frenzy over the maltreatment of Mrs Dean's charges. Then on Monday 13 May, when the police returned for their third day of digging and the usual crowd of onlookers gathered to watch, a constable noticed the little children clinging to the skirts of one of Minnie's neighbours. 'Mother not coming back any more,' they cried. 'Can we go home with you?'[6] But the police took them to Invercargill and placed them in a Charitable Aid Board home instead.[7]

Tuesday's papers told of the discovery of the skeleton of a four-year-old child at The Larches. '. . . it is possible, even expected, that other bodies may be unearthed . . .' the *Southland Times* reported breathlessly, and added, stating the obvious, 'The terrible charges against the woman have caused intense excitement in the district, and indeed, a profound sensation throughout the colony.'

Wednesday's papers reported that inquests into the two infant bodies had been opened and adjourned. The members of both coroners' juries were named. To late-twentieth-century readers such information may seem of little import. In New Zealand coroner's juries were abolished in 1951, and anyway, inquests just determine the cause of death, don't they? Surely, even back in the 1890s, when someone was charged with murder the key people were the magistrate (who decided whether there was a case to answer), the grand jury (a body that, until it was abolished in 1961, reconsidered the evidence and either threw out the case or passed it on to trial) and the judge and common jury of the Supreme Court (who decided on the guilt or innocence of the accused person). Not so. Those men may have been powerful in theory, but in practice the men that comprised the coroners' juries were the most powerful of all.

§ *A note concerning nineteenth-century coroners' inquests*

From medieval times coroners have investigated violent and unnatural deaths. Nineteenth-century coroners were charged with enquiring into 'the manner of death of a person who is slain or drowned or who dies suddenly or in prison or while detained in a lunatic asylum'.[8] Twentieth-century descriptions of the coroner's role are similar in wording, but over the intervening decades interpretations of the phrase 'manner of death' have changed dramatically. Nowadays New Zealand coroners determine the cause of death in medical terms and make recommendations concerning the health and safety issues involved. They do not apportion individual blame. As the handbook accompanying the 1951 Coroners Act states:

... it is contrary to natural justice to condemn a person in proceedings
to which he is not a party and in which his conduct is not in issue ...
[The coroner] is concerned solely with the cause of death.[9]

But back in the nineteenth century determining the 'manner of death' also
meant determining whether a crime had been committed. An 1895 handbook
for Justices of the Peace (who could also act as coroners) even supplied a
sample murder verdict for inquest juries:

That one A.B. of [description] on the ... day of ... one thousand ... at
... hour in the night of the same day, at ... aforesaid, in and upon the
aforesaid C.D., then and there did [stating the facts] of which said mortal
wound to aforesaid C.D. then and there instantly died: and so the said
A.B. then and there feloniously killed and murdered the said C.D.
against the peace of our said Lady the Queen her crown and dignity.[10]

To their credit, some Victorians were concerned that finding a person guilty
of murder before he or she had been tried was a breach of natural justice. At
least two murder inquest juries prior to the Dean case (the Hall case in Timaru
in 1886 and the Chemis case in Wellington in 1889) declined to name the person
believed responsible on the grounds that to do so would prejudice the right of
the suspect to a fair trial.

Prior to the passage of New Zealand's 1893 Criminal Code, if a person was
found guilty of murder at a coroner's inquest no further preliminary court
hearing was required; the person named as murderer was simply sent straight
to trial in the Supreme Court. With the introduction of the Criminal Code,
coroners lost this awesome power. After 1893, whenever an inquest jury
identified a murderer, all the coroner could do was issue an arrest warrant (if
the accused person was free) or a 'detainer' (if the accused person was already
in gaol). Then the prisoner had to go through the normal court procedure:
magisterial inquiry, grand jury, Supreme Court trial.

In theory the 1893 Criminal Code reduced the power of inquest juries. But
they were still expected to determine culpability and to name those
responsible; they were still expected to announce their verdict prior to the
accused person's trial, and their inquests were still open to the public and
widely reported in the press. So in practice inquest juries remained essentially
as powerful as ever.

§ *The story of Minnie Dean resumes*

In the early 1890s there were usually two or three inquests per year in
Invercargill and most of them involved accidents. Until the Dean case hit the
headlines there hadn't been an inquest involving suspected murder in town
since a madwoman drowned her toddler under the wharf back in 1893. On
Tuesday 15 May 1895, readers of the *Southland Times* would have perused the

names of the men appointed to the coroner's juries in the Dean case with riveted attention and been left in no doubt that these were the two most important inquests ever to be held in Invercargill.[11]

The jury for the Eva Hornsby inquest was the first to be sworn. It was the important one. Minnie Dean had been arrested for the murder of Eva Hornsby and those six good and lawful men would be the first to hear the evidence and pronounce on her guilt. The second jury was important too, but at that stage the police did not know who the second child was or when, where or how she had died. (But of course, as with Eva Hornsby, they suspected murder.)

As befitted the importance of the occasion, the man sworn in as foreman for the Eva Hornsby inquest was James Walker Bain. During his thirty-five years in Invercargill, Mr Bain had owned both the *Southland News* and the *Southland Times*. He had been president of the Southland Building Society since its inception in 1869. He had served his community as borough councillor, mayor and member of the House of Representatives. When he died in 1899 the *Southland Times* observed, 'Mr Bain's name is probably more familiar over Southland than that of any other present citizen.'

James Walker Bain wasn't the only juror for the Hornsby inquest to have served his community well, or at least conspicuously. Three of the six jurymen were former mayors of Invercargill (J. W. Bain, Nicholas Johnson and David Roche), five were present or former borough councillors (J. W. Bain, N. Johnson, D. Roche, Archibald McEwan and James Arthur Lennie) and two were Justices of the Peace (J. W. Bain and Anthony Christophers).

The jury for the inquest into the death of the second child was also headed by a Justice of the Peace who had served Invercargill as mayor and councillor (William Horatio Hall), but by the time Mr Hall was sworn in, one begins to suspect, the ranks of available former mayors and councillors were becoming depleted. The remainder of the second jury was made up of two future borough councillors (James Erskine Watson and James Duncan McGruer), the son of a former mayor (John Henry Kingsland) and two men (Robert Erskine and Walter Searle) whose business premises were in the same central Esk-Dee-Tay Street block as those of the other jurors.

The last-named, Walter Searle, was a man of experience. He had served on two of the five previous coroner's juries empanelled in Invercargill. Mr Roche, Mr McGruer, Mr Hall and Mr McEwan had each served on one. Mr Bain must have gained his inquest experience at an earlier time; when the coroner sent the Hornsby jurymen out to consider their verdict he assured them that in their foreman they had 'a gentleman of great experience and eminently capable of assisting them'.[12] But doesn't this mean — I hear you cry — that those coroner's juries were hand-picked? Yes. Or as James Walker Bain would probably say — of course. So how were nineteenth-century inquest juries supposed to be chosen?

§ *Another note concerning nineteenth-century coroners' inquests*

According to the 1895 JP's handbook,[13] when an inquest was required the coroner had to direct the local constable to summon six good and lawful men of the neighbourhood. No instructions were given as to how those men were to be selected. The Act on which the handbook was based (the Coroners Act of 1867) is no help. It says that the coroner should instruct the constable to summon 'jurors of the same number and description as have been used and accustomed to make such inquests or inquiries before the coming into operation of this Act'.

Prior to 1867, the Coroners Act of 1858 ruled. It says that New Zealand coroners shall have 'all such powers and privileges, and be liable to all such duties and responsibilities, as Coroners by Law have, or are liable to, in England'. So how were coroners' juries supposed to be chosen in England? In a burst of diligence and determination I worked my way back through every English Act and Amendment concerning coroners, starting in the reign of Queen Victoria and ending up in the reign of Edward I ('the Lawgiver'), but nowhere did I find any directions as to how inquest juries should be chosen. No requirement for a coroner's jury roll. No requirement for a ballot to select jury members. No directions of any sort. Nothing. As W. R. Cornish noted in his book on the English jury:[14] 'Coroners' juries have never been subject to precise qualification rules and it was formerly quite common for the Coroner's Office to . . . use the same jurors time and time again.'

Well it didn't matter anyway. Not at first. Not in the early days of the New Zealand colony when the population was thinly spread. Back then inquest juries had to view the body and authorise burial, so they had to be summoned quickly. Usually when a suspicious death occurred the coroner took the first six (or, prior to 1885, the first twelve) men he could find. In sparsely populated regions it was not unknown for witnesses and even suspected murderers to be co-opted onto juries inquiring into deaths for which they were directly responsible. As the 1895 handbook explained, 'The jury may find a verdict upon their own knowledge; but they ought to inform the Court that they have knowledge of the matter . . .'

No records remain of how the Invercargill coroner and the Invercargill police chose the inquest juries in the Dean case. Maybe Mr Pardy, the district Inspector of Police who came from Dunedin to oversee the inquests, lent a hand. As they mulled over the names of potential jurors they presumably used a list of some sort — something like the Invercargill grand jury roll — as a starting point.

§ *A note concerning nineteenth-century grand juries*

The Juries Act of 1880 provides instructions for the preparation of a grand jury roll. It says that the Sheriff should extract from the common jury roll:

> ... all men who shall be described in such lists as esquires, gentlemen, merchants, managers of banks, civil engineers & architects, and also such other persons whose names appear on such lists as shall be known to him to be of the best condition, so as to make up such a number of special jurymen as he shall consider to be necessary.

So when the Invercargill coroner consulted with the police over the selection of inquest jurors for the Dean case, the grand jury roll would be a good place to start, wouldn't it?

§ *The story of Minnie Dean resumes*

On Thursday 16 May the papers of the colony were again filled with news and gossip about the Deans, but in Milton the people had no need for newspapers; history was being made before their very eyes.

The police could have — should have — taken Minnie from the Milton railway station to the Milton court-house by carriage, but as if to show off their trophy to the crowds they escorted her on foot through the jeering throng that lined the half-mile route.[15] At the court-house men and women pushed and fought for a glimpse of the prisoner, but her appearance was brief. Detective McGrath explained that the case had been remanded to Milton in the expectation that Eva Hornsby's body would be found at nearby Clarendon, but the body had been discovered at Winton. The case was therefore remanded back to Invercargill.

When Minnie Dean and Detective McGrath left later that day, the biggest crowd ever assembled at the Milton railway station pressed around their compartment window. Some hotheads climbed aboard and fought for standing room in the narrow corridor. Some even opened the compartment door and stared in. And when the departure whistle blew some stayed aboard as far as Clarkesville and walked the two miles back home.[16] By comparison, Charles Dean's court appearance in Invercargill the same day, at which he too was remanded for a week, went almost unnoticed. Thereafter, between a series of tumultuous court appearances, Charles and Minnie were housed separately in the relative tranquillity of the Invercargill gaol.

The jury for the inquest on the skeleton was sworn in on Tuesday 21 May with Mr Thomas Perkins, JP, serving as acting coroner. None of the jurymen were former mayors or councillors, but one (Henry Wilson) was a JP and two (John Thompson, the foreman, and William Wade) had served on inquest juries during the previous year. The other three (Thomas Muir, Charles Fairweather and Robert Wesney) had their businesses in the same central Tay-Esk-Dee Street block as the other men on the three inquest juries in the Dean case.

If Thomas Muir (Jury 3), had set up his tripod at the intersection of Esk and Dee Streets he could have photographed, using only four glass plates, the business premises of fifteen of the eighteen men on the three inquest juries. He could have produced a set of four 'Muir and Moodie'[17] postcards entitled 'Street scenes of Invercargill, 1895':

Postcard A, 'The west side of Dee Street, looking north from Esk St' would show the businesses of James McGruer (Jury 2), William Wade (Jury 3), David Roche (Jury 1), James Lennie (Jury 1), Nicholas Johnson (Jury 1) and Henry Wilson (Jury 3) all together in the block between Esk and Spey Streets.

Postcard B, 'The east side of Dee Street, looking north from Esk St' would show the businesses of William Hall (Jury 2) and Robert Wesney (Jury 3) in the first block, and the drapery of Archibald McEwan (Jury 1) one block further along.

Postcard C, 'The south side of Esk Street, looking east from Dee St' would show Muir's own studio and, side by side a few doors along, the businesses of Robert Erskine (Jury 2), James Walker Bain (Jury 1) and James Watson (Jury 2).

Postcard D, 'The east side of Dee Street, looking south from Esk St' would show the Albion Hotel owned by Walter Searle (Jury 2) halfway along the block and the Bank of New South Wales, of which Antony Christophers (Jury 1) was manager, on the far corner.

The only businesses of inquest jurymen in the Dean case that Thomas Muir could not have photographed from the intersection of Esk and Dee Streets would have been those of John H. Kingsland (Jury 2), Charles Fairweather (Jury 3) and John Thomson (Jury 3).* They were just around the corner in the first block of Tay Street.

Over the following three weeks all the inquests were adjourned at least twice. The lower court hearing before the Invercargill magistrate was also deferred twice, pending the outcome of the inquests. As the Crown solicitor kept explaining, the police had to bring witnesses from as far away as Christchurch and Professor Black of Dunedin had to carry out special tests on the organs of the deceased. It all took time.

The police search for witnesses would have been easier if the newsmongering newsagent on the Dunedin to Invercargill express had agreed to give evidence but, as he indicated to the Minister of Justice when he wrote to claim a reward, he was a police informer of cowardly disposition:

> I got Inspector Pardy to keep me out of all that . . . I did not wish my name to be messed up with it . . . in my occupation as newsagent on the train I meet perhaps many of her friends and as I am of service on many

---

* There are four John Thomsons in the directory, but I'm fairly sure our man is the draper in Tay Street.

occasions to the police force in the exercise of their duty it's not necessary to make known the name . . .[18]

By Monday 27 May the men who had given up their valuable time to sit on the Hornsby inquest jury were becoming impatient. Their impatience was probably compounded by the belated discovery that, thanks to the 1893 law change, they no longer had the power to send murderers directly to the Supreme Court. As the *Otago Daily Times* reported on 28 May:

> . . . coroners' inquests in such cases are almost absolutely futile . . . there is no power to commit for trial . . . the verdict is simply to show cause of death . . . A verdict of natural death or wilful murder is simply the opinion of so many people, and has no legal effect whatever.

The latest rumours concerning the other baby, now identified as Dorothy Edith Carter, would have fed the jurors' frustration. If the rumours were true the Carter inquest would almost certainly upstage the Hornsby inquest as the key inquiry in the Dean case. The *Otago Daily Times* was agog:

> . . . rumours are rife . . . startling revelations will be made. It is said that the purchase of laudanum has been traced to Mrs Dean, and that the same drug had been found in the body of one of the children. [19]

So when the Hornsby inquest jury reassembled on Monday 27 May, they did not take kindly to a request for yet another adjournment; this time so that Mr Hanlon of Dunedin could attend. Mr Bain protested that there was no need. He complained that the jury had come prepared to do its work and was being put to a great deal of inconvenience. He demanded that they be discharged. Mr Roche endorsed his foreman's request. He said it was a disgrace that they should be put to this trouble to suit a Dunedin lawyer when there were plenty of perfectly good ones available in Invercargill.

The coroner, Mr Rawson, was also impatient to finish. If it wasn't for the adjournments, and for the fact that the bodies had been discovered on the eve of his transfer to another district, he would have been spared all this stress. In view of his previous dealings with Mrs Dean he probably found the case particularly unpleasant. Four years earlier, at Winton, he had investigated the death of Bertha Currie and despite police suspicions he had found Mrs Dean blameless. Then in 1894, in his role as Stipendiary Magistrate, he had infuriated the police by fining Mrs Dean one penny for a breach of the Infant Life Protection Act. Now he was presiding over inquests which suggested that the police may have been right all along. There was probably a discomforting air of 'I told you so' in the way the police laid their evidence before him.

Mr Rawson declined the foreman's request for a discharge and adjourned the inquest until Monday 3 June. He appealed to the common sense of the rebellious jurymen, explaining that if a new jury was empanelled Eva

Hornsby's body would have to be exhumed.* Then he issued the jurors with bonds to sign requiring their continuing attendance.

'What if I don't sign?' fumed Mr Roche.

'I will send you to prison.'

'And what if I don't appear?'

'You will be fined £25.'

Next morning Alf Hanlon arrived from Dunedin and the inquest into the death of Dorothy Edith Carter began in earnest. Minnie and Charles Dean sat together on a bench in front of the dock, surrounded by a swaying, twisting crowd of curious onlookers. What was Mrs Dean like? Some newspapers described her as 'showing signs of insanity'. Others said she was 'cheerful and chatty'. So what was she *really* like? In reality both Minnie and Charles were probably numb with stress, but the *Otago Daily Times* reporter, like most spectators in court, interpreted their impassivity as cool composure: 'The accused persons were perfectly calm and self-possessed throughout the day, never betraying any anxiety or emotion . . .'[20]

Mr T. M. Macdonald, Crown Solicitor, examined the witnesses. Messrs Hanlon and Hanan watched on behalf of the Deans. There wasn't a lot they could do. Coroners' inquests didn't follow normal courtroom rules. The lawyers involved had no right to challenge the appointment of jurors or question the admissibility of evidence.

The orderly sequence of witnesses provided a near-seamless account of Minnie's travels and transactions between Monday 29 April, when she left Winton for Bluff, and Saturday 4 May, when she returned from her round trip to Clarendon. Some could identify Minnie Dean as the woman whose movements they observed, some could not. On the first day the witnesses were:

♦ Mrs Cox, who gave her granddaughter Dorothy Edith Carter to a 'Mrs Gray' at a Bluff hotel on 30 April.

♦ Mary Cameron and her sister Margaret, daughters of the Bluff hotelier, who confirmed Mrs Cox's story and added a few details of their own.

♦ George Froggatt, the Bluff chemist, who sold laudanum to a 'Mrs Gray' on 30 April.

♦ Esther Wallis, who described Mrs Dean's comings and goings between Monday 29 April and Saturday 4 May.

♦ William Everett, guard on the morning train from Winton to Lumsden on Thursday 2 May.

♦ John McKellar, a passenger on that train.

♦ Thomas Baker, who carried a lady's hat box from the Dipton railway station to the Dipton hotel on the morning of Thursday 2 May and carried it back to

---

* Inquest juries were required by law to view the body.

the railway station that evening ('It was light . . . The lady had a baby . . .').

♦ George Aylin, landlord of the Dipton hotel.

♦ Charles Davis, guard on the evening train from Dipton to Lumsden.

♦ James Aitken, who carried a lady's hat box from the railway station to the Lumsden hotel in the evening ('It was heavy . . . The lady had no baby . . .').

♦ Catherine Healy and Eveline Powell from the Lumsden railway hotel; one carried the lady's hat box upstairs in the evening, the other carried it downstairs next morning ('It was heavy . . . The lady had no baby . . .').

♦ Willie Crosbie who carried the lady's hat box from the Lumsden hotel to the morning train on Friday 3 May ('It was heavy . . . The lady had no baby . . .').

♦ Thomas Martin, guard on the train from Lumsden to Gore on Friday 3 May.

The chronological sequence was then broken by the demands of the railway timetable; three guards scheduled to give evidence had to leave to catch trains. The flow of witnesses continued with:

♦ Jenny McKay, from the Clinton boarding house where the lady now in court stayed for the night of Friday 3 May ('She had no baby . . .').

♦ Catherine Cameron of the Mataura hotel, where the lady now in court had breakfast on Saturday 4 May ('She had no baby . . .').

♦ Joseph Limbrick, gardener at the Mataura Hotel who prepared a parcel of flowers and cuttings for the lady now in court.

At 4. 40 pm Mr Macdonald proposed an adjournment until the following morning; the police witnesses were yet to be heard — their evidence would be long — it would be inconvenient to have to break off in the middle.

'Do you think you will finish tomorrow?' asked Mr Rawson anxiously.

'Oh yes, I think so,' Mr Macdonald assured him.

Next morning women's bonnets bobbed up and down in the crowded court as spectators struggled to glimpse the Deans and the exhibits on display: a tin hat box, a bundle of baby clothes, a piece of oilcloth, three medicine bottles, a bunch of flowers.

First the police (Constables Barrett, Detective Herbert, Constable Rasmussen and Sergeant Macdonnell) described the search of Mrs Dean's garden and the precautions taken to ensure that the bodies discovered there were not tampered with prior to the post-mortem examinations.

Then Mr Macdonald requested another adjournment. He appealed to the patriotism and good sense of the jury. He explained that the most important witness, Professor Black of Dunedin, was unable to attend until the following week. He wanted to save the rest of the medical evidence until then. An adjournment was granted until Tuesday 4 June at 2. 30 pm, by which time, it was expected, the inquest into the death of the other child, Eva Hornsby, would be completed.

[140]

After another adjournment of the magisterial hearing, followed by three days out of the public eye, Minnie and Charles were back in the crowded courtroom on Monday 3 June for the much delayed inquest into the death of Eva Hornsby. According to the *Otago Daily Times* Minnie was showing signs of strain:

> Mrs Dean appeared much paler and more haggard-looking than when last seen in court. The reading of her letters and the other evidence produced today seemed to considerably affect her hitherto complacent demeanour — more than anything else has done since the commencement of the inquiry. Towards evening she showed marked signs of prostration and weariness, and leant her head heavily on the shoulder of her husband.[21]

The proceedings began with Esther Wallis and Willie Crosbie repeating the evidence they had presented at the Carter inquest. Next Charlie Simmonds, a railway guard, told of seeing Mrs Dean on Friday 3 May travelling north, second class, on the express from Gore to Clinton, and on Saturday 4 May, travelling south, first class, on the early train from Clinton to Mataura. He couldn't remember much about her luggage. James Hay, who replaced Charlie Simmonds at Clinton on Friday 3 May, was also vague about the details. He saw Mrs Dean when he joined the train at Clinton. He saw Mrs Hornsby with something in her arms on the Milburn platform. Later he noticed her alone on the train near Waihola. But he didn't see Mrs Dean and Mrs Hornsby together and he didn't see Mrs Dean alight at Clarendon. How unobservant. Newsagent Nicol — who was no doubt following the news as avidly as he was selling it — must have been disgusted.

Mrs Hornsby told the court that in early April she had replied to an advertisement seeking a child to adopt. She produced a letter from the ensuing correspondence with Mrs Dean. To those convinced of Minnie's guilt the letter was proof of cold-blooded hypocrisy and premeditated murder. To Minnie, at the time of writing, it may have been what she believed or hoped was the truth:

> . . . please understand I wish the child to be entirely my own. I wish her to grow up in the belief that I am in truth her mother. I wish to put it out of anyone's power to tell the child that I am not her mother, or that the stain of illegitimacy is on her birth. So I wish no one of those interested to know where the child has gone. I will do my best, with God's help, to train the child to become a good and useful woman. I pledge the word of a mother who has loved and lost her own that I will be a mother to the child. In weal or woe, in sickness or in health, a mother's loving, watchful care will be bestowed on her . . . the little one will have plenty of milk and will soon grow up to be a big fat girl.
>
> Truly yours,
> M. Dean

Mrs Hornsby was followed onto the witness stand by Alice Bennett, a widow of Port Chalmers whose house was registered under the Infant Life Protection Act. She had cared for Eva Hornsby from 2 April (when she was two days old) until 2 May (when her grandmother took her away). She had identified Eva's body at the morgue and the clothes found at The Larches.

'Alice Bennett, her mark,' wrote the coroner beside the large X at the end of her statement.

Then a series of witnesses traced Mrs Dean's journey from Clarendon to Winton:

♦ William Gibb, guard on the late train south from Dunedin on 3 May saw Mrs Dean join the train at Clarendon, without a baby.

♦ Constable King of Milton saw her in the first-class compartment of the southbound train that evening. He did not see a child with her.

♦ Jenny McKay of Clinton, and Catherine Cameron and Joseph Limbrick of Mataura, repeated the evidence they had given to the Hornsby inquest.

♦ Detective McGrath told of Mrs Dean's arrest, and Detective Herbert, Sergeant Macdonnell, and Constables Barrett and Rasmussen, repeated the evidence they had given to the Hornsby inquest about the discovery of the bodies.

The proceedings adjourned at 5.15 pm and resumed the following morning to hear the post-mortem results presented by the medical officer in charge of the Southland Hospital, Dr Roderick Macleod, and his assistant Dr James Young. Dr Macleod graduated from Glasgow University in 1887 with the degree of MB CM with honours in medicine. As a student he would have studied under Dr Joseph Coats, one of the most distinguished pathologists of the age.[22] Dr Young, MD and Doctor of Surgery from Royal University, Ireland, was also well qualified.

The doctors reported that Eva Hornsby's body seemed generally healthy. The organ samples analysed by Professor Black showed no traces of poison. They were uncertain about the cause of Eva Hornsby's death, but the appearance of the skin led them to suspect asphyxiation. They found nothing abnormal about the position of the tongue and the windpipe was clear. There were no external marks of violence, but under the scalp, behind each ear, they discovered a small deep bruise. If someone had gripped the back of the baby's head with a thumb and forefinger, suggested Dr Young, that could explain the bruises. And if that same person had pressed the baby's face into a cloth, that could explain the asphyxiation.

After examining the medical report nearly a hundred years later, Dr A. G. Dempster of the Pathology Department, University of Otago School of Medicine, concluded: 'In the light of contemporaneous reports, Dr Macleod's postmortem examinations were generally thorough and his interpretations of the findings were probably reasonably accurate.' What Dr Macleod didn't know (because cot deaths were unrecognised at the time) was that the post-mortem appearance of a cot death victim is almost indistinguishable from that of a very young victim of asphyxiation; nowadays supporting evidence, such as marks of violence, are usually required before a firm diagnosis of asphyxiation can be made. So could Eva Hornsby have died of cot death? Probably not — firstly because cot death victims always die in their sleep, and secondly because the deep 'finger tip' bruises on Eva's scalp, which were probably caused by pressure applied externally to the back of her head, support the hypothesis that Eva was forcefully smothered.

When all the witnesses had testified the coroner reviewed the evidence and complimented the police and the Crown solicitor on their work. He told the jurymen that the time taken and the adjournments involved were justified by the gravity of the case. He reminded them that if the evidence reasonably led them to the conclusion that any person or persons feloniously murdered the child, it was their duty to say so.

After a half-hour retirement the foreman, Mr James Walker Bain announced to a hushed court: 'The jury are of the opinion that the child Eva Hornsby was wilfully murdered within the Colony of New Zealand on or about the third day of May 1895.'

'Is that all?' asked Mr Rawson. Despite his careful directions the jury had failed to name the culprit.

'The jury are aware that a magisterial inquiry will take place at any rate, and consider that they have sufficiently discharged their duty,' said Mr Bain. The magistrate recognised the reply for what it was — a complaint that the 1893 Criminal Code had robbed the jury of its power to commit the culprit directly to trial in the Supreme Court.

'There's no need for an explanation,' he snapped.[23]

After a break for lunch the spectators rushed back to court to hear the long-promised 'startling revelations' concerning the death of Dorothy Edith Carter.

Dr Macleod said that the child's body was well nourished and showed no signs of disease. He said that the slightly engorged appearance of the organs was not inconsistent with opium poisoning.

Professor James Gow Black, Doctor of Science from Edinburgh University, Professor of Chemistry at the University of Otago and Government Analyst, then described his analysis of Dorothy Edith Carter's stomach, intestines and kidneys. 'In my opinion the quantity of opium found in the organs would decidedly produce death in a child of that age,' he said.

When Professor Black had completed his evidence, Mr Rawson again complimented the police and the Crown prosecutor, and (according to the *Otago Daily Times*) 'traversed the evidence at considerable length strongly against Mrs Dean'. After a fifteen-minute retirement the jury foreman, Mr W. H. Hall, returned what Mr Rawson must have regarded as a highly satisfactory verdict:

'That Dorothy Edith Carter met her death on the 2nd May, between Winton and Lumsden, through poison administered by Minnie Dean.'

'Then you find that Minnie Dean has been guilty of murder?' asked Mr Rawson, making sure that this time the identity of the culprit was absolutely clear.

'Yes,' said Mr Hall.

The announcement had no visible effect on either of the Deans.

At the inquest into the death of Thomas Hall's father-in-law Captain Cain, which began in Timaru on 18 November 1886, the inquest jury was more sensitive to the suspect's right to a fair trial. After a jury of Hall's peers had heard the evidence of more than sixty witnesses concerning his interest in poisons, his purchases of antimony and his constant attendance on his father-in-law; and about Captain Cain's last illness and the presence of antimony in his organs, the foreman reported:

> The jury are of the opinion that Captain Cain's death was accelerated by poison, but by whom administered there is not sufficient evidence to show. They therefore return the verdict of 'wilful murder against some person or persons unknown'.[24]

On Thursday 6 June 1895 the magisterial hearing into the Dean case began. The court room was so packed that the railing around the dock threatened to collapse under pressure from the surging crowd.

Minnie and Charles Dean were jointly charged with the murder of Dorothy Edith Carter. Mr T. M. Macdonald, Crown Prosecutor, told the new magistrate, Mr J. W. Poynton, that he would present the facts through the testimony of his witnesses. He expressed confidence that by the end his Worship would see it his duty to commit at least one of the accused for trial. There must have been no doubt which of the accused he had in mind.

Twenty-two of the thirty-seven witnesses had already given evidence at one inquest, a further twelve had given evidence at two. During the three-day hearing only three new witnesses were heard, but thanks to the vigorous cross-examination provided on behalf of the Deans by Alf Hanlon and Josiah Hanan, the onlookers were never bored.

Josiah Hanan was twenty-seven years old, Alf Hanlon was twenty-nine. In the years ahead Hanan would go on to a distinguished political career and Hanlon would become one of New Zealand's most celebrated and successful criminal lawyers, but in 1895 both were virtually unknown. Alf Hanlon was the New Zealand-born son of an Irish policeman. During the previous seven years in his one-man Dunedin law practice he had built up a reputation as a vigorous and effective defender of the poor. He already had one relatively straightforward murder case under his belt when Josiah Hanan asked him to defend Minnie Dean. Hanlon must have known there was no money to be made from the case. It was probably the chance of being launched into prominence by the accompanying publicity, even if he lost, that the young lawyer found irresistible.

A new witness took the stand first — Dot Sarah Izett of Christchurch, the agent who had arranged for Minnie to take Dorothy Edith Carter. She presented her correspondence with the woman who signed herself 'M. Cameron'. The letters showed the same concern for secrecy that had been revealed in Minnie's correspondence with Mrs Hornsby.

Then Alf Hanlon rose to cross-examine the witness. He was over six foot tall, theatrical and commanding. His voice was rich, his vocabulary expressive. The crowd was enthralled. His questions to Mrs Izett and the next witness, Mrs Cox, established an important point: Minnie Dean had received no money for Dorothy Edith Carter.

There were no gains for the Dean case from the rest of Mrs Cox's cross-examination. Dorothy Edith had never been out of her grandmother's house from the day she was born until the day she left for Bluff eleven months later. Mrs Cox was able to assert with authority that her granddaughter was a placid, healthy baby who took her food well and had never been given laudanum.

Hanlon let pass the evidence confirming that Mrs Dean had received Dorothy Edith at Bluff, but the Crown claim that she had bought laudanum there did not go unchallenged, especially when Maggie Cameron assured the court that the signature 'M. Gray' in the Bluff chemist's poison book was the work of Mrs Dean.

'You have no doubt that these letters are in Mrs Dean's handwriting?' he asked.

'I have no doubt about it.'

'It is comparatively easy to form an opinion from several pages of manuscript, but the case is different when there are only five letters. Do you mean to tell the court that those five letters were penned by Mrs Dean.'

'Yes.'

'Beyond all doubt?'

'Yes.'

'You swear that? What about the capital M?'

'She always made an M that way.'

'And what about the G?'

'She always made a G like that.'

'But that is not her name.'

'It is somebody else's name, but her handwriting.'

'You will swear positively that no other person wrote those words?'

'Yes.'

To underline the doubt Hanlon recalled George Froggatt, the Bluff chemist, who conceded that he could not identify in court the woman who had bought laudanum from him that day.

After lunch the chronological sequence of witnesses was broken so that Professor Black could give his evidence before leaving for Dunedin. He assured Mr Hanan that the tests for opium he had used were recommended by the highest authorities.

Then, after Esther Wallis had told her story of Minnie's travels for the third time, Hanan subjected her to a lengthy and wide-ranging cross-examination. She assured him that Mrs Dean was fond of children and they were fond of her. She insisted that Mrs Dean had cared well for Dorothy Edith despite the child's constant crying, and with Hanan's prompting she recalled a specific example:

'You remember going home from Gap Road with the child?'

'Yes.'

'Do you not remember that Mrs Dean took off her cloak and wrapped it around the child?'

'Yes.'

'You remarked that she would catch cold and she replied, "No matter." '

'Yes.'

Hanan then asked Esther about Charles Dean. She recalled conversations between the Deans indicating that Charles believed that Dorothy Edith had been adopted, and that his wife's hat box contained bulbs. Esther assured Mr Hanan that Mr Dean never opened his wife's mail, never dug in her flower garden and was often away from home. In fact he took no part in his wife's adoption activities and didn't approve of her taking children at all.

Hanan's last questions to Esther were about the three medicine bottles seized from The Larches. She said that the one labelled 'Laudanum' was used by Mrs Dean as an eye wash (when seized it contained half a teaspoon of liquid, which Professor Black had analysed and found to be extremely weak laudanum); the ones labelled 'Chlorodyne' and 'Neill's Cholera' (patent medicines containing opium) were used by Mr Dean for diarrhoea.

After Esther's long session there was time for only two more witnesses (railway guard William Everett and passenger John McKellar) before the case was adjourned for the night.

Next morning Thomas Baker, George Aylin, Charles Davis, Catherine Healy, Evelyn Powell, William Crosbie and Thomas Martin recounted for the second or third time their observations of Minnie's fateful train journey from Lady Barkly to Dipton, Lumsden and Gore. Two new witnesses also appeared: Christina Duncan, a servant at the Dipton hotel, and Mrs Crosbie, wife of the landlord of the Lumsden hotel. When challenged by Hanlon some witnesses became less certain; others revealed that their evidence had been contaminated by information obtained later. Mr Aylin said, 'I did not remember the date till the constable came to me', and Christina Duncan admitted that she had read the age of the child in the newspaper.

Though Hanlon exposed flaws in the evidence, the overall picture of Minnie Dean's journey held firm. There could be no doubt that she left Lady Barkly on the morning of 2 May with a baby and a light hat box, arrived at Lumsden that evening with a heavy hat box and no baby, and travelled on to Gore next day.

Just before lunch Mr Macdonald announced that he proposed to introduce a new line of evidence. His aim was to show that on 3 May Mrs Dean had another infant entrusted to her, and that she murdered that infant.

This was a touchy legal point. It was a long-established principle of British justice that while all evidence relevant to a particular case was admissible in court, evidence linking the accused to other crimes normally was not. After all, evidence that a person has committed one crime does not prove that he or she has committed another, but if admitted such evidence could so prejudice a jury that a guilty verdict may be inevitable. In response to Hanlon's protest the Crown prosecutor referred to the precedent-setting Makin baby farming case in Sydney. The legal arguments involved would have been of little interest to the spectators, but Macdonald's mention of the notorious Makin case must have electrified them. He reminded the court that infants were entrusted to the Makins for adoption, that a sum insufficient to support the children was paid them and that the bodies of infants were found buried in their garden. In addition, Macdonald said, evidence was adduced to show that the Makins had obtained other children on similar representations. Such evidence had been tendered to show that the death of the infant the Makins were charged with murdering was not accidental. He proposed to tender evidence on the same grounds. He wished to demonstrate that the death of Dorothy Edith Carter was not accidental by introducing 'the whole of the facts' to show that the accused, Minnie Dean, had murdered another infant named Eva Hornsby.[*]

The magistrate noted that the Appeal Court ruling in the Makin case (that evidence of other crimes was admissible for the purpose of showing that a crime had occurred by design rather than by accident) had been endorsed by the Privy Council. He therefore ruled that the evidence was admissible.

Next a procession of witnesses (Charlie Simmonds, Joseph Kay, Jane Hornsby,

---

[*] Another advantage of admitting the Hornsby evidence as part of the Carter murder inquiry was that the Crown prosecutor could then present indictments for both murders to the Supreme Court without the need for two separate magisterial hearings.

Alice Bennett, William Gibb, Constable King, Jenny McKay, Catherine Cameron and Joseph Limbrick) traced Minnie's travels from Gore to Clarendon to Clinton.

Unlike Mrs Cox, who had cared for her illegitimate granddaughter for eleven months, Mrs Hornsby had handed Eva to a baby minder within two days of birth, and had retrieved her one month later, the day before she set off by train to meet Mrs Dean. When she admitted under cross-examination that she had made no enquiries concerning the character of Mrs Dean, Hanlon commented:

'I suppose you just wanted to be rid of the child.'

'I wanted a home for it.'

'You had a home of your own.'

'Yes.'

'But no room in it for one little baby?'

'No — I have seven children already.'

Then came the police witnesses: Detectives McGrath and Herbert, Constables Barrett and Rasmussen, Sergeant Macdonnell. Constable Rasmussen reported a comment made by Charles Dean, 'Had I known the bodies were there I should have removed them to screen her — I certainly should.'

That day the hearing continued into the evening. The *Otago Daily Times* noted that Mrs Dean's 'dejected appearance in court has excited a good deal of sympathy'.

Next morning Dr Macleod stated, with far more confidence than he had done at the earlier inquest, that Eva Hornsby had died of asphyxiation. Mr Hanan asked him for a detailed description of the child's organs and then challenged the certainty of his conclusion:

'That impression was not surrounded by perplexity in any way?'

'No, not in any way.'

'You were quite satisfied that asphyxia was the cause of death?'

'The child died in a condition of asphyxia. That was the condition of death.'

'Why did you send the intestines to Dunedin for analysis?'

'The bodies were in the hands of the police. They asked me to do so.'

'Was it not on account of a doubt in your mind as to the cause of death?'

'No.'

'What experience have you had in regard to cases of death produced by asphyxia?'

'Naturally I have not got a record of every case with me, but I have had three during the past year, and during the seven years I have been at the hospital that would be a fair average. Dying by asphyxia is a common way of dying.'

'That way may be an innocent way?'

'It may be.'

Mr Hanan then explored the possibilities of an innocent explanation for the death of Dorothy Edith Carter.

'What may laudanum be used for innocently,' he asked.

'It is a very dangerous drug to deal with. It ought not to be given to children unless under medical supervision.'

'Is it not popularly used often?'

'Yes, it is given often, but it is a dangerous drug.'

'To alleviate pain?'

'Yes, that is the great cause of its use in adults.'

'To induce sleep?'

'Yes.'

'It may be given, doctor, in small doses without injury?'

'It is quite possible to give it in small doses without injury, but it is a dangerous drug.'

'Are not all drugs dangerous?'

'No, this is peculiarly dangerous.'

When all the evidence had been presented Alf Hanlon addressed the court. He acknowledged that a prima facie case had been made against Minnie Dean, but suggested, measuring his words for dramatic effect, that Charles Dean was entitled to an immediate acquittal. He paused significantly, and was about to launch into a full-scale oration when the magistrate commented that he intended to acquit Mr Dean. Hanlon said he still wished to say a few words on Dean's behalf — he wished to point out that there was not only no evidence against him, but some facts were strongly in his favour. Mr Poynton said that he had intended to do that too, but, presumably because Hanlon wanted to perform and his performances were always worth watching, the young lawyer was allowed the floor.

Hanlon reminded the court that Mrs Dean was anxious to conceal the hat box from her husband, that Mr Dean believed the child Carter had been adopted and that the hat box contained bulbs, that he had no involvement with, and indeed disapproved of, his wife's child care activities. Furthermore, despite his declared wish to shield his wife and despite the two days that elapsed between his wife's and his own arrest, he did not remove the bodies from the garden or the child Carter's clothes from the house. There was not a tittle of evidence against Dean, Hanlon said. He suggested that in fairness and justice His Worship might say that Dean left the court without a stain on his character.

The magistrate said he intended to do that, and Charles Dean was duly discharged. Hanlon intimated that his other client would reserve her defense for the Supreme Court. Minnie Dean was then committed to trial.

At the end of the lower court hearing into the attempted murder of Mrs Hall, Thomas Hall and Margaret Houston were also committed to trial. Hall's lawyer immediately requested that his clients' Supreme Court trial be held in Christchurch 'as with the strong feelings entertained in Timaru it would be impossible to obtain a fair trial.'[25] His request was granted.

After an eight-day trial in Christchurch in October 1886, Thomas Hall was found guilty of the attempted murder of his wife and sentenced to life imprisonment, and Margaret Houston was discharged 'without a stain on her character'. * In December, after the inquest into the death of Captain Cain and the subsequent magisterial hearing, the Timaru magistrate sent Thomas Hall to trial for the murder of Cain. 'I earnestly ask that you not commit my client to Christchurch,' his lawyer pleaded, pointing out that since Hall had already gone through a trial in that city (for the attempted murder of his wife) the public there would be biased against him. A second change of venue, this time to the court of Judge Joshua Strange Williams in Dunedin, was granted.[26]

According to a story passed down in the Hanlon family, Alf Hanlon requested a change of venue in chambers soon after Minnie Dean's magisterial hearing. He wanted her trial held in Christchurch so that she could escape both the Invercargill public and Mr Justice Joshua Strange Williams, the Otago-Southland Supreme Court judge. This story may come as a shock to members of the Otago-Southland legal fraternity, among whom the memory of Judge Williams is revered to this day. Indignant lawyers will probably rush to defend His Honour with quotations from Hanlon's *Random Recollections*[27] or W. Downie Stewart's *Portrait of a Judge*[28]. A word of explanation is in order.

Firstly, Alf Hanlon did not write *Random Recollections*. It was ghost-written by Ronald Jones, a reporter from the *Otago Daily Times*. According to the Hanlon family the book is bereft of both Hanlon's eloquence and Hanlon's opinions. Hanlon was sympathetic to Minnie Dean; the book depicts him as hostile. Hanlon had reservations about Judge Williams; the book depicts him as an unctuous admirer.[29] Secondly, Judge Williams was not as flawless as the work of Ronald Jones and William Downie Stewart suggests.

When Joshua Strange Williams[30] arrived in Christchurch in 1861 his distinguished parentage and his education at Harrow and Cambridge gave him ready entry into the ranks of the gentry. In his memoirs, Judge O. T. J. Alpers added his voice to the chorus of adulation:

---

* The library Dr T. M. Hocken gifted to the nation in 1910 contained published material on the Hall case and this hand written note: 'There is little doubt but that Miss Houston was an accomplice in the attempt to murder, or at least that there was knowledge of what was going on. When Hall's goods were sold there were found amongst his photographic slides many pictures of Miss Houston taken in various attitudes & quite naked. T. M. H.'

The very name Judge Williams is redolent of the law. He was a son of Joshua Williams, Q.C., the great conveyancer and historical jurist, whose *Law of Real Property* has been for so long the classical authority upon that topic. One felt instinctively that New Zealand was honoured in having such a man as a member of its judiciary.[31]

Between 1862 and 1870 Williams served on the Canterbury Provincial Council and the Provincial Executive. In 1871 he became district land registrar. In 1872 he was appointed registrar general of land. Among his acquaintances during his fifteen years in Christchurch was the influential South Canterbury pastoralist and politician, Sir John Hall, uncle of the future poisoner, Thomas Hall.

In 1875, despite his dearth of experience as a barrister, 39-year-old Joshua Strange Williams became the youngest judge ever appointed to the New Zealand Supreme Court. His posting to Dunedin did not impress the *Otago Daily Times*:

> the chief judicial centre of the Colony is too precious a bauble to be toyed with . . . that an inexperienced tyro in forensic combat — one unused to the ways and customs of a Court of Justice — should be vaulted from the quiet post he now so well fills into the most important and responsible judgment seat in the Colony is to our mind an absurdity so stark that we feel bound to protest vehemently against it.[32]

After this shaky start Williams's reputation grew steadily during his thirty-nine years on the Otago-Southland Supreme Court bench. 'What was the secret of the esteem, affection and veneration in which this great man was held . . . ?' wrote William Downie Stewart in his 1945 hagiography. '. . . he was my ideal of a perfect judge, and a noble citizen.' Williams's secret seems to have been his patient kindness to nervous or befuddled barristers and his unfailing courtesy to all. 'Time after time he would lead young lawyers through their cases, suggesting . . . which questions they should ask next, which points of argument they wished to make.'[33] His admirers also wrote of his considered and balanced judgments, but the examples given were few and unconvincing. As Iain Galloway observed in *Portrait of a Profession* (a centennial history of the New Zealand Law Society): 'One might wish . . . that some of Sir Joshua's contemporaries had compiled a more factual account of his life and cases.'[34]

A brief search beyond the eulogies suggests that the reluctance of Williams's contemporaries to discuss his judgments in detail may have been prompted by a desire to protect the great man's reputation from the damage such scrutiny could cause. Sir Hubert Osler wrote of Williams in *Portrait of a Profession*, 'I often heard from the elder men who practised before him that in his earlier years he was by no means a good Judge.'

Here are some of the controversial cases over which Judge Williams presided ◆ The Robert Butler murder trial in 1880 ('This verdict caused consternation in Dunedin: the judge's summation was held to be "extremely unsatisfactory" and, in some aspects, "entirely misleading". But the Minister of Justice William Rolleston* advised against a second trial.')[35] ◆ The action by Southland Frozen Meat against Nelson brothers in 1895 (Williams's judgment was overturned by the Court of Appeal on the ground that the judge had misdirected the jury).[36] ◆ The 1896 application for court approval of a bid to save the J. G. Ward Farmer's Association from collapse (when politician Ward came south following a savaging from Williams, 2000 indignant Ward supporters met his train in Dunedin and 3000 met his train in Invercargill)[37] ◆ The 1897 bid to save Ward from bankruptcy (after another savaging from Williams, Acting Premier Jock McKenzie declared that Ward would have received better treatment had he been a Tory).[38] ◆ The 1909 complaints of malpractice against a Dunedin lawyer (after dismissing the charges on somewhat dubious grounds, Williams congratulated the lawyer on having his character completely cleared).[39] ◆ Then there were the murder trials of Thomas Hall and Minnie Dean, but we shall hear more of them later.

Williams's ancestry and education fitted him well for a professional life in the administration of justice and a social life among the pastoralists and merchant princes of Canterbury and Otago. He was too well bred to allow his friendships to influence his judgments, but there was a hint of unconscious bias in his controversial decisions in favour of the well-connected Thomas Hall and the well-educated Robert Butler, and against the likes of baby farmer Minnie Dean and politician Joseph Ward (a swashbuckling Southland entrepreneur of Irish working-class stock).

Like Ward, Alf Hanlon was a self-made man of humble Irish parentage. His relationship with Judge Williams would have lacked the natural affinity enjoyed by men who shared a common background. Also, the silver-tongued Hanlon would have learnt during his seven years at the Dunedin bar that Williams's sympathy towards inarticulate barristers was matched by a dour suspicion of articulate ones. Williams made his views clear in a pamphlet he wrote in 1894 in protest at a legislative attempt to restrain judges from giving juries the benefit of their opinions in their summing up:

> His [the judge's] duty is to see that justice is done, and that a party, so far as he can help it, shall not suffer by the inexperience of his own counsel, or the cleverness of counsel on the other side. If the proposed alteration is carried, this will cease to be the judge's duty. When the judge is muzzled, the most able, or rather the least scrupulous lawyer will have it all his own way.[40]

---

* A member of the Canterbury gentry and close friend of Joshua Strange Williams during his years in Christchurch.

Alf Hanlon's oratory was his greatest strength, but in the court of Mr Justice Williams the more fluent and convincing his arguments the more likely they were to be ignored or belittled by the judge in his summing up. This was almost certainly the reason Hanlon sought to have Minnie Dean's trial held outside Judge Williams' jurisdiction, though he would not have said as much to the judge. When he asked for a change of venue he probably spoke only of the prejudicial pre-trial publicity. At all events, Judge Williams declined his request.

After the magisterial hearing Minnie had one day out of the public gaze. Then on Monday 10 June she was back in the crowded court for the inquest into the skeleton. The mystery over the identity of the skeleton gave the police an excuse to introduce evidence indicating that several children had disappeared in Mrs Dean's care.

Of all Minnie's public appearances this was the most harrowing. She no longer had her husband at her side, she could no longer clasp his hand as she had done so often during the preceding weeks, but his presence in the body of the court would have given her some comfort.

Charles Dean was supportive in other ways too. Immediately after being discharged by the magistrate he had forced his way into the home where Esther Wallis was staying, despite being warned to stay away, and had spoken with her. According to the police, Esther subsequently showed a marked disinclination to give evidence against Mrs Dean. Minnie thought otherwise. Minnie was convinced that the evidence presented at the inquest into the skeleton by her adopted daughters, Esther Wallis and Maggie Cameron, was the result of police coaching. Of Maggie she wrote:

> The sight of her in the witness box giving evidence against me on the night of the inquest on the skeleton, and Sergeant Macdonnell standing at the side of the box and putting the questions to her and grinning like a hyena in triumph, will be with me while memory last. If he could have changed places with me and suffered for one five minutes what I then endured, I think that even his hard and callous heart would have been touched. I have no teeth in the upper jaw and when I recovered a little I found my teeth embedded in the gums and had to pull my mouth open with my hands. And for days afterwards my gums felt as if I had had teeth newly extracted. What arguments he used, what threats or persuasions he had resource to, before he got that girl persuaded to traduce her mother is best known to himself . . . I do not believe in all the Police Court records throughout the colonies a more cruel, heartless or shameful proceedings is to be found. There was during the first part of it no restraining hand and the police ran riot, their one aim being to incite public feeling and torture me. No victim on the rack or tied to the stake

suffered what I suffered that night. I was pierced to the heart, slain by the hand I had cherished. God forgive them for they knew not what they did. After Maggie stepped out of the box Sergeant Macdonnell turned and grinned in my face in triumph. All the way back to the jail and in my lonely cell all night long was the one cry — how can I bear it? How can I bear it? I knew, none knew better, the girl's proud sensitive nature and I knew the torture it cost her. The police discovered her weak points and played on them . . . Poor girl, after the first shock was over I have never cherished a hard or bitter thought against her. I have loved her too well for that. Nor have I blamed her.[41]

Minnie was more deeply embittered by Esther's testimony at the inquest:

> . . . truth was never in her. She would swear to anything that suited her, and the police found her an apt pupil. To hear how glibly she came out with the name they had given to the boy Sydney, a name I had never heard until I heard it in court. Sydney McKernan I think was the name. I wonder how the police would have looked if the question had been put to her as it ought to have been. *Who told her* that was the boy's name? It was the police. She never heard it from me. I sat lost in amazement at her cunning in denying all knowledge of the youngest child, when she knew almost as much about it as I did. It was her that always posted the letters, called for letters and sent telegrams.[42]

Despite the stress, Minnie's dark eyes betrayed no emotion. The *Otago Daily Times* reported that Mrs Dean, ' . . . seems to take matters as coolly as ever, though some of the evidence this afternoon was most sensational'.

The inquest opened with Maggie Cameron, and then Esther Wallis, recounting their memories of Cyril Scoular, Henry Cockerill (also known as John Clark), Sydney McKernan and William Phelan. The girls gave vague, and sometimes conflicting, information on the ages of the children, when they arrived and when they left, and whether or not Mrs Dean received any money with them. On at least two occasions Mr Hanan protested to the apparently ineffectual acting coroner, Mr Perkins, JP, about Sergeant Macdonnell's treatment of Maggie Cameron, and though the policeman's questions were never recorded their shadow remains imprinted on her statement. Here's what Maggie said about Mrs Dean's care of Cyril Scoular (you'll have to fill in the policeman's questions for yourself):

'Cyril was well treated.'

'Mrs Dean did not treat all the children alike — she treated some better than others.'

'Sometimes she was very kind to Cyril Scoular and at other times she smacked him as he needed it.'

'He was a good child.'

'I don't think Mrs Dean particularly liked him.'[43]

Maggie also said that Mrs Dean did not particularly like Sydney McKernan. She may have meant that Minnie actively disliked Cyril and Sydney, or she may have meant that those two children were not her special favourites. But with Willie Phelan there was no doubt. Both Maggie and Esther agreed that Mrs Dean did not like Willie Phelan.

An important point regarding Willie that did not emerge at this inquest, or at the Supreme Court trial that followed, was that the boy was mentally retarded. Much was made of the problem two years earlier when Minnie sued Willie's mother, Mrs Olsen, for maintenance costs for her son. At that hearing Minnie's counsel (who was Josiah Hanan on that occasion too) said that Mrs Dean had refused to adopt Willie because, though the child had been represented to her as strong, healthy and intelligent, he was an imbecile. Hanan submitted that when Mrs Dean complained Mrs Olsen said the boy would not live to seven years of age because he had water on the brain.[44]

In the nineteenth century terms like 'imbecile' and 'water on the brain' were used more loosely, and predictions of early deaths were made more freely, than they are today. It would be prudent to consider Minnie's description of Willie's behaviour before we draw any conclusions about the child's mental state.

In August 1893, when Willie was four and a half years old, Minnie left him with his mother in Dunedin for ten days. The following month she wrote to Mrs Olsen about their return to The Larches:

> Directly we got in sight of the house he saw Mr Dean outside, and he called out, 'There's the guv'nor,' and he ran to him. Then the other four came, and if you only heard how their tongues went.[45]

The Willie described in this letter — a child who could talk, run and relate freely to adults and children — was clearly not severely handicapped. However, in her last statement Minnie referred to Willie's 'dirty habits', which may mean that he was developmentally delayed to the extent that he was not toilet trained by the age of four.

Both Maggie and Esther said that Mrs Dean sometimes took Willie by the hair and banged his head on the floor, and Minnie herself admitted the violence in her last statement: 'If I got in a temper and punished the child severely sometimes on account of his dirty habits I allowed no one else to lift a hand to him.'

The girls said that Mrs Dean was always sober when she punished the children, though she sometimes got drunk at home alone, a claim that Minnie vigorously denied:

And as for me being a drunkard, there are three hotels in Winton and the keepers can each and all say if Mrs Dean was a drunkard she did not get drink from here. The extent of my libations never exceeded a sixpennyth of beer, and they could not say that that was bought even once a month. If anything else was sent for it was for medicine or for some other purpose, for spirits I rarely took.[46]

Later, during the seven weeks and three days that would elapse between the end of her trial and her execution, Minnie was offered, and at times urged, to partake of whatever alcoholic beverages she desired, but she steadfastly refused to touch a drop.

Even more disturbing was the evidence given by Maggie and Esther concerning the disappearances of Cyril, Henry, Sydney and Willie. The overall pattern was always the same: on a day when her husband was away Mrs Dean would tell Maggie and Esther that adoptive parents were coming to collect one of the children (from Gore for Cyril, from Wallacetown for Henry, from Woodlands for Sydney, from Limehills for Willie). Then she would send the girls away for several hours. By the time they returned the child was gone. Neither girl ever saw adoptive parents coming or going from The Larches.

Some details seemed particularly sinister: before Cyril vanished both Esther and Maggie saw Mrs Dean give him laudanum, supposedly so that he would not fret when his new parents came to collect him; after Cyril and Willie had gone Esther saw their clothes at The Larches, Mrs Dean said that the adoptive parents brought new clothes and left the old ones behind; after Henry and Cyril left Mrs Dean showed the girls what she said were recent photographs of the departed children. Neither Maggie nor Esther was sure whether the photographs, presented in court, really were of the missing boys.

Both girls saw the skeleton unearthed at The Larches. They thought the skull (which had a piece of scalp and hair attached) looked like the head of Willie Phelan.

The next witness to take the stand was Sydney's mother, Caroline McKernan. She told of handing over her two-week-old baby to a woman in Dunedin, a woman who called herself Minnie McKellar and who claimed to be the daughter of a clergyman of the First Church of Scotland. Then she told of going to The Larches nineteen months later in a fruitless search for her son.

Margaret Olsen confirmed that her son Willie Phelan had been placed in the care of Mrs Dean, and Mrs Hogan, a fruiterer of Invercargill, denied the claim (reportedly made by Mrs Dean to Maggie Cameron) that she had adopted Willie.

Constable Rasmussen was probably looking forward to recounting his dealings with Mrs Dean but he had to be brief; the evening was growing late and there were more witnesses to be heard. He said that he had frequently called at The Larches but, except for one occasion, Mrs Dean had refused to give him information about the children. This statement was untrue; Minnie had twice (in 1891 and 1893) given him full details of the backgrounds of the children in her care. He also said that none of the children that had disappeared from The Larches had been traced. This was also untrue. In 1893 Minnie told him that the child who appeared on the 1891 list as 'no name' had been adopted and taken to Australia. The police later found the infant in the care of his own mother in Southland.

Next Constable McDonough and Detective Herbert described the discovery of the skeleton. The detective also produced a letter seized from The Larches in which Cyril's mother, Ellen Scoular, advised Minnie of the death of Cyril's father, Colin McLachlan, in January 1895. 'P. S. — Trusting the wee fellow is a good boy', she wrote, obviously unaware that Cyril had vanished from Minnie's care two years earlier.

The final witness was Dr Macleod, who judged the skeleton to be that of a four-year-old child. He was unable to determine the sex or the cause of death.

The coroner asked Mrs Dean whether she wished to give evidence, but she made no reply. He then reviewed the case and complimented the police on the able and fair manner in which they had conducted the inquiry. It was after 10 pm before the jury returned their verdict:

> That of the name and identity of the said child unknown, the subject of this inquest, and of the cause, time, and place of the occurrence there is no evidence; but they are strongly of opinion that the body of the said child unknown is that of a male child by name Willie Phelan of Russell St Dunedin.

The verdict may have been vague, but that didn't matter. In building up the case against Minnie Dean the inquest served another purpose entirely — it allowed the police to convey to the public and the press the impression that Minnie Dean was engaged in a large-scale, cold-blooded, mercenary scheme of systematic, premeditated murder. Minnie Dean may have been hanged for the murder of Dorothy Edith Carter, but in the eyes of the public it was the evidence that emerged at this inquest that determined her guilt.

Reader, this inquest was crucial. We must re-examine it carefully and I know just the place to do it. Come with me to Bad Minnie's Café in Invercargill. It's said to be on the very spot where Minnie Dean was hanged (but it isn't.) * Let's take this table by the window. We'll order a meal, open a bottle of wine and talk through the issues.

---

* If you must know, the old Invercargill gaol where Minnie Dean was hanged was on the south-west corner of the Leven and Spey St intersection, where the railway yards are now.

The testimony presented at the inquest into the skeleton was widely interpreted to mean that each missing child was killed by Minnie Dean, and that she planned their deaths in advance. But surely that's not the only interpretation. Even if she did invent that adoption story to cover up their deaths, that doesn't mean that she murdered them, does it? I know she could be careless, violent and neglectful under stress. I wouldn't rule out the possibility that she killed some children accidentally — perhaps Eva Hornsby, perhaps Dorothy Edith Carter, perhaps Willie Phelan. But what about all the evidence (from her neighbours, from the children in her care, from Minnie herself) that she was well-meaning, kind-hearted and loving. Do you really believe such a woman was capable of cold-blooded murder? Consider the five well-fed, happy, well-cared-for little children at The Larches at the time of her arrest. Consider the fact, acknowledged by Judge Williams himself, that Minnie's adopted daughters, Maggie Cameron and Esther Wallis, were well brought up. Consider Minnie's long-drawn-out efforts to return Baby O'Brian to one of his parents. Why didn't she just kill him, if that was her habit? Consider 'no name' from Invercargill: Minnie told the police he'd been adopted and taken to Australia, then they found him with his own mother in Southland. Doesn't this indicate that some of the babies Minnie claimed were adopted could still be alive? Consider John Brookland: Minnie didn't like him, and since his payments weren't being kept up she asked Sergeant Macdonnell to put him into state care, which he did. Wouldn't it have been easier for Minnie to murder the child, if she was a murderer? Consider the fact that Henry Cockerill spent nine months at The Larches before he disappeared, Sydney McKernan spent a year, Cyril Scoular spent more than two years and Willie Phelan spent more than three. If Minnie intended to murder them why did she waste all that time and money feeding, clothing and sheltering them first? Why did she bother to nurse them when they were ill? Do you really believe that this demonstrably caring woman was capable of premeditated murder?

More wine?

Minnie admitted in her last statement that the skeleton found in her garden was that of Willie Phelan, but she continued to insist that Cyril Scoular, Sydney McKernan and Henry Cockerill were adopted, though she refused to say by whom. Could they have been adopted? Well frankly, I doubt it. There was a surplus of unwanted babies in Victorian New Zealand, and eugenically-conscious childless couples probably favoured the children of relatives over the bastards of strangers. To find willing adoptive parents Minnie would have had to advertise vigorously. She certainly advertised vigorously for babies, but I have found no evidence that she ever advertised for adoptive parents at all. And why wouldn't she tell the police who the adoptive parents were when her life depended on it? She had no hesitation in directing them to people who could prove she wasn't a drunk. Also the police had little trouble prising the names of natural parents out of her — if keeping secrets was important to Minnie she should have concealed those identities; in colonial society the shame of bearing an illegitimate child was far greater than the shame of adopting one. I suppose there is an outside chance that some of the missing children may have been adopted, but I think it's far more likely that they died, probably as a result of spontaneous violence, illness, accident or neglect.

This soup is delicious.

So you think the evidence given by Esther and Maggie points strongly to premeditation? Well, in the light of current knowledge about the reliability of eye-witness testimony[47] I think we should look at their evidence again. Sure they testified with poise and conviction, and they probably believed every word they said, but that doesn't mean they were telling the truth. Their conviction was more than likely a by-product of the number of times they had to tell their stories in court. That was certainly the case with Dr Macleod: he wasn't at all sure about the cause of Eva Hornsby's death when he took the stand at her inquest, but by the time he gave evidence at the magisterial hearing he was in no doubt; Eva Hornsby had been asphyxiated.

Another problem with the girls' testimony relates to the difficulty we all have in separating out memories of similar, repeated events. 'One Christmas was so much like another . . .' wrote Dylan Thomas, 'that I can never remember whether it snowed for six days and six nights when I was twelve or whether it snowed for twelve days and twelve nights when I was six.' Those of us who have trouble recalling which of our children was immunised against which disease at what age will appreciate the problem. Could Esther and Maggie have confused the details of the separate disappearances of the missing children? Could they, with a little prompting from the police, have moulded the vaguely remembered details of children disappearing at different times and under different circumstances into a recurring pattern that was not evident in the original events? More importantly, were some of their memories reconstructed from Minnie's later explanations of the events in question, rather than directly remembered from first-hand observation? Such reconstructions are certainly possible; as an adult the educationalist Piaget discovered to his astonishment that his vivid and detailed childhood memory of being abducted had no basis whatever in fact; the supposed memory had simply grown in his imagination from a story told by his nurse.[48]

How's your chicken?

In her last statement Minnie admitted that she told Maggie and Esther that Willie had been adopted in order to explain his disappearance. She may have done the same thing for the same reasons with the other missing children. (We can imagine her saying — remember, I told you last week that he was going to be adopted, his new mother came to collect him while you were out . . .) If she repeated that story often enough, with whatever details she chose to throw in, her fiction would have soon become Maggie and Esther's reality. Here's Minnie's account of Willie's death:

> The boy was leaving me, and daily expected, and all the arrangements had been made for his leaving. It was a Mrs Norris that was adopting him. My time is now short as not only my days but hours are now numbered, and to go into the details of what befell is more than I can do. On the word of a woman standing on the verge of eternity, what befell the boy was an accident. I wrote to the mother three days after I received my sentence as I thought it cruel to go away and leave her in a state of uncertainty as to the boy.[49] If I got in a temper and punished the child severely sometimes on account of his dirty habits I allowed one else to lift a hand to him. If he was sick I nursed him and he would put his arms about my neck and kiss me the same as the others. If I liked one child more than another it made no difference in my treatment of them. Esther was at home when it occurred, but did not know about it as I sent her and the other children away. I tried to restore animation but was too late. Not twenty minutes before I found him drowned he had brought me in some chips and I said he was a good boy. That was the last I saw of Willie alive. He went outside, dancing with glee at being praised. I did not bury him that day but on the following one. The knowledge that the boy was leaving me made [the children] already believe that he was gone. I buried him as I did to escape the inquest — the first one had cost me dear — and on account of Maggie — her dread and horror of having to be put in a witness box again amounted to almost a frenzy. To save her pain I would have imperilled my soul's salvation.[50]

Well I don't know. This explanation of Willie's death seems disturbingly vague, and the passing reference to her violence seems worryingly reminiscent of Minnie's account of Eva Hornsby's demise. But regardless of how Willie died, Minnie's statement confirms that she instilled in Maggie and Esther the erroneous belief that Willie had been adopted.

Despite having her adoption scenario disproved by the discovery of Willie Phelan's body, Minnie insisted to the end that the other missing children had been adopted. Perhaps she was like Dr Larch, the kindly head of St Cloud's orphanage in John Irving's *Cider House Rules*.[51] On the rare occasions when a child died in his care, Dr Larch comforted himself and shielded the other children from the sad finality of the event by creating a happy ending instead. He recorded in his diary the details of the vanished children's adoptions. He described each member of their adoptive families, and over the following years he created ongoing fictional accounts of their careers. Could Minnie, out of sheer soft-heartedness, have taken the same approach?

Let's open another bottle.

The big question concerning the adoption scenario is this: did Minnie tell Esther and Maggie that the missing children had been adopted before or after they vanished? If she gave the girls the adoption details before each child disappeared it is hard to avoid the conclusion that the adoption scenario was a cover for premeditated murder. If, on the other hand, she convinced the girls after the event that she had discussed the details with them beforehand, even if she hadn't, then the adoption story seems more like the cover for an unplanned death. Of course we can never know the answer to this question.

But let's face it, knowing what we know about Minnie, the chances of the missing children dying as a result of spontaneous violence, accident, illness or neglect was surely much greater than the chances of them dying from premeditated murder. According to Minnie, Willie died by accident, but I'm not sure whether I believe her. I think he may have died an unplanned violent death. Henry probably died of illness (on at least five occasions Constable Rasmussen told his superiors that Henry had a chest ailment and Dr Hunter did not expect him to live). Esther testified that Willie and Henry were in bed when she last saw them. Perhaps they were already dead. I don't know what happened to Sydney and Cyril, but we should not forget that the chances of a small child surviving a serious illness in the cramped and squalid Larches were not great. If Henry, Cyril and Sydney did die, I don't know what Minnie did with the bodies. Maybe she buried them in the soft earth of a recent grave in the nearby Winton cemetery. The cemetery records show that some old plots, when reopened for later burials, were found to contain the remains of unrecorded children.

Yes thanks — just half a glass.

Just between you and me, I can think of another explanation for the disappearances (apart from spontaneous violence, accident, illness or neglect). This explanation doesn't involve cold-blooded premeditation, but it does involve a dangerous level of mental disturbance on the part of kindly Mrs Dean. What I have in mind is the mirror-image of the phantom pregnancy syndrome. Let's call it the phantom adoption syndrome. Look at Minnie, a woman living on the emotional edge and stressed beyond reason, trapped in a life of misery and squalor with a houseful of children — some of them real honeys and some of them little monsters. She probably longed to get the monsters adopted. She may have even used adoption as a threat — if you don't stop grizzling I'll get you adopted. With every increase in her stress level such adoption talk probably became more frequent, more emphatic. Then, like a woman who convinces herself she is pregnant for nine months and then feels compelled to steal a baby to maintain the fantasy, the pressure on Minnie to translate her talk of adoption into action may have eventually become overwhelming. So she sends the household away for the day, all except for the chosen child, and in numb, urgent desperation she gives him an overdose of laudanum, speeds his demise with a pillow and hides his body. Maybe. Maybe not. We'll never know.

Coffee?

The gentlemen of the press drew only the most sinister conclusions from the evidence presented at the inquest into the skeleton. The Southland correspondent of *Otago Daily Times* reported:

> The police at yesterday's inquiry clearly proved that four children had disappeared from the Larches in a most mysterious and unaccountable manner and in quick succession, whilst all of the belongings of the poor unfortunate children remained in the house. I have said *four* children, but the police, I believe, could have gone on all night producing evidence of a similar character, showing that a great many other children disappeared in a like manner. It was most painful to witness at yesterday's inquiry the distress, agony, grief, and shame of some of the poor mothers, who in that court probably for the first time heard of the treatment their little ones had received.[52]

The weekly *New Zealand Graphic* carried an article illustrated with photographs of the police at work in the Dean garden. 'The story does not bear thinking of,' wrote the reporter. 'To imagine the terror of the poor doomed children "left alone" with a woman now charged with the murder must shake even the stoutest nerve.'[53]

The day after the inquest into the skeleton ended, the Dean case went before an Invercargill grand jury.[54] In his address to the jurors Judge Williams noted that the cases before them were, with one notable exception, very much the same as usual. There was a case of assault, a case of forgery, a case of theft, a case of carnal knowledge and a case of perjury; and there was a case in which a woman was charged with the murder of two children. He reminded the jurors that their function was not to determine guilt or innocence but to decide whether the evidence laid before them in the bills of indictment established a prima facie case against the accused. Two of the grand jurors (Nicholas Johnson and Walter Searle), as members of the Hornsby and Carter inquest juries, had already found Minnie Dean guilty of murder. A third grand juror (Robert Wesney) had served on the skeleton inquest jury. Not surprisingly, the grand jury took no time at all to determine that a case had been established against Mrs Dean. By contrast, the Dunedin grand jury that considered the evidence of murder against Thomas Hall eight years earlier took an usually long time — nearly three hours — to decide that the accused had a case to answer.[55]

Minnie Dean's trial in the Invercargill Supreme Court was set down to begin on Thursday 18 June 1895.

Chapter XVI

———— ❧ ————

THE TRIAL

The trial of Minnie Dean opened in the Invercargill Supreme Court at 10 am on Tuesday 18 June 1895 before Mr Justice Joshua Strange Williams. At that time official records of court proceedings were deemed to be unnecessary,[1] but the judge took extensive notes and, thanks to the apparently insatiable appetite of Victorian newspaper readers for scandal and tragedy, virtually every detail of the four-day drama was reported in the local press.[2]

The prisoner was charged with having murdered a female child named Dorothy Edith Carter, and with having murdered 'a second female infant whose name is unknown'. There was presumably some esoteric legal reason for not naming the second child, but everyone following the case would have known it was Eva Hornsby. The Crown intended to deal with the Carter case first and then, depending on the outcome, follow with the Hornsby case. Mr T. M. Macdonald and Mr Y. H. Hall, both of Invercargill, appeared for the prosecution. Mrs Dean was defended by Mr A. C. Hanlon of Dunedin. According to the *Otago Daily Times* the prisoner was 'perfectly calm in her demeanour during the whole of the proceedings . . .'[3]

The jury was drawn from a roll containing the names of men between the ages of twenty-one and sixty living within a twenty-mile radius of Invercargill. The total population of the district was about 6,000, but many of that number were too young or too old, or were otherwise disqualified or exempted from jury service. New Zealand women won the right to vote in 1893 but they did not win the right to serve on juries until 1942. Maori, aliens, convicts, undischarged bankrupts and persons of bad fame were also disqualified. Members of Parliament, judges and magistrates, clergymen, schoolmasters, lawyers, government employees, coroners, policemen, shipping masters and pilots, members of Her Majesty's Army, Navy, Militia and Volunteer Force, firemen and railway employees were exempt. All things considered, the Invercargill common jury roll cannot have been unduly long.

Eight years earlier in Dunedin, when Thomas Hall was tried before Judge Williams for the murder of his father-in-law Captain Cain, he had the advantage of a jury of his peers.[4] Under the Juries Act of 1880 any party in a case before the Supreme Court could apply for a special jury instead of a common jury. If the application was granted the twelve-man jury would be drawn from the local grand jury roll. No criteria for the use of special juries were given in the Juries Act of 1880, but the provision probably had something to do with the misgivings felt by the then Premier, Sir John Hall, about the move towards electoral democracy that had taken place the previous year. To Sir John Hall (New Zealand Premier 1879–82), and many other class-conscious colonists, the extension of the franchise to all adult New Zealand males in 1879 must have seemed like the beginning of the end.

And it was. At each election that followed the balance of power shifted further away from the landed gentry. Finally, in 1890, the scales tipped and a group of liberals committed to land and labour reform (most notably John Ballance, Richard John Seddon, William Pember Reeves, Jock McKenzie and Bluff's own Joseph Ward) were swept to power on the votes of working men. Following the 1890 election Sir John Hall complained to a friend about 'the loafing single men who held a great voice in the last election'.[5*] It was probably the prospect of having such men sitting in judgment on wayward members of propertied élite that in 1880 prompted Sir John and his colleagues to make provision for the use of special juries.

On Tuesday 4 January 1887 in the Dunedin Supreme Court the Crown prosecutor applied for a special jury for the trial of Thomas Hall.

'I would not have done it on my own motion,' Mr Haggitt explained apologetically. 'But I have been instructed to do so by the Crown solicitor at Timaru.'

Judge Williams replied sagely, 'If criminal cases are to be tried by special juries at all . . . this certainly is a proper case. This is one of the kind of case the Legislature contemplated when it authorised the trial of criminal cases by special juries. There should be no difficulty. I will make the order.'

There would have been no point in Minnie Dean's lawyer applying for a special jury. Such a body would have had even less resemblance to a jury of her peers than the common jury that assembled to consider her case. On the morning of the trial the common jurors' names were drawn from a barrel in the proper manner. Ten prospective jurymen were challenged by Mr Hanlon; nine were stood aside by Mr Macdonald. The twelve men duly selected and duly sworn (and duly named in the newspaper the next day) were drawn from a far wider

---

* The antidote to this appalling state of affairs, as Sir John saw it, was the civilising influence of women's votes. During the 1890s he became a leading advocate of female suffrage.

range of occupations and locations than the gentlemen who had served on the inquest juries. The trial jurors were: George Smyth (foreman), storekeeper; William Hyndman, labourer; Ebenezer Johnson, Bluff Harbour Board employee; Robert Instone, storeman; Thomas Donaldson and James Ferguson, carpenters; William Fryor, bullock driver; Patrick Joyce, farmer; William Brown, blacksmith; Thomas Lewis, striker; and one of the four James Andersons and one of the two Alexander Jenkins in the district.[6]

During the six weeks leading up to the trial, two inquest juries comprising the most important men in town had found Minnie Dean guilty of murder (in one case implicitly, in the other explicitly); the local magistrate had ruled that Minnie Dean had a case to answer; a third inquest jury — also composed of important men — had heard evidence suggesting that Minnie Dean was engaged in a long-term scheme of mercenary, systematic, cold-blooded murder; the Crown solicitor had compared Minnie Dean to Australia's most evil baby farmers, the Makins; a grand jury comprising some of the same men as had sat on the inquest juries had endorsed the magistrate's ruling. Righteous matrons had knitted their indignation into their woollens and stirred it into their stews. Steaming clouds of outrage had poured from the mouths of their menfolk as they went about their business in the wintery town. The trains that clattered through the land mumbled and screamed the repetitious rumours. Day after day the story filled the newspapers. So when Mr T. M. Macdonald, Invercargill Crown solicitor, opened the case for the prosecution in the crowded court room, he impressed on the twelve common jurymen the importance of discarding from their minds all statements with regard to the case which they had previously read or heard, of approaching the evidence free from bias and prejudice and of doing their duty without fear or favour — and he really seemed to believe that such a thing was possible.

'You have met this day to enquire into a charge against a woman of murdering a female infant,' he said. 'These few words, I think, will suffice to impress upon you the extreme importance of the case, and to remind you of the responsibility that rests upon you.' In fact in those days there was nothing unusual about a woman murdering a baby. It happened all the time. Admittedly most of the people responsible for the dead infants found abandoned under hedges or floating in waterways were never traced, but those that were nearly always turned out to be women. The culprit was often the mother or grandmother of the dead child. The charge was usually concealment of birth, and the culprit could face up to two years in prison.

Of course the Dean case was different. Minnie's business was an affront to contemporary ideals of motherhood and the family. Instead of upholding the moral standards of the age as all good women were expected to do, in the eyes of respectable folk Minnie Dean was undermining them. Trapped in the distorting mirror of public exposure, Minnie Dean had been transformed between her arrest and trial from a poor woman engaged in a running battle with the police to a scapegoat for all the immorality, crime and infanticide that plagued the anxiety-wracked colony. The whole country was watching, and waiting transfixed to see if one of the greatest evils of the age could be disposed of and atoned for in one dramatic prosecution.

The Crown prosecutor defined murder as the unlawful and deliberate taking of a human life. He said that people who committed premeditated murder rarely did so in the presence of witnesses and took great care to avoid detection. The Crown had to rely on a series of linked facts to prove its case. It was the duty of the jury to consider the facts as a whole and to say not only whether they were consistent with the prisoner's guilt, but also whether they were inconsistent with her innocence. He reminded the jury of the ease with which an adult responsible for the care of a child could murder it undetected. He said that society relied, and wisely relied, greatly upon maternal affection; there was no higher, more intense affection than that of a mother for a child. But when from stress or circumstances, misfortune, or other causes to which he need not refer, a mother found it necessary to part with her offspring, the Legislature deemed it necessary to step in and protect infant life.

Mr Macdonald then outlined the evidence to be presented: the accused had left The Larches with the child on 2 May but by the time she reached Lumsden the child had disappeared; she had purchased laudanum at Bluff two days earlier; laudanum was later found in the organs of the dead child. 'What inference can you draw from that,' he said, 'but the inference that accused administered laudanum to the child and caused her death?' He went on to review the evidence of 'deliberate design, contrivance and concealment . . . which went to show that this laudanum was wilfully and deliberately given by Mrs Dean for the purpose of disposing of the child'. Why had she taken the child away from The Larches, he asked, except for the purpose of destroying it on the journey? Why had she taken a near-empty hat box, except for the purpose of concealing the body inside? Why had she buried the body in her garden and placed plants on top, except for the purpose of concealing the burial? The motive, he said, was perfectly obvious; she wanted to rid herself of the expense of maintaining the child and of the risk of incurring a fine for breaching the Infant Life Protection Act. However, he added, motive was not a neccessary part of the case. Regardless of motive, if the jury was satisfied after considering the evidence that Mrs Dean was guilty of wilfully causing the death of the child, it was their duty to find her guilty of murder.

After Macdonald's one-hour address a procession of twenty witnesses, familiar to the spectators from their appearances at the inquests and the magisterial hearing, traced Minnie Dean's travels concerning Dorothy Edith Carter, first from Bluff to The Larches, then from The Larches to Lumsden and Gore. The only new face was that of the surveyor brought in to describe the location and dimensions of the Dean property. To add weight to the Crown case, two sandbags were produced; one weighing 14^1/$_2$ lb to represent Dorothy Edith Carter, another weighing 7^1/$_2$ lb to represent Eva Hornsby. Every witness who testified to carrying Mrs Dean's hat box was invited to lift the hat box in court with or without the appropriate sandbags. Yes, they all agreed helpfully, it was about that weight when I carried it.

As he had done at the earlier hearing, Hanlon worked his questions into the gaps and uncertainties in the evidence, and elicited details which he would later use to argue for the innocence of his client.

When Mrs Dean's movements had been traced as far as Clinton, Mr Macdonald asked His Honour for permission to call evidence detailing her actions after leaving Gore on 3 May. He said he intended to prove that she murdered a child obtained from Mrs Hornsby at Milburn. The purpose of introducing this evidence, he explained, was to show that the death of Dorothy Edith Carter was not accidental.

Mr Hanlon objected to the admission of the evidence, and asked that discussion of the matter be allowed to stand over until morning. He did not need to spell out the reason for his objection. The judge and the lawyers involved knew that the issue was 'collateral facts'. * Hanlon's concern was that though evidence that Eva Hornsby had died under suspicious circumstances in Minnie Dean's care did not in itself prove that Minnie had murdered Dorothy Edith Carter, if admitted such evidence could seriously prejudice the jury. As Oscar Wilde might have said (had he not been so preoccupied with his own trial in London at the time), 'To have one child die on a train journey may be regarded as misfortune, to have two die looks like carelessness — or worse.'

In his search for arguments to support his objection Hanlon studied the appeal decision in the case of *Makin* v. *Attorney General of New South Wales*. He must have been dismayed by what he found. A summary of the case[7] states:

> Makin and wife were convicted of the murder of an infant. It appeared that the child which they had undertaken to adopt for a small premium was found buried in their back garden under circumstances which pointed to the conclusion that the child had been murdered. At the trial evidence was adduced to shew that the prisoners had adopted other infants upon payment of sums inadequate for their support, and that the bodies of infants had been found buried in a similar manner in the gardens of several houses occupied by the prisoners. *Held*, on appeal to the Privy Council, affirming the decision of the Full Court, that such evidence was rightly admitted.

---

* Thanks to changes in terminology, what were known in the nineteenth century as 'collateral facts' are nowadays known as 'similar facts' (and nowadays the term 'collateral facts' refers to something else again).

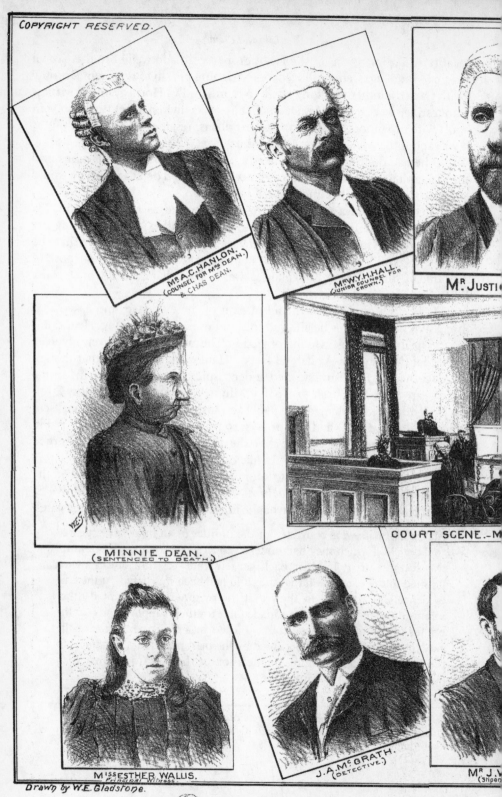

Mr A.C. HANLON.
(COUNSEL FOR Mrs DEAN.)
& CHAS DEAN.

Mr W Y. H. HALL
(JUNIOR COUNSEL FOR CROWN.)

Mr JUSTI

MINNIE DEAN.
(SENTENCED TO DEATH.)

COURT SCENE.—M

Miss ESTHER WALLIS.
(Primeval Witness)

J. A. McGRATH.
(DETECTIVE.)

Mr J. W.
(Stipen

Drawn by W.E. Gladstone.

The Child Murders Case.

Mr. T. M. MACDONALD
(CROWN PROSECUTOR)

Mr. J. A. HANAN.
(COUNSEL FOR CHAS DEAN)

—AMS.

—EAN'S TRIAL.

CHARLES DEAN.
(DISCHARGED IN LOWER COURT.)

P. HERBERT.
(DETECTIVE.)

MISS M. CAMERON.
Principal Witness.

—TON.
—afe)

Lithographed by W. Craig & Co. Invercargill.

Winton, Southland, N.Z

Next morning, before the puffing and steaming crowd that crushed in from the snow-dusted Invercargill streets, Judge Williams invited Hanlon to expand on his objection. The young lawyer confessed that it was very difficult to argue that the Makin case did not apply. Realising that he could not stop the evidence being admitted, Hanlon made the best of a bad situation by asking Judge Williams to rule that the question of the admissibility of the evidence be reserved. A favourable ruling would guarantee a hearing in the Court of Appeal, but Hanlon must have sensed that the judge was disinclined to grant his request. He went on to quote a subsection of the Act which stated that if the Court refused to reserve a question it 'shall nevertheless take a note of such objection, unless it considers the application frivolous', and another subsection which stated 'If the Court refuses to reserve the question the party applying may, with leave in writing of the Attorney-General, move the Court of Appeal as hereinafter provided.' The 'hereinafter provided' referred to a further subsection which stated that if the Attorney-General's response was positive the request for leave to appeal would then go before the Court of Appeal, at which time 'the Court of Appeal may . . . grant or refuse such leave'.

Judge Williams directed his reply to the Crown prosecutor:

> I don't want to trouble you, Mr Macdonald, I have no doubt whatever that this evidence is admissible and that it is admissible apart altogether from the decision of the Privy Council in Makin's case. It is certainly relevant to the present enquiry that the jury should know everything done by Mrs Dean between the time she left The Larches with the child on Thursday until the time she returned to The Larches on Saturday with the child. Everything she did and said during that time is part of the *res gestae.** If the evidence of what she did and said between Lumsden and Clinton on Friday was admissible, then there can be no reasonable doubt for excluding anything she did or said between the time she left Clinton for Milburn and the time she returned to Clinton. That is, I say, altogether apart from the decision in Makin's case. That decision, however, seems to me to completely cover the whole ground of the objection to the present evidence . . . I hesitate to say that the objection is frivolous, but it appears to me to have no solid foundation. I think my duty will be to refuse to reserve the question and to take a note of the objection.

'That is all I ask,' said Mr Hanlon.
'You have plainly done your duty,' said the judge.[8]

---

* *Res gestae* (the thing done). The facts surrounding or accompanying a transaction which is the subject of legal proceedings; or facts so connected with a fact in issue as to introduce it, explain its nature, or form in connection with it one continuous transaction. (*Jowett's Dictionary of English Law*, Sweet & Maxwell, London, 1977).

Eight years earlier, before the same judge, at the trial of Thomas Hall for the murder of his father-in-law Captain Cain, Hall's lawyer objected to the admission of evidence that Hall had earlier been convicted of the attempted murder of his wife. On that occasion Judge Williams was less certain. After mulling over the question he decided to admit the evidence but reserve the point.

Thus in the Hall case Judge Williams, without being asked, assured Hall's lawyer of an automatic Appeal Court hearing, while in the Dean case he placed two obstacles (the need for prior permission from the Attorney General, and from the Court of Appeal itself) in the way of Hanlon's wish to appeal.

After the question of admissibility had been argued, witnesses to Minnie Dean's travels and transactions concerning Eva Hornsby were called. The only witness who had not appeared before was George Findlay, a commercial traveller who shared the first-class carriage with Minnie Dean between Gore and Mataura on 4 May.

Mrs Hornsby did not stand up well to Hanlon's vigorous cross-examination. She claimed to have given Eva fresh milk at Milburn, but when Hanlon asked her why she had not said so at the earlier enquiry she replied lamely that she couldn't remember whether she'd been asked. When he asked her why she had not used her own name in her correspondence with Mrs Dean she was equally vague. 'I don't know,' she said.

Mrs Hornsby had cared for her granddaughter for only three days of her month-long life (two days after birth and one day prior to being handed over to Minnie Dean) and her unfamiliarity with the child soon became apparent. Hanlon asked her how she identified Eva's body at the Southland Hospital morgue. 'By the look of it,' she said. When pressed for details she suggested that Eva's head was a peculiar shape. 'I couldn't explain it,' she added vaguely. 'The shape of head was similar to that of Eva Hornsby.'

Mrs Hornsby's credibility suffered a further blow when Mrs Bennett, the Port Chalmers baby minder who had cared for Eva for most of her short life, took the stand. Mrs Bennett assured Alf Hanlon that there was nothing peculiar about the shape of Eva Hornsby's head; she had identified Eva's body at the morgue by its general appearance and by the presence of two distinctive marks (a small burn on one finger and a mark below the navel) — marks that Mrs Hornsby never noticed.

After the Hornsby evidence had been presented, the police witnesses gave their reports and Drs Macleod and Young described their findings. Under cross-examination Dr Macleod conceded that laudanum was commonly given by mothers to stop crying and induce sleep in their infants, and that the time a small child may take to die from an overdose of laudanum could not be predicted in advance. He also admitted that Mrs Dean had taken children to him when they were sick.

Professor Black then gave a full account of his investigations. He explained that the stomach and intestines of the two infants had been sent to him intact. In Dorothy Edith Carter's stomach he found a quantity of undigested meat and carrots; in his professional opinion it was either corned beef or Irish stew.* He found Eva Hornsby's stomach and intestines to be completely empty. He said he had never seen such empty intestines. Further tests revealed that Dorothy Edith Carter's stomach, liver, kidneys and intestines contained poisonous levels of the opium constituents, morphia and meconic acid. His analysis of a sample from the Bluff chemist's stock bottle revealed that it contained average strength laudanum. In response to Hanlon's cross-examination he described his analysis methods in lengthy technical detail.

'We are none the wiser,' sighed the judge when he had finished.

The Professor's detailed explanation was not entirely wasted. After studying Black's report in 1991 Professor F. N. Fastier, Emeritus Professor of Pharmacology at the University of Otago, confirmed that the results of the tests used by Black provided strong evidence of the presence of morphine.

The point should also be made that the bodies and organs of Dorothy Edith Carter and Eva Hornsby were kept under close security and handled with great care from the time they were discovered in Minnie Dean's garden through to the post-mortems at the Southland Hospital morgue and the analyses of the organs by Professor Black in Dunedin. The chances of their being tampered with or accidentally contaminated were extremely remote.

On the third morning of the trial Mr Macdonald polished up the Crown case by introducing the Southland Hospital Dispenser (who confirmed that the bottles in which the child's organs had been sent to Professor Black were prepared and sealed in the proper manner) and two bank accountants (who declared that the letters to Mrs Izett signed 'M. Cameron', the letters to Mrs Hornsby signed 'M. Dean' and the signature in the Bluff chemist's poison book were the work of the same hand).

Then Mr Macdonald delivered another blow. Referring to the precedent-setting Makin case he announced that he wished to call evidence to show that the accused received infants into her charge, that they disappeared, and that the skeleton of one was found buried in her garden, the object being to show that the death of Dorothy Edith Carter was not an accident.

Hanlon again objected, and asked the judge to reserve the point or note the objection; and Judge Williams again said he saw no foundation for the

---

* Presumably from the meal of corned beaf, carrots and potato served to Minnie Dean at the Dipton Railway Hotel.

objection but under the circumstances he could not say it was frivolous. He therefore noted the objection.

By the time evidence concerning the disappearances of Sydney McKernan, Willie Phelan, Cyril Scoular and Henry Cockerill had been presented, and Inspector Pardy had testified that Mrs Dean was not registered under the Infant Life Protection Act, a total of forty-seven witnesses had taken the stand and thirty-five exhibits (press advertisements, letters and telegrams, baby clothes, a chemist's poison book, a plan of the Dean property, a handbag, a hat box, dress pieces, oilcloth, a receipt, flowers, medicine bottles, train tickets, sand bags) had been discussed. At that point Mr Macdonald announced that he had reached the conclusion of the evidence for the prosecution.

Hanlon was faced with a difficult choice. According to the Criminal Code of 1893 a defence counsel may call witnesses or address the jury, but he may not do both. The key defence witness was Minnie Dean herself. How would she conduct herself? How would the Crown prosecutor treat her in cross-examination? Though she was on trial only for the murder of Dorothy Edith Carter, if she entered the witness box she would be called upon to explain the deaths of Eva Hornsby and the skeleton, and the disappearances of Sydney McKernan, Willie Phelan, Cyril Scoular and Henry Cockerill. Could she convey her innocence more effectively in person than Hanlon could by summoning all his powers of oratory? Could she enter the witness box and say with simple conviction — *Yes, gentlemen, I was responsible for these deaths. And yes gentlemen, I lied. But what follows is the truth, the whole web of circumstances that brought me to this place. Gentlemen, I will tell you what happened to Dorothy Edith Carter, Eva Hornsby, Willie Phelan, Sydney McKernan, Cyril Scoular, Henry Cockerill. Hear my story that you may understand I am no different from you. I am not evil. And all along I acted only for what I took to be the best.* But it was not to be.

When the opportunity came Hanlon did not put Minnie Dean in the witness box. Why he made that decision, and whether or not it was the right one, has been debated in legal circles for decades. Now, thanks to Sergeant Macdonnell's curiosity and an archive system that occasionally throws up something really useful, we have an insight into Hanlon's dilemma. This is Sergeant Macdonnell's report on his post-execution conversation with Josiah Hanan about why Mrs Dean was never allowed to testify:

Her own solicitors could not depend upon anything she said unless they really knew it to be true independently of her. For instance, when the two bodies of the infants were found in her garden, she was asked if it was possible for the police to find any more, she again and again assured them there was no other to find. When the skeleton was found two days afterwards they told her they could not believe a word she said, and that they had very little chance in defending her unless she told them the truth. She promised she would.

Before her trial she was anxious to give evidence re the deaths of the two infants, and also of the skeleton. She was to account for the death of Dorothy Edith Carter as appeared since in the papers viz: an overdose of laudanum. And that of Eva Hornsby by falling in Clarendon Railway Shed. She admitted that the skeleton was that of Willie Phelan and she told her solicitors he accidentally fell in a large tub of water and was of course drowned. She thus wished to explain how each of the three children named came by their deaths. She was told that if she gave evidence at all she would have to explain what became of the other children not accounted for. She said she would do so. She was then asked where were they to be found &c, she said, 'in different places in Australia'. She was told it would be necessary to name the people and the exact places where they were. She said she could give names. She was told if not true it would never do, but she urged that the police would not have time to find out whether it was true or not. She was told they would *cable* and find out in no time. She still urged that supposing the police could not find the persons named, how could they (the police) prove her statement was not true. It was pointed out that the police had photos of children which she said were those of some of the missing children and that any statement made by her inconsistent with that would tell against her, and that the photographers were said to be interviewed. She made no answer to this. She was then told that if she could satisfactorily account for *even one* of the missing children it would go a long way in her favour — if she could for instance say, 'Go to such a person and you shall find such a child,' it would be most important for her, and she might be able to give the evidence she wished, but if not, she would have to keep silent in court. She then decided not to give evidence.[9]

Which is why, after all the evidence for the prosecution had been presented, Hanlon announced that he did not intend to call any witnesses for the defence. All that remained was for Mr Macdonald and Mr Hanlon to put their arguments, for the judge to sum up and for the jury to consider the verdict.

At 2 pm Mr Macdonald began his eighty-minute address. He told the jury that the real question before them was — did the accused intentionally cause the death of Dorothy Edith Carter? He said that the child was handed over to Mrs Dean by Mrs Cox with the sum of £10 less expenses.[10] This statement must have confused the jury; they had already been told by Mrs Cox that Minnie Dean had received no money with the child. Mr Macdonald did not repeat the error during his address, but neither did he correct it.

Early in his speech he alluded to the evidence relating to Eva Hornsby and thereafter linked the two children in most of the arguments he presented:

> So far then it has been shown that Mrs Dean leaves Lady Barkly and goes to Lumsden, during which journey one child disappears; that she proceeds to Milburn and gets possession of another child which also disappears; that she comes back to The Larches without the children; that she has something in the tin box corresponding with the weight of the dead children; and that the bodies of the two children are found buried in her garden. What is the inference you are bound to draw from these facts? The inference you are bound to draw is that Mrs Dean killed those two children; that they died while in her charge and she was the cause of their death. I now come to the *gravamen** of the charge. If the jury are satisfied that these children died under Mrs Dean's charge and that they were killed by her, the question arises as to whether or not they were intentionally killed by her.

In attempting to establish intent, the Crown prosecutor raised six points. The first concerned Mrs Dean's reported claim that she took Dorothy Edith Carter away from The Larches to give to a lady. No such lady met the accused on her journey and no such lady was produced to give evidence. Furthermore, if the child died by misadventure why did Mrs Dean not inform the authorities?

> I think I am justified in asking the jury to come to the conclusion that Mrs Dean's story is untrue, and that, looking at the whole of the facts, she had no other motive when she took the child than to do away with it.

His second point was that Mrs Dean took a near-empty tin hat box with her. 'For what object had she taken the box with her except that of putting bodies into it?' he said.

His third point concerned laudanum:

> Mrs Dean purchased laudanum at the Bluff; the child disappeared during the course of a journey upon which Mrs Dean had taken her for no apparent reason; the body had been found buried in her garden; and an examination of certain organs showed that a poisonous dose of morphia was in the body. What other conclusion can the jury come to other than that the laudanum had been bought for the purpose of being administered to, and had been administered to, the child.

His fourth point was that Mrs Dean buried the bodies in her own garden: 'That in itself was an unlawful act. Why did she run the risk of incurring a penalty if there was not some greater reason for concealment than an accident or misadventure?'

---

* *Gravamen*: that part of an accusation weighing most heavily against the accused. (*Collins Concise Dictionary*, 1990).

Mr Macdonald's fifth point concerned the lies told by Mrs Dean. She lied to Esther about the contents of the hat box and the fate of Dorothy Edith Carter. Her claim that the child was sick at Dipton, he suggested, was a lie — Esther said that Dorothy Edith took her breakfast well that morning and Dr Black testified that the child's stomach contained food from the meal served to Mrs Dean at Dipton. Mrs Dean also lied to the police and Mrs Hornsby when they confronted her about the fate of baby Eva — 'What inference can you draw from that fact, taken in conjunction with the other facts, but that the accused has been guilty of murder?'

The Crown prosecutor's final point concerned the discovery of the skeleton and the disappearances of other children from The Larches. His closing words were:

> I do not think I would be doing my duty if I do not tell the jury that in my opinion this doing away with children has been part of a system prosecuted by this woman. If the jury came to that conclusion their duty is obvious and they will have no difficulty in arriving at a verdict. If, on a consideration of the whole of the facts which have been proved by the evidence — not individual facts, but the whole of them and linked together as they have been — you entertain a reasonable doubt that the death of the child was intentionally caused by the accused, then, gentlemen, you must acquit her. But if, on the other hand, a full, fair and careful consideration of the evidence forces you to the conclusion that she wilfully and designedly caused the death of Dorothy Edith Carter, you would not be doing you duty to yourselves, to your consciences or to your God if you do not find her Guilty.

Alf Hanlon was faced with the daunting task of convincing the jury that his client's guilt had not been proved beyond reasonable doubt. Unlike the Crown prosecutor, whose best chance of securing a conviction lay with persuading the jury to consider 'the whole of the facts', Hanlon's best chance of having the charge reduced or dismissed lay with persuading the jury that only the evidence concerning the death of Dorothy Edith Carter was relevant, and that her death was an accident. His learned friend had said, declaimed Hanlon, that murder might be defined, for the purpose of the present charge, as unlawfully and intentionally taking the life of a human being. He had said further that if he proved to the jury that Mrs Dean had intentionally caused the death of Dorothy Edith Carter, then it would be their duty to convict her of murder. Had his learned friend proved that? Hanlon submitted he had not. What evidence had been adduced to show that she premeditated killing the child and actually did kill it?

Hanlon's careful summary of the evidence concerning Dorothy Edith Carter made the Crown case sound flimsy. When he offered alternative explanations for his client's actions the public gallery became unusually still. Throughout the rest of his ninety-minute address the crowd listened in silent, spellbound sympathy.

It was neccessary to bear in mind, he said, that Mrs Dean was continually getting babies to nurse, and a business of trafficking in children had to be conducted with secrecy. Mrs Hornsby herself had adopted secrecy in signing herself A. B. C. and in not giving her address. What did such things show? They showed that if an unfortunate girl had an illegitimate child she had to hide her shame because the world looked aghast at what was perhaps the one mistake of her life — and so the poor little child of love had to be sent away, no matter where, so that its mother could hold her head up again. This showed the rottenness of society, but still it was true. This showed that when a woman took children to nurse she had to keep the secret and hide the names from enquiry. Could they blame her for that? He could not deny that Mrs Dean had told many lies but she had done so to shelter her clients. She had divulged information in one case and had received a letter of complaint from the father of the child, and from that time forth she would not give any information. Could they blame her?

Hanlon then discussed the death of Dorothy Edith Carter, weaving through his address alternative explanations for all the apparently incriminating evidence (Mrs Dean bought the laudanum to replenish her home supply, she alighted at Gap Road to keep her activities secret, she took the hat box because she had no valise, she said she was getting the child adopted because that was her intention, she buried the bodies in her garden because she was carrying on a secret business). But his primary concern was with the evidence in his client's favour:

> At Bluff the child was seen only by the two girls at the hotel — if she wanted to murder it why did she not do so before it was seen by any more people? Why did she not kill it between Bluff and Invercargill? She had the poison and she had the child. Why did she take it home where people she knew would see her with it? The Crown claim of premeditation is absurd. At Gap Road she wrapped her cloak around the child to keep it warm. Was this the action of a murderess? She carried the little child home, put it to bed, lifted it up in the morning and each day bathed and clothed, fed and nursed it; was that the action of a murderess? Are you going to allow the suggestion that she intended all the time to murder the child to be thrust upon you? It is positively and absolutely absurd. Mrs Dean took food for the child when she left The Larches. She took things to sustain the child's life, not to annihilate it.

Hanlon noted the evidence that the child was crying and looked sick at Dipton, and disappeared between Dipton and Lumsden. He conceded that the death could have been caused by laudanum administered by Mrs Dean, but argued that the drug, in a much stronger solution than she was used to using at home, was given either to allay pain (in which case the child died by misadventure and his client should be acquitted) or to keep the child quiet (in which case his client may be guilty of manslaughter). He said that without evidence of premeditation they could not find her guilty of murder, and he reiterated that the Crown claim of premeditation was absurd:

> If she wanted to murder the child why go to Dipton to do it? What was easier than for her to dispose of the child at The Larches if she wanted to, as the Crown has tried to show that she has done before? She only had to get rid of Esther Wallis. Why go to the expense? Why go where people would see her? Why take the body home at all? There were plenty of rivers to dispose of it in. And after the burial, was the placing of plants on the grave the action of a murderess? The Crown says she stuck them in to hide the traces but that is preposterous. They didn't hide the grave. Ashes or dry earth would have done that.

Hanlon then discussed the death of Eva Hornsby. Undeterred by the fact that Dr Macleod had found no evidence that Eva had vomited or choked, Hanlon suggested that Eva had died by choking on her own vomit. He pointed out that, though Mrs Hornsby claimed to have fed the baby, Professor Black found her stomach to be completely empty; that proved she must have vomited, he said. What Professor Black actually said was that Eva Hornsby's stomach *and* intestines were completely empty. This finding is significant. The empty intestine suggests that not only did Mrs Hornsby not feed Eva at Milburn as she claimed, she may not have fed her at all from the time she picked up her granddaughter from Mrs Bennett on 2 May, to the time she handed her over to Minnie Dean twenty-four hours later. One person who could have testified about Mrs Hornsby's care of Eva during this period was Mrs Dryden, the Milburn woman with whom Mrs Hornsby and Eva spent the day while awaiting Minnie's arrival on the evening train. Mrs Dryden was not called as a trial witness, but she was interviewed by Constable King two days after her visit from Mrs Hornsby. He reported to his inspector:

> ... the child, she (Mrs Dryden) said, was about a month old and seemingly neglected as it was cold when she brought it to her place and did not appear to trouble much about it. She also said she did not think Mrs Hornsby was up to much.[11]

Perhaps Eva was frantic with hunger by the time Minnie carried her into the Clarendon railway shed. Perhaps she was too weak to feed. Perhaps Mrs Hornsby's neglect contributed to Eva's demise.

But Hanlon did not want to dwell on the death of Eva Hornsby, or for that matter on the disappearances of the other children. His aim was to convince the jury that all such evidence was irrelevant:

> If the Crown has a strong case, why do they want to prop it up with evidence of this sort? — because they know it is perfectly possible that Dorothy Edith Carter died by accident. They have brought in evidence to show that two or three children disappeared from The Larches; have they not done so because their case is so weak that without such evidence it must fall to the ground? This additional evidence does not prove that the death of Dorothy Edith Carter was not accidental — every circumstance of her death is consistent with misadventure. I do not care if other children have been murdered,* my client is on trial for the murder of Dorothy Edith Carter. If Dorothy Edith Carter was accidentally killed what became of the other children is irrelevant.

He asked the jurors to confine themselves solely to the evidence concerning Dorothy Edith Carter. He said that if they had any shadow of doubt as to whether or not Mrs Dean had killed that child then she was entitled to the benefit of it, and they were bound to acquit her. Then he returned to the question of motive:

> The Crown can assign no motive because there is none. No money was paid to Mrs Dean. She had no security that she would get the money. So long as she kept the child alive all she had to do was take it back, but once she disposed of the child she could not enforce her claim. She kept Mrs Olsen's child Willie Phelan, and when the £20 was not forthcoming she sent it back. That experience would make her keep the child.

Finally he tackled the Crown claim that Mrs Dean was systematically taking children for money and doing away with them. That was a bold statement and was disproved by the evidence, he said.

> There were five children living with Mrs Dean. Why had they not been murdered? The system seems to have fallen short somewhere. The children were well nourished though poorly clad, but lots of children are poorly clad and any amount of them are not so well fed. Look at Miss Cameron! Is this the kind of girl you would expect to be dragged up in the home of a murderess? Does she not give you the impression of being well reared and well cared for? Is Esther Wallis not well cared for and fairly well educated? How could these children be brought up like that if it was a murderess that raised them? Does it not strike you as exceedingly strange? A woman who could rear children in this way cannot be all bad.

---

* A startled *Otago Daily Times* reporter heard Hanlon say that he did not care if forty children had been found buried in her garden, but no other reporter, no matter how detailed the account, recorded that statement.

In closing Hanlon said, 'If I were blessed with the ability to stir your blood I might be able to touch your sympathy.' Then he proceeded to do exactly that:

> I don't ask for sympathy or pity — I am not entitled to it. I ask only for justice — and justice I am entitled to get. You have before you today a woman fast declining into the vale of years who has stood for a month accused of these crimes. I ask you to think of what her feelings must have been sitting listening to these harrowing details. I submit to you that you should hesitate before putting a hangman's rope around her neck upon such evidence as has been submitted by the Crown. Her life is in your hands. It behoves you to give the case your gravest attention. I ask you to acquit her if you find that the child has died of misadventure, or if by negligence to convict her of manslaughter, but not murder. I have said all I can say. I ask you to do your duty conscientiously, and I trust that when you leave that box each one of you will be able to go to your separate avocations feeling in your own bosom that you have done your duty, and brought in a verdict in accordance with your conscience, and in accordance with the evidence — feeling that you have done that which each of you called upon God, when you took the oath, to help you to do, namely 'to harken to the evidence and a true verdict give accordingly'.

There was a moment of stunned silence. Then a great burst of applause erupted from the public gallery. While shocked court officials suppressed the disorder, Judge Williams considered his next move. It was not yet five o'clock. He had time to address the jury and send them out to consider their verdict, but under the circumstances that seemed unwise. 'I do not propose to sum up this evening,' he announced. 'I shall adjourn the court until 10 am tomorrow, by which time the minds of the jury will be fresh to consider the important issues which will come before them.' Years later Williams admitted to a colleague that he adjourned the court that afternoon to reduce the emotional impact of Hanlon's eloquent and impassioned address on the jury.[12]

Next morning light rain was falling on a ground still icy with frost when Minnie crossed the slippery pavement outside the gaol and set off by carriage for her last day in the densely thronged court.

The crowd was on tenterhooks. Through three days of damning evidence the prisoner's guilt had seemed assured, then Hanlon's address had changed everything. The *Otago Daily Times* reporter said that after hearing Hanlon 'many were inclined to think it not unlikely that a verdict of manslaughter would be returned'.[13]

But a verdict of manslaughter was not what Judge Williams had in mind. The *Otago Daily Times* reporter continued:

> The judge summed up strongly against the prisoner, and his remarks were

evidently directed with the distinct object of counteracting any influence that the speech of the learned counsel for the defence might have been expected to exert on the minds of the jury in determining them to come to an erroneous conclusion.

So anxious was Judge Williams to counteract the influence of Hanlon's address that during his two-and-a-half-hour speech he not only reiterated the Crown arguments and either refuted or ignored the points made in Minnie Dean's defence, he also offered the jury some incriminating interpretations of the evidence that were apparently of his own devising. He began by stressing the importance of looking at 'the evidence as a whole':

> The issue you have to determine is as to the death of Dorothy Edith Carter, but because that is the only issue you have to determine you have no right to neglect evidence as to transactions with other children which has also been given. That evidence has been admitted, and properly admitted, and has in many respects an important bearing upon the direct issue which you have to determine.

On the vexed question of adoption, his Honour introduced a point that was probably inspired by arguments proffered in the Makin case. He suggested that adoptions normally took place as pecuniary transactions or because the woman concerned had no children of her own: 'Could this latter have been the motive of the accused in the present case?' he asked. 'If it was not, then what sort of business transaction was entered into?' In his view the small sum of money involved was highly sinister:

> If £10 is a wholly inadequate consideration for maintaining a child from the age of twelve months till it might earn money for itself, what possible motive could be suggested for a woman in poor circumstances taking over a child and undertaking to rear and maintain it from that early age? Does not even that suggest that there was some improper motive?

If this argument had been presented earlier, Hanlon could have offered a rebuttal. He could have drawn the jury's attention to three obvious points: firstly, that no figures were presented in court regarding the real cost of raising a child at that time (and as far as I have been able to find out none were available out of court either) — Judge Williams's statement that Mrs Dean's adoption fees were inadequate seems to have been based on opinion rather than fact; secondly, that according to contemporary newspaper reports Minnie's fees were not unusually low (some advertisements asked only £5 for adoptions) but were set at standard market rates; and thirdly, that it was unrealistic to suggest that a sum equivalent to the total cost of raising a child from birth to independence should change hands at the time of adoption.

Another point made by Judge Williams that had apparently not been previously presented in court concerned Mrs Dean's desire to protect her clients:

> It is quite understandable that when girls have the misfortune to have an illegitimate child their relations should be anxious to conceal their shame. But . . . there is no shame or disgrace in wanting to adopt a child.

He also offered a new, sinister explanation for the fact that Mrs Dean broke her journey in Dipton:

> It might be suggested that if accused had a criminal intention, and if accused had made up her mind to go to Lumsden that night, that it would have been better for her to arrive at Lumsden in the dark than in broad daylight.

If Hanlon had had the chance he would probably have ridiculed this suggestion. He would probably have said something like: if my client wanted to arrive at Lumsden under cover of darkness why did she not take the evening train from Lady Barkly to Lumsden? On the evening train she could have made the entire journey in the dark. If my client had criminal intent why did she take the morning train in broad daylight and then spend all day at Dipton? Why alert everyone at Dipton to the fact that she was travelling with a baby? The suggestion that she stopped at Dipton in order to arrive at Lumsden under cover of darkness is absurd. But of course the jury never did hear those arguments; on that last day of Minnie Dean's trial the only arguments the jury heard were those of Mr Justice Joshua Strange Williams.

In his address the judge also outlined the significance, as he saw it, of the evidence relating to Eva Hornsby, arguing that while the death of one child may be innocent, the deaths of two infants under similar circumstances strongly suggested that both children had been murdered. He was so confident of the validity of this theory that he went on to argue:

> Even if no opium had been found at all, supposing that the body had been found and there was no direct evidence from the post mortem . . . the death may have been either naturally or wilfully caused — even then there would have been plenty of evidence for the jury to consider whether the death had been wilfully caused . . . because of the almost simultaneous disappearance of the other infant, Eva Hornsby, and of that infant having apparently died by suffocation.

Then there was the evidence that other children had disappeared under suspicious circumstances in Mrs Dean's care:

> An accident may happen once, but if there are a number of cases of a similar class it is difficult to suggest that all of them were the result of accident, and if they were not was this particular one a result of accident?

In fact there was nothing unusual about a New Zealand household losing two or more infants to childhood illnesses and accidents, but that detail did not concern the judge. If the parents were legally married the rosy Victorian vision of motherhood and the family protected them from any suspicion of wrongdoing.

The judge did not attempt to explain the presence of the five well-fed and well-cared-for children at The Larches at the time of the prisoner's arrest.

On Hanlon's key point, that the accused had no motive because she had received no money for Dorothy Edith Carter, he said:

> The parents of Dorothy Edith lived a long way away — they lived in Christchurch — and it was exceeding unlikely that they would come down here to visit the child. If Mrs Dean thought that the £10 was practically safe, whether the child was living or dead, there was the motive ... With respect to Eva Hornsby, of course, she had the money. The motive in that case is obvious, and as I have said it is very difficult, in fact it is impossible, to dissociate the circumstances attending the death of one from the circumstances attending the death of the other.

He went on to distinguish between 'fair doubt' and 'shadow of doubt' and to caution the jury that: 'such phrases as a shadow of doubt, and so on, are altogether out of the question'.

His closing words were:

> I warn you, gentlemen, against returning a verdict of manslaughter unless you are satisfied that that conclusion is fully justified by the evidence. Looking at the evidence as it came before the court, I must say that it seems to me such a verdict would indicate a weak-kneed compromise. It seems to me that the real honest issue in this case is whether the accused is guilty of intentionally killing the child, or is innocent altogether.

The *Otago Daily Times* reporter observed, 'When his Honor had finished summing up there could hardly be any doubt in the minds of any what the verdict would be, however the jury may have been previously influenced.'

Then as now, misdirection of a jury by a judge was grounds for appeal, but Hanlon did not pursue that option. He had already indicated his intention to appeal on the grounds of inadmissibility of evidence, and he was probably constrained from extending his appeal by memories of a debate the previous year over the extent to which judges should be allowed to give juries the benefit of their opinions. Judge Williams himself had been outspoken in his opposition to the abortive 1894 attempt to restrict judges to ruling on the admissibility of evidence, explaining points of law and summarising the evidence presented. In his pamphlet entitled *The Supreme Court Act*

Amendment Bill, 1894. Remarks by Mr Justice Williams on the Proposal to Restrain a Judge in Charging a Jury from Commenting on the Evidence,[14] he argued that a jury given the full benefit of a judge's comments and opinions was far more likely to reach a correct conclusion than one receiving a more restricted briefing. Under the circumstances Hanlon probably thought that any challenge to the judge's direction of the jury would be futile.

The jury retired at 12.30 pm and returned after only half an hour. The buzz of conversation gave way to hushed expectation as the formal, chilling words were exchanged:

'Have you agreed as to your verdict?'

'We have.'

'Do you find the prisoner guilty or not guilty?'

'Guilty, your Honour.'

'So say you all?'

'So say we all.'

All eyes turned to Minnie.

'Prisoner, what is your age?'

'Forty-eight.' (Which happened to be a lie — her true age was fifty.)

'Have you anything to say why the sentence of the court should not be passed upon you?'

'No,' said Minnie in a low, clear, firm voice. 'I only wish to say that I thank Detective McGrath for his kindness.' Judge Williams then donned the black cap and passed sentence:

> Prisoner at the bar, the judgment of the law is that you, Minnie Dean, be taken from the place where you now are to the prison from whence you came, and thence to the place of execution, and that there, in the manner and form by law appointed, you be hanged by the neck until you are dead. And may God have mercy on your soul.

Minnie stood calmly while the sentence was delivered, then she left the court attended by the gaoler with a firm, unfaltering step.

Chapter XVII

———— ∼ ————

SOUTHLAND TIMES
24 JUNE 1895

After a long and careful trial, presided over by a most just-minded Judge, whose instincts are always towards mercy, Minnie Dean has been convicted of the murder of Dorothy Edith Carter, an infant placed in her charge for the purpose of adoption. Apart from the particular crime brought home to her the evidence disclosed the systematic prosecution by the convict of a truly fiendish business, only paralleled in the criminal annals of Australasia by the terrible Makin case in New South Wales.

There is reason to believe that for some years this unhappy woman has been receiving in her obscure cottage near Winton, for pecuniary considerations, children themselves the offspring of moral guilt, and when all the money which could be obtained on their account was secured, putting them out of the way with cold-blooded atrocity.

The poor babe for whose foul murder the woman Dean has been sentenced to the extreme penalty of the law is only one among many victims. More than twenty children have already been traced to her residence, of whom at least two-thirds have disappeared, no sign of their existence being left.

The words of the Psalmist, when speaking of a certain class of wicked people, have been exemplified: 'Privily, in their lurking dens, do they murder the innocent.'

Resting, as the case for the prosecution in charges of murder almost invariably does, upon purely circumstantial evidence, it is always satisfactory, when the result is a conviction, that this evidence should be so clear and convincing as to leave no reasonable doubt as to the guilt of the person convicted. Happily, in one sense of the word, the evidence, taken as a whole, admits of no other conclusion than that the death of Dorothy Edith Carter was intentionally caused by the convict. The admirably lucid and exhaustive summing up by the Judge placed the points of the case so distinctly before the jury that we are not surprised at their agreeing unanimously to a verdict of 'Guilty' after very brief deliberation.

Circumstances piled upon circumstances, all tending to establish the guilt of the accused, were substantiated until the indictment was driven home with such force that it could not be the least shaken by the efforts of the counsel for the prisoner, whose able conduct of the defence excited general admiration. No twisting and turning, however, of demonstrated facts and the natural deductions there-from, no ingenious theories to account for action inexplicable except on the hypothesis of guilt, could break the chain of damning circumstances in which not a link was weak.

The motive for the murder — a paltry

mercenary motive it is true — was, as the Judge pointed out, clearly established. That the death of the child had been caused by misadventure his Honour conclusively showed was a theory altogether untenable in the face of the evidence, direct and corroborated. Fortunately for society murderers frequently display a want of judgment in the perpetration and concealment of their crimes which borders on insanity and seals their doom. The extraordinary railway manoeuvres of Mrs Dean in this case were suspicious in themselves, and entirely inconsistent with the theory advanced by her counsel that there was no premeditation and no doing away with the infants, but that their death was due to accidental causes beyond her control. Then again, it was nothing but sheer madness that could have induced her to bring the bodies home and bury them in her garden. Consciousness of her criminality must surely have affected her reason.

It is to be noted that throughout the trial the utmost consideration was extended to the accused. The counsel for the prosecution in his opening speech, setting forth facts he was in a position to prove, and in reply to the speech for the defence, was conspicuously moderate in tone, and whilst confuting the arguments advanced was evidently anxious that the jury should consider them on their merits and give the prisoner the benefits of any reasonable doubt.

It is unnecessary to refer to the absolutely impartial conduct of the Judge; no prisoner ever had a fairer trial than Minnie Dean. The deplorable circumstances brought to light, and the proceedings of this trial point a moral as to the inequitable treatment under the present social system of women who may be led into temptation, or by the arts of the seducer into a breach of the moral laws and suffer the natural consequences. For these unfortunates there is no social redemption if once their fair fame is tarnished, and not unreasonably they resort to questionable means to hide their shame. In the dread of public reprobation and absolute ruin of their prospects they consign the fruits of their sin to the care of strangers, desirous at all hazards to conceal their dishonour. Hence arises the opportunity of the professional baby farmer, whose direct interest it is to carry a business with as little trouble and as much profit as possible.

How many poor children are done to death, or at the best miserably ill-treated by these harpies can never be known. The fault unmistakably lies with society which, tolerant of any amount of immorality in man, has no sympathy or pardon for the woman, but for one fault condemns her irretrievably.

Before dismissing this painful subject it is only fair to the police to express our sincere concurrence in the compliment paid them both by the Stipendiary Magistrate and the Judge of the Supreme Court.

Chapter XVIII

───── ∼ ─────

THE END OF THE LINE

In Dunedin in 1887, when Judge Williams summed up at the end of the trial of Thomas Hall for the murder of his father-in-law Captain Cain, he took care to distinguish between facts and inferences, and to impress on the jury that inferences should be treated with great caution. The facts of the case were that Thomas Hall bought a book of poisons and purchased antimony. Antimony is a toxic metallic element used to strengthen alloys; it has no household use. Hall could provide no satisfactory explanation for his purchase of antimony.[1] It was established that Hall had attended Captain Cain at his midday and evening meals and was frequently alone with him. At these times the deceased suffered severe vomiting attacks. Cain was free of such symptoms at breakfast. At the time of Cain's death Hall was in financial difficulties and stood to benefit from his wife's inheritance from her stepfather. Cain's body was found to contain a poisonous amount of antimony. Six months after Cain's death Hall was convicted of the attempted murder of his wife with the same poison. However, as the judge pointed out, none of this proved that Hall murdered Cain. The questions were: was Cain's death accelerated by antimony? If so, was antimony administered by the accused (bearing in mind that other people had access to the food and drink taken by Cain)? Could Cain have taken antimony of his own accord? Could antimony have been administered accidentally? The judge closed by telling the jury that they were free to draw whatever conclusion they wished, but regardless of the outcome he would refer to the Court of Appeal the question of admissibility of evidence concerning Hall's attempt to murder his wife. After deliberating for almost an hour and a half the special jury returned a verdict of guilty.

'As I have already intimated to you, prisoner,' said Judge Williams. 'The legal question connected with your case will be considered by the Court of Appeal. If there is anything in the point you will have the benefit of it.' Then he assumed the black cap and passed sentence.[2]

In terms of the 1882 Court of Appeal Act ('The Judges of the Supreme Court of the said colony for the time being shall be the Judges of the Court of

Appeal') there was nothing strange in the fact that Judge Williams sat in judgment on his own case as a member of the five-man Court of Appeal. What was strange was that, after a three-day hearing, the Appeal Court decided *unanimously* that the evidence concerning Hall's attempted murder of his wife had been improperly admitted. Hall's conviction for the murder of Captain Cain was therefore quashed.

The verdict was delivered on behalf of the Court of Appeal by Judge Johnston. In attempting to explain the decision, he said:

> Viewed in the light of science, philosophy, or common sense, there is without doubt a nexus between the two events . . . We are aware that in cases like the present the application of the rigid principle of the common law must often result in what the public may regard as a failure of justice. That is really not our concern. It is our duty to see that justice be administered according to law.[3]

'There is widespread feeling that there has been a miscarriage of justice in Hall's case,' wrote the Dunedin correspondent of the *Southland Times*. 'Intense indignation is felt here at the result.' It was claimed that 'had Hall been an ordinary member of the community, related in no way to the "upper ten", it is in the last degree improbable that he would now be alive.'[4] Newspaper editorial opinion was divided. The *Otago Witness* supported the Appeal Court ruling and deplored the 'indignant and sometimes hysterical letter writers who have rushed into print.'[5] The *Timaru Herald* poured scorn on Judge Williams's claim that there was insufficient evidence to convict Hall for the murder of Cain without the admission of the evidence regarding Hall's wife and concluded, 'The mildest adverse comment is that the trial was a farce, the Crown bungled the prosecution and a murderer of the vilest stamp escaped on a technicality.'[6] The *Lyttelton Times* urged the Crown to take the case to the Privy Council,[7] but no further action was taken. Thomas Hall served a twenty-one year prison term for the attempted murder of his wife. On his release he was paid a £200 annuity by his uncle, Sir John Hall, on the condition that he never returned to New Zealand.[8]

Six years later, when a similar question of admissibility was argued before the New South Wales Court of Appeal in relation to the Makin case, the New Zealand Appeal Court decision in the Hall case came in for vigorous criticism. In the opinion of the Australian judges the law was supposed to be the epitome, not the antithesis, of common sense.[9]

After receiving the Attorney General's consent, Hanlon's application for leave to appeal the Dean case was considered by the New Zealand Court of Appeal at a hearing in Wellington on Saturday 27 July 1895. In the absence of any official record of the trial, the court accepted as evidence a printed transcript of the Judge's Notes, the *Southland Times* report of the trial and a statement of the facts of the case prepared by the prisoner's counsel and approved by Mr Justice Williams.[10] As in the Hall appeal, Judge Williams sat in judgment on his own case. The other appeal judges were Chief Justice Sir James Prendergast and Justices C. W. Richmond, E. T. Conolly and J. E. Denniston. For those interested in coincidences the gossip columnist of Milton's *Bruce Herald* reported that, 'It is said that she [Minnie Dean] attended college at the same time as Justice Denniston.'

Alf Hanlon did not attend the appeal application hearing. The previous year he had married Mary 'Polly' Hudson, daughter of Richard Hudson (a Dunedin manufacturer of biscuits and chocolates). Their first child was due at the time of the Wellington hearing and according to his descendants Hanlon was a great family man — an indulgent father to his four children and a devoted son who, except when he was out of Dunedin, visited his mother every day of her life. The imminent birth of his first child and the exciting possibility that the infant might arrive on 1 August (the birth date shared by Alf Hanlon and his father William)* was probably enough to keep Hanlon at home. There would also have been financial considerations. Most of Hanlon's clients were poor and his one-man practice was far from prosperous. There was little chance that he would receive any payment for his work on the Dean case. So instead of making the long, expensive trip to Wellington, he asked a former Dunedin barrister Dr J. G. Findlay of the Wellington firm Stout, Mondy, Sim and Findlay, to present his application for leave to appeal.

Findlay was a close friend of Premier Richard Seddon. Later he became Attorney General under Premier Joseph Ward. During the 1890s he helped draft the Liberal government's labour and land reform legislation.[11] To Hanlon, Findlay's interest in social equity would have made him a good man to represent Minnie Dean at the Court of Appeal. The Crown was represented by Mr T. M. Macdonald of Invercargill and the Wellington Crown solicitor, Mr Gully.

Perhaps because he knew the application was unlikely to succeed, Dr Findlay opened by saying that he proposed to argue the matter fully at the application stage, then if leave to appeal was granted he would simply submit to the Court of Appeal the arguments he had already delivered. This approach ensured that Minnie Dean's appeal could not be dismissed before it was heard.

The appeal judges' later comments[12] suggest that Dr Findlay argued his case at careful length, but all that now remains of his presentation is the summary reported in newspapers at the time. According to the press account, Dr Findlay did not dispute the introduction of evidence relating to Eva

---

* The baby, a boy, did indeed arrive on 1 August.

Hornsby. His concern was with the improper admission of evidence concerning the disappearances of other infants and the discovery of the skeleton at The Larches. He argued that the Makin case did not apply. 'To make evidence of other acts admissible they must appear to be part of a series of similar occurrences and to be part of one scheme,' he said. He went on to claim that in the present case there was little to connect the separate events. The bodies of the children allegedly received by Mrs Dean had not been found, and there was nothing to identify the skeleton as a child taken in by the prisoner. When he had finished, the Chief Justice adjourned the court for the weekend. Mr Macdonald was not called to present the Crown case, either that day or when the court resumed the following Monday. As Judge Denniston noted in his written judgment, 'The invalidity of the grounds on which the application for leave to appeal are based is to my mind so clear that it would I think be unfortunate to allow such a suggestion of doubt as might be created by calling on counsel for the Crown.'

When the court reopened on Monday Sir James Prendergast announced that the members of the Court of Appeal were unanimously of the opinion that leave to appeal should be refused. Two days later all the judges, with the exception of Judge Richmond,* released their reasons in writing.[13]

Judge Prendergast interpreted the Privy Council-endorsed New South Wales Court of Appeal ruling in the Makin case to mean that if the accused took other children on the claim of adoption for sums inadequate to support them, and if some of those children disappeared, such evidence was admissible even if no bodies were found. He further ruled that if bodies were found under similar circumstances such evidence was admissible — even if the bodies were not identified, even if the causes of death were unknown, even if it could not be proved that the infants had previously been in the care of the accused and even if the deaths and disappearances were years apart. 'The motive is brought out much more certainly when several instances of pretended adoption and of undertaking support on inadequate terms are proved,' he explained.

Judges Richmond and Williams were the only members of the New Zealand Court of Appeal in the Dean case who had also sat on the Hall appeal. Judge Richmond was probably too ill to care about the apparently contradictory appeal verdicts — one in favour of the admission of collateral fact evidence, the other against — or about the criticism of the New Zealand Court of Appeal ruling in the Hall case by the New South Wales Court of Appeal in its ruling on the Makin case, but Judge Williams took the opportunity to defend himself.

He sought to play down the importance of the Makin decision by arguing

---

* Judge Richmond attended the hearing only on the Saturday. The following Monday he was indisposed. Five days later he was dead.

that the collateral fact evidence in the Dean case was admissible for reasons quite apart from the Makin ruling. After quoting from the 1893 edition of *Stephen's Digest of the Law of Evidence* ('When there is a question of whether an act was accidental or intentional the fact that such act formed part of a series of similar occurrences in each of which the person doing the act was concerned is deemed to be relevant') he argued that,

> The receipt by the prisoner of other infants on somewhat similar terms and their mysterious disappearance, accounted for by the prisoner in the same way, and the discovery of the skeleton of another infant in the prisoner's garden, form together a series of similar occurrences to the one in question in each of which the prisoner was concerned. They are therefore under the above rule admissible to shew that the act of the prisoner in administering opium which may have been already proved by other evidence was done with criminal intent.

He added that 'the case of *Regina* v. *Hall*, decided by this court, in no way conflicts with the rule laid down by Sir J. F. Stephens' and went on to argue, without a trace of irony, that the collateral fact evidence about Hall's wife — which he himself had admitted — was inadmissible.

Judge Denniston also had a connection with the Hall case; he had been one of the defence lawyers. He endorsed the New South Wales judges' ruling on the Makin appeal and suggested that their criticism of the Hall ruling was caused by 'an obvious misapprehension of the reasoning and effect of the judgment'. Of the Dean appeal he said that the collateral fact evidence was clearly admissible to show 'that her motives were not philanthropic and benevolent but sordid and mercenary'.

Judge Conolly, a seventy-three year old with a reputation for crabbiness,[14] argued that there was enough evidence concerning the deaths of Dorothy Edith Carter and Eva Hornsby to convict the accused without the admission of the other evidence, but since it was tendered simply to corroborate evidence already presented he failed to see how it could be inadmissible. For good measure he added that he agreed with his colleagues' comments on the Hall case.

With leave to appeal denied her, Minnie's only remaining hope of escaping the gallows lay with the Executive Council, who had the power to recommend that the Governor of the colony commute her sentence to life imprisonment. On Saturday 3 August, Premier R. J. Seddon, Sir P. A. Buckley and Messrs W. P. Reeves, J. McKenzie, A. J. Cadman, J. G. Ward and J. Carroll met to consider her case. Though they were liberals in matters of land and labour reform, they were conservatives when it came to law and order. Their resolve was probably strengthened by memories of the public outcry two years earlier when the death sentences pronounced by Judge Denniston on the baby-murdering Flanagan women were commuted to life imprisonment. Another troublesome case was that of convicted murderer Louis Chemis, but with Chemis the outcry was against execution. The Governor had commuted his death sentence, but for many people that wasn't enough. The government was being bombarded with petitions demanding that Chemis be retried or freed. And on top of all that, some sections of society were agitating for the abolition of capital punishment. The beleaguered Executive Council may well have felt it was time to take a stand. A hand-written note dated 3 August 1895 reads:

> Case of Minnie Dean convicted of murder and under sentence of death — After giving the matter every consideration, Ministers see no reason for advising His Excellency's interference with the ordinary course of the law. (signed) R. J. Seddon.[15]

His Excellency the Governor signed the neccessary papers on 5 August, and Minnie Dean's fate was sealed.

The newspaper editorial writers who manned the moral barricades of the nation were, for the most part, well satisfied with the Executive decision. An *Otago Witness* columnist wrote approvingly:

> We cannot doubt that the decision was a right and proper one . . . there was no redeeming feature in the case — nothing at all that could be urged as a plea for mitigation of the sentence . . . The man who commits the foulest murder in a paroxysm of anger, or even of avarice, is not so lost as the woman who is constantly on the lookout for infants to murder at so much a head.[16]

According to the *New Zealand Graphic*, hanging was too good for the infamous Minnie Dean:

> One wishes there were some punishment twice as terrible as death for a monster capable of such crime. Hanging is too severe a punishment for some murders. But for such murders as these, it is a perfectly inadequate punishment.[17]

The *Southland Times* declared:

> The cruel killing of helpless innocents, systematically perpetrated as a matter of business, is murder in so aggravated a form that sympathy for the wretched woman now awaiting execution would be misplaced.[18]

Despite the fulminations of editorial writers, sympathy for Minnie Dean did exist. The unusually high proportion of women spectators in court, much commented on by the press, may have been the first sign. After the trial the

Cabinet memo advising the Governor not to interfere with
the sentence passed on Minnie Dean.
National Archives, Wellington

signs became more explicit. On 29 June a columnist in Invercargill's *Southern Cross* commented on the community agitation to have Mrs Dean's sentence commuted. The same day Christchurch suffragist, Ada Wells, penned a letter to the Minister of Justice on behalf of the Canterbury Women's Institute:

> That this Institute is in favour of the abolition of Capital Punishment (1) as the State has no right to commit murder; (2) as it has not proved a deterrent; & that therefore the Minister of Justice be petitioned in the matter of the Dean Case, in which sentence of death has been passed, that the sentence be commuted to imprisonment for life.[19]

'Mother' of Christchurch wrote directly to Minnie, a Dunedin woman gave £40 towards her defense costs, the congregation of St Paul's Presbyterian Church in Invercargill said a prayer for her and other sympathisers wrote to the press. On 1 July a letter from Edwin Rutland to the *Southland Times* opened timidly with, 'Please allow me a little space to say a few words about the poor woman Mrs Dean, who now lies under sentence of death in the Invercargill gaol.' He suggested that if her sentence were commuted to life imprisonment, 'she would have time to repent of her sins and be made in a fit state to enter heaven'. The following week 'Mercy', wrote to the *Southland Daily News* to complain of the unfairness of hanging Mrs Dean before the Bill for the abolition of capital punishment had been considered by Parliament, while in Dunedin's *Evening Star*, 'Justicia' urged that women be appointed to charitable and other boards because 'It takes a woman to understand a woman's woes.' 'The terrible case of Mrs Dean should raise Dunedin women to a sense of their duty,' 'Justicia' wrote, and went on to press for the provision of foundling wards in hospitals. This was too much for 'Mother'. 'In my opinion such resources only foster the crime that causes the misery,' she wrote. 'It would be far better for the country if there was State punishment for the crime of illegitimacy.'

The expressions of sympathy were to no avail. On 5 August the Superintendent of Prisons telegramed the Invercargill gaoler Mr Bratby:

> Please inform prisoner Minnie Dean that His Excellency the Governor sees no reason to interfere with the sentence passed upon her and it will therefore be carried out in due course.[20]

As far as the authorities were concerned, carrying out the hanging was a matter of urgency; delays often provoked embarrassing public outcries for clemency and with the prisoner being not only a woman, but a refined woman, the chances of an outcry were probably greater than usual. They would have been mindful that in Melbourne the previous year the passing of the death sentence on baby farmer Frances Knorr had provoked an alarming wave of petitions and public meetings culminating in a march on Government House on the eve of her execution that had 'given the impression that an attack might possibly be made on the premises'.[21]

According to New Zealand law, executions had to take place within a week of the local sheriff receiving notice that the Governor would not interfere with the sentence, but by the time the Invercargill sheriff received his notice in the mail on Thursday 8 August most of the arrangements had already been made by telegram: the scaffold was on its way from Dunedin, the hangman was on his way from Wellington and the date and time of the execution had been fixed.

The search for the hangman had begun soon after Judge Williams pronounced sentence. Despite the apparent popularity of the verdict, the authorities feared that finding someone willing to hang a woman would not be easy. In this matter too they were probably mindful of the Australian experience; in Victoria 'Jones the Hangman' was reported to have committed suicide by cutting his own throat because of his

> unwillingness to execute Mrs Knorr, the baby farmer, and that unwillingness was the result not so much of conscientious scruples or of sympathetic feeling for the condemned woman as a shrinking from the contemptuous jeers and the persecutions of his neighbours, who, he believed, would be still more hostile if he hanged a woman.[22]

The most likely candidate for hangman in the Dean case was intemperate Tom Long, an old soldier, nearly sixty years of age, who had in the course of his life hanged over a dozen felons. On 6 July an urgent and confidential memo was issued by the Wellington Police Office:

> The Commissioner directs that immediate enquiries be made for the whereabouts of Tom Long, known as the 'hangman' ... If found a telegram to be at once sent to this office. Report results of enquiries without delay.[23]

By 6 August Tom Long had been located at Wanganui, taken to Wellington, locked in prison and presented with an agreement to sign:

> To the gaolers at Wellington, Dunedin and Invercargill & all whom it may concern —
> I Thomas Long do hereby agree to act as hangman in the case of Minnie Dean, for the sum of £25. 0. 0, twenty five pounds. I further agree to be taken to Invercargill under escort, sleeping in any prisons that may be necessary en route, and that, on arrival in Invercargill I shall allow myself to be enclosed within the walls of the prison, and be fed on prison fare, until the execution is over and I hereby agree to bring no action against any person for so shutting me up in prison, as it is my own wish and request that I shall be so treated. The Prison Department are to pay my fare from Wanganui to Invercargill and back, and if the hanging is

satisfactorily carried out I am to receive the £25. 0. 0, twenty-five pounds, on my arrival in Wellington when returning from Invercargill.[24]

With the success of the hanging resting on Tom Long's unreliable shoulders, the Under-secretary for Justice was understandably anxious. *'I wish particularly to impress on you the great necessity of taking every precaution to prevent the occurrence of any hitch or bungle,'* he wrote to the Invercargill sheriff. 'Will you be good enough to telegraph to me whether he has given satisfaction. '[25]

News that her sentence would not be commuted was relayed to Minnie by the Reverend George Lindsay of St Paul's Presbyterian Church, Invercargill, who had attended her daily since her conviction. She responded, as always, with composure. She said she hoped she would not be a coward, but would face the end like a brave woman. She even remained calm when the sheriff informed her, on 7 August, that he had fixed the time of execution for 8 am on Monday 12 August. Only when he brought her the news that she would not be buried in the gaol yard like a common criminal, because her husband's request to take her body to Winton for burial had been granted, did she sob briefly.

Throughout her three months in the Invercargill gaol, Mr Bratby the gaoler and his wife the matron did their best to make Minnie comfortable. They provided her 10 foot x 12 foot gas-lit prison cell with a neat wooden bedstead, a table, two wooden stools, a strip of carpet, a Bible, a fire in the grate and a vase of spring flowers on the mantelpiece. Minnie wrote:

> From the gaoler and the matron I have received every care, attention and kindness that was in their power to bestow. From the matron I have received the affectionate consideration of a sister and she has tried in every way to alleviate and lighten the heavy burden that has been laid on me. May God's blessing rest on both of them, may they live to a ripe old age and may their end be peace.[26]

Charles Dean visited his wife for the last time on Saturday 10 August. After that Minnie spent her time praying, reading the Bible, writing the statement that she was never allowed to make in court, preparing herself for her fate and asking repeatedly to see the little children from The Larches:

> The one yearning wish of my heart has to remain ungratified — I have been refused to be let see the children. The thought and hope of being able to see them only once has sustained me in all my bitter trouble. And surely I have been punished enough without inflicting this worst of all troubles on me. What is to become of them now? Who is to love and care for them as I have done? Oh it is cruel to have to go to the grave with the only ray of comfort denied me, a fond last look at the faces of my little ones.[27]

The evening before her execution Minnie sat up late finishing her statement and writing letters. She slept from 11.30 pm until 3.00 am, then rose and again engaged in writing. She refused breakfast but accepted a few sips of tea. She also cut a lock from her fine, soft iron-grey hair, tied it with a ribbon, and left it on the mantelpiece beside the small vase of snowdrops and violets.

Shortly before seven thirty the Reverend Lindsay came to pray with Minnie and hold her hand. Dr Macleod also called, and on learning that Minnie had taken no breakfast he ordered a glass of whisky and water for her. 'For goodness sake doctor,' she said. 'Get it over quickly.' But she left the whisky untouched.

At three minutes to eight the gaoler, the sheriff, the doctor and the executioner entered her cell. The sheriff formally demanded from the gaoler the body of Minnie Dean. Then he turned to the hangman and said, 'Executioner, do your duty.' Minnie stood quietly as the hangman strapped her upper arms to her sides, bent her arms forward, crossed her wrists and pinioned them to a strap around her waist.

The gaol bell tolled slowly as the procession to the scaffold began. At the head walked the gaoler and the doctor, then came the Reverend Lindsay, reading from the Presbyterian burial service. Behind him walked Minnie, erect and dignified, with a prison warder on either side. Next came the hangman followed by the sheriff. At the foot of the broad sloping stairs Minnie dropped one hand, lifted her skirt and ascended gracefully to the gallows. While the hangman pinioned her ankles, adjusted the noose around her neck and placed the white calico cap over her head and face, she held tightly to the hand of the warder beside her and took a few deep breaths.

'Do you wish to say anything before you leave this world?' asked the sheriff.

'I have nothing to say,' said Minnie. 'Except that I am innocent.'

As the warder beside her released his hand she swayed a little and seemed about to fall. Then she straightened herself and murmured, 'Oh God let me not suffer.' At that moment the sheriff gave the signal. The hangman drew the trapdoor bolt. Minnie Dean dropped from sight. The rope jerked taut. Minnie Dean was dead.

TO *Under Secy Justice*

Wellington —

Dean executed at two minutes past eight Execution most successful Executioner performed duties entirely satisfactorily —

W. Martin

Sheriff

Invercargill

Telegram confirming Minnie Dean's execution.
National Archives, Wellington

Author's Note

Not only did Minnie Dean live all but the last five years of life in near-anonymity, during most of that time she concealed her true past and laid a false trail. Historical researchers, frustrated by the problems of uncovering the largely undocumented private lives of Victorian women, may take heart from my discovery that fragmentary information, when closely studied and placed in context, can be surprisingly revealing. The relatively well-documented final years of Minnie Dean's life also presented difficulties. After almost a century a few gaps in the record are to be expected, but in the Dean case important archives have vanished completely. For example, the Trial File, supposedly containing indictments and depositions, is nowhere to be found. Contemporary newspaper accounts indicate that prior to the trial the press was given free access to documents seized by the police and, judging by F. G. Hall-Jones's notes from the 1940s, police evidence also circulated among the public after the trial. In 1985 an Invercargill resident found the 'bluey' summoning Charles Dean to court on a charge of murder in the pages of a borrowed book. All this suggests that over the years many official Minnie Dean papers have fallen into private hands. Some papers may have been destroyed but other could still exist in old cartons or suitcases, on top of wardrobes, in attics and drawers. I urge anyone who comes across documents concerning Minnie Dean to pass them into safe keeping at their nearest branch of National Archives without delay.

I am indebted to scores of people and institutions for their assistance with my research. Ellen Ellis pursued Minnie tirelessly at National Archives. At the Dictionary of New Zealand Biography, Betty Iggo solved the mystery of Minnie's Scottish origins and Diana Beaglehole helped to trace New Zealand records and coordinate overseas research. Awards for outstanding helpfulness should also go to Alan Bryce and Johanna Massey of the Invercargill Public Library, Alan Edwards, Law Librarian at the University of Otago, David McDonald and the staff of the Hocken Library, Katherine Dolby of the Otago District Law Society and Mrs Couperwhite of the Watt Memorial Library in Greenock. Other institutions deserving special mention are the Otago Early Settlers Museum, the Dunedin Public Library, the New Zealand Police Museum, the National Library of Scotland, the Scottish National Archive, the Mitchell Library in Sydney, the Australian National Library and the State

Archives of New South Wales, Victoria and Tasmania. Many individuals provided research assistance (most notably John Hall-Jones, Jack Tourelle, Phil Lister and Fergus More of Invercargill, Vince Boyle of Winton, the Turners of Etal Creek, Jim Conradson, Jim Dangerfield and countless genealogists in Dunedin, members of the History and other Departments at the University of Otago, Derek Dow and Judith Bassett of Auckland, Jen Glue, Margaret Martin and Joan Stedmond of Christchurch, Rosalind Maclean and Melanie Mills of Wellington and Kathy Laster, Helen Harris and Phyllis Bhogal of Victoria). W.G.P. allowed me to use his poem and many people provided folklore and gossip (you know who you are). Others supplied welcome hospitality. My husband and children shared four years of their lives with the ghost of Minnie Dean with good humour and generosity. A thousand thanks to you all.

During the preparation of the manuscript I received legal advice from Donna Buckingham, Kevin Dawkins, Kathleen Weatherall, John Weatherall and Judith Meddlicott. My other 'expert witnesses' were Alex Dempster (pathology), Fred Fastier (pharmacology), Julia Faed and Sarah Romans (psychiatry) and John Clarkson (paediatrics). Anna Marsich, Alex Dempster, Julia Faed, Kathleen Weatherall and Donna Buckingham read the draft manuscript. None of these people are responsible for my interpretations of the life of Minnie Dean — for this I accept full responsibility.

Assistance with funding for this four-year project came from a Robert Burns Fellowship at the University of Otago, a Claude McCarthy Fellowship and grants from the Literature Programme of the Queen Elizabeth II Arts Council of New Zealand and the Altrusa Club of Dunedin. These sources provided one third of the total cost of reseaching and writing the book. The remaining costs were met from my own pocket.

Notes and References

Abbreviations

BDM	New Zealand Regional Registrar of Births, Deaths and Marriages
BH	*Bruce Herald* (Milton)
DNZB	*Dictionary of New Zealand Biography*
ES	*Evening Star* (Dunedin)
GRO	General Register Office for Scotland
MDLS	Minnie Dean's last statement
NA	National Archives
NZRGO	New Zealand Registrar General's Office
ODT	*Otago Daily Times* (Dunedin)
OW	*Otago Witness* (Dunedin)
SC	*Southern Cross* (Invercargill)
SDN	*Southland Daily News* (Invercargill)
ST	*Southland Times* (Invercargill)
WS	*Western Star* (Riverton)

Chapter II

1. F. Preston, *A Family of Woolgatherers*, McIndoe, Dunedin, 1978, p. 29.
2. A. D. McQuillan, 'Prestonville pioneers had tough struggle', *Southland Times*, 14 April 1990.
3. From a colonial diary quoted in E. Soper, *The Otago of Our Mothers*, Otago Centennial Historical Publications, Dunedin, 1948, p. 35.
4. A Niven family tradition recorded by S. Natusch in *At the Edge of the Bush* (Craig, Invercargill, 1986, p. 51). This version contrasts with Hocken's claim (*Contributions to the Early History of New Zealand, London, 1898*) that Dugald Niven was drowned.
5. Letter from Wohlers to Tuckett quoted in F. G. Hall-Jones, *Kelly of Inverkelly*, Southland Historical Committee, Invercargill, 1944, p. 31.
6. J. Hall-Jones, *The South Explored*, Reed, Wellington, 1979, p. 71.
7. A. Anderson, 'Tuhawaiki, Hone', in *Dictionary of New Zealand Biography (DNZB)*, Vol. 1, W. H. Oliver (ed.), Allen & Unwin/Dept. Int. Affairs, Wellington, 1990.
8. Quoted in F. G. Hall-Jones, *Kelly*, p. 30.
9. F. G. Hall-Jones, *Kelly*, pp. 132–3.
10. *ST*, 13 May 1895.

Chapter IV

1. Reprint of Reginald Scot's sixteenth-century treatise *The Discoverie of Witchcraft*, Dover, New York, 1972.
2. C. Hibbert, *The Roots of Evil*, Weidenfeld & Nicholson, London, 1963. M. Kunze, *Highroad to the Stake*, U. Chicago Press, Chicago, 1987, p. 182. L. Radznowicz, *A History of English Criminal Law*, Vol. 1, Stevens, London, 1948.
3. J. Westwood, *Albion*, Paladin, London, 1987, pp. 156–57.

Chapter V

1. Two versions of Minnie Dean's last statement are extant. The original, in Minnie Dean's own hand-writing, is held at National Archives in Wellington. It is unpunctuated and unparagraphed, contains a few spelling errors and uses capital letters apparently at random. A copy, taken from the original for her Invercargill lawyer, Josiah Hanan, is held by the Otago District Law Society. In the copy the punctuation and spelling have been corrected but the words, and the word order, have not been changed.

2. K. Catran, *Hanlon — a casebook*, BCNZ Enterprises, Auckland, 1985, p. 51.

3. In 1990 Betty Iggo, Edinburgh-based researcher for the *Dictionary of New Zealand Biography*, uncovered Minnie Dean's origins by tracing Granny Kelly (having nothing in her past to hide, Granny Kelly proved relatively easy to trace). Betty discovered: Granny Kelly's sister Elizabeth married John McCulloch, an engine driver from Greenock; the McCullochs had a family of girls; their daughter Williamina was born in 1844; Elizabeth died of cancer in 1857. Most newspapers at the time of her trial reported that Minnie Dean was the daughter of a clergyman from Edinburgh, but I found two that confirmed Betty's findings, gave Minnie's home town as Greenock, and reported that her father was an engine driver. Granny Kelly died four years before Minnie's trial — the newspapers must have got their information from someone else.

Chapter VI

1. J. Wallace, *Observations on the causes of the great mortality in Greenock*, Orr Pollock, Greenock, 1860. Jordanhill College Local History Archives Group reprint, Glasgow, 1977, pp. 3–4.

2. Quoted in T. W. Hamilton, *How Greenock Grew*, McKelvie, Greenock, 1947.

3. *Groome's Gazetteer of Scotland*, 1905, p. 220.

4. R. M. Smith, *The History of Greenock*, Orr Pollock, Greenock, 1921.

5. R. M. Smith.

6. *Greenock — Housing, Health & Social Conditions 1860–1885*, Local History Archives Project, Jordanhill College, Glasgow, 1978, p. 3.

7. T. C. Smout, *A Century of the Scottish People 1830–1950*, Fontana, London, 1987, p. 35.

8. *Reports on the Sanitary Conditions of the Labouring Population of Scotland*, Clowes, London, 1842. Jordanhill College Local History Archives Group reprint, Glasgow, 1977, p. 251.

9. 'Dr Buchanan's Report on Fever in Greenock', *Greenock Advertiser*, 22 June 1865. Reprinted in *Greenock — Housing, Health & Social Conditions*, pp. 16–22.

10. *Reports of the Sanitary Conditions of the Labouring Population of Scotland*.

11. 'Dr Buchanan's Report'.

12. A. Wohl, *Endangered Lives*, Dent, London, 1983, pp. 166–204.

13. *Shaws Water*, Local History Archives Project, Jordanhill College, Glasgow, 1979.

14. *Reports on the Sanitary Conditions of the Labouring Population of Scotland*, p. 251.

15. Wallace, p. 3.

16. *Greenock — Public Health 1800–1860*, Local History Archives Project, Jordanhill College, Glasgow, 1978, p. 16.

17. T. C. Smout, *A History of the Scottish People*, Fontana, London, 1983, pp. 259–60.

18. The cholera epidemic struck only three years after the sensational Edinburgh trial of Burke and Hare for body-snatching and murder.

19. *Greenock Telegraph*, 11 September 1871. Quoted in *Greenock — Housing, Health and Social Conditions*, p. 25.

20. *Greenock Advertiser*, 27 January 1952. Quoted in *Greenock Public Health*, p. 17.

Chapter VII

1. Smout, *Century of the Scottish People*, p. 12.

2. J. Monteith & J. McCarroll, *Greenock from Old Photographs*, Vol. 2, Inverclyde District Libraries, Greenock, 1983.

3. Original documentation of the McCulloch family (births, deaths and marriage registrations and census returns) from GRO.

4. Smout, *Century of the Scottish People*, p. 135.

5. R. M. Smith.

6. Smout, *Century of the Scottish People*, p. 50. The infant mortality statistics would have been more alarming had certificates been required for stillbirths and babies dying within a few days of birth. This loophole meant that the quick death of a weak or unwanted baby saved the trouble of an inquest and the burial fee charged for a normally certificated child.

7. F. B. Smith, *The People's Health 1830–1910*, Holmes & Meier, New York, 1979, p. 79.

8. L. Rose, *Massacre of the Innocents*, Routledge & Kegan Paul, London, 1986, p. 38.

9. Rose, pp. 79–84, 93–107.

10. Smout, *Century of the Scottish People*, p. 125. Maternal malnutrition in Scotland was exacerbated mid-century by a dietary shift from oatmeal, salt herrings, buttermilk and potatoes to a cheaper, less nutritious diet of tea, sugar and bread. Meat was an occasional luxury reserved for men.

11. Wohl, pp. 20–26.

12. Wallace, *Observations on . . . the great mortality in Greenock*, pp. 17–18.

13. F. B. Smith, p. 97.

14. Wohl, p. 35.

15. F. B. Smith, p. 99.

16. A. S. Taylor, *Poison in Relation to Medical Jurisprudence and Medicine* (Taylor on Poisons), Churchill, London, 1859.

17. F. B. Smith, p. 98.

18. Between 1840 and 1860 the average length of employment for railway workers was $2^{1}/_{2}$ years. (P. Kingsford, *Victorian Railwaymen*, Cass, London, 1979.)

19. *Greenock Advertiser*, 30 March 1841.

20. F. McKenna, *The Railway Workers 1840–1970*, Faber, London, 1980, p. 151.

21. R. M. Smith.

22. *Greenock Academy 1855–1955*, a publication held by the Watt Library, Greenock.

23. By the 1861 census Thomas McNeill had become a master watchmaker employing two boys. That year he and his wife and their baby girl had a three-roomed apartment all to themselves.

Chapter VIII

1. Synod of Glasgow & Ayr, Vol. 3, *Fasti Ecclesiae Scoticanae — the Succession of Ministers in the Church of Scotland since the Reformation*, H. Scott, Oliver & Boyd, Edinburgh, 1920.

2. Smout, *Century of the Scottish People*, p. 188.

3. J. Smith, *Our Scottish Clergy*, Oliver & Boyd, Edinburgh, 1849.

4. Documentation of the Rev. J. M. McCulloch and his family (births, deaths and marriage registrations and census returns) from GRO.

5. Smout, *Century of the Scottish People*, p. 182.
6. 'Dr Buchanan's report'.
7. *Greenock Advertiser*, 24 October 1865. Reprinted in *Greenock, Housing, Health & Social Conditions*.
8. Rose, p. 2.
9. Smout, *History of the Scottish People*, p. 75.
10. Kirk Session Minutes 1840–1865, West Parish of Greenock.
11. Smout, *History of the Scottish People*, p. 76.
12. Obit. *Sydney Morning Herald*, 11 October 1901, and *Australian Dictionary of Biography*, D. Pike, (ed.), Vol. 3, p. 328, MUP, Melbourne, 1969.
13. Documentation of Paterson and How families from birth, death, marriage and shipping records, and from business directories, of Scotland and New South Wales.

Chapter IX

1. F. G. Hall-Jones notes.
2. BDM, Riverton.
3. *ES*, 13 May 1895.
4. The records searched are held at the State Archives and State Libraries of Tasmania (Hobart), New South Wales (Sydney) and Victoria (Melbourne).
5. R. Hughes, *The Fatal Shore*, Pan, London 1987, p. 161.
6. See B. Philp, *Whaling Ways of Hobart Town*, Lindisfarne, 1935, and L. Norman, *Haunts of the Blue Whale*, OBM, Hobart, 1978.
7. James How, Insolvency Papers 1865, State Archives of New South Wales.

Chapter X

1. M. H. Holcroft, *Old Invercargill*, McIndoe, Dunedin, 1976.
2. F. G. Hall-Jones, *Historical Southland*, Southland Historical Committee, Invercargill, 1945, p. 196.
3. F. G. Hall-Jones notes.

4. F. G. Hall-Jones, *Historical Southland*, p. 197.
5. F. G. Hall-Jones, *Historical Southland*, p. 196.
6. BDM, Dacre.
7. Register of baptisms solemnised in the Parish of New Norfolk in the county of Buckingham, Van Diemen's Land, in the year 1837.
8. V. G. Boyle, *Mossburn*, Mossburn Centennial Book Committee, Mossburn, 1987, p. 52.
9. At that time Southland was part of Otago. It became a separate province in 1861 and rejoined Otago in 1870. Provincial government in New Zealand was abolished in 1876.
10. Boyle, p. 52.
11. Boyle, p. 52.
12. The photograph is dated 1872.
13. NZRGO.
14. Minnie's sister Christina married a man named Selby in Greenock in 1870. When Minnie's younger daughter died in New Zealand in 1949 her mother's maiden name was recorded on her death certificate as Selby. This familiarity with the name Selby suggests that Minnie maintained contact with her family in Greenock at least until the time of her sister Christina's marriage.
15. T. Simpson, *Shame and Disgrace*, Penguin, 1991, p. 58, 81–84.
16. W. J. Gardner 'A Colonial Economy' p. 78, in W. H. Oliver (ed.) *The Oxford History of New Zealand*, Oxford, Wellington, 1981.
17. Sheep returns 1884–85, *NZ Gazette* 1886.
18. J. H. Beattie, *The Southern Runs*, Southland Times, 1979.
19. BDM, Winton.
20. Descendant information, M. Cameron.
21. D. Milligan, *Moonlight Ranges*, Dipton Centennial Committee, 1977.

22. MDLS, J1 1895/917 (NA).
23. *Mercantile & Bankruptcy Gazette*, July–December 1884, January–June 1885. *ST*, 13 and 20 December 1884, 28 January and 28 May 1885.
24. *WS*, 1 August 1885.

Chapter XII

1. F. G. Hall-Jones, *Historical Southland*, p. 196.
2. Holcroft, p. 97.
3. J. Sheehan, *Famous Murders in New Zealand*, Waverley, Wellington, 1933.
4. Catran, p. 51.
5. J46 Cor 1908/1016, (NA).
6. RGO, Wgtn.
7. According to the *Mercantile & Bankruptcy Gazette*, 27 August 1887, Christina Kelly lent Minnie Dean £200 at 8%, with '13 cows, furniture &c, on sections 15, 16 & 17, Block I, East Winton [i. e., The Larches]' as security.
8. Invercargill Magistrate's Court Register 1887. The smaller claim was made by a Winton watchmaker. I have been unable to determine the identity of the other claimant.
9. *ST*, 30 April 1888.
10. *ST*, 10 October 1888.
11. *ST*, 17 May 1895.
12. Descendant information.
13. S. Eldred-Grigg, *Pleasures of the Flesh*, Reed, Wellington, 1984.
14. In New Zealand's sister colony of Victoria there were 391 coroner's inquests in 1893. Of these, 101 cases concerned the deaths of infants, with the coroner returning a finding of infanticide in thirty-two. K. Laster, 'Frances Knorr: She killed babies, didn't she?' in *Double Time*, ed. M. Lake & F. Kelly, Penguin, Melbourne, 1985.
15. *Stone's Otago & Southland Directory, 1895*, Stone, Dunedin, 1895.

16. Letter (Ltr): Dunedin coroner to Minister of Justice. J 89/277 (NA).
17. Ltr: Inspector of Police, Dunedin, to Commissioner of Police, Wellington. J 89/299 (NA).
18. Ltr: Inspector of Police, Wellington, to Commissioner of Police, Wellington. J 89/277 (NA).
19. MDLS.
20. The information in this book concerning the children in Minnie Dean's care was collated from fragments of data found in police letters, telegrams and reports, and from MDLS.
21. E. Olssen, 'Towards a new society' in *The Oxford History of New Zealand*, 2nd ed. , G. W. Rice (ed.), OUP, Auckland, 1992.
22. Rose, p. 23.
23. Known deaths: May Irene Dean I, Bertha Currie, May Irene Dean II, Willie Phelan, Dorothy Edith Carter, Eva Hornsby. Known survivors: Maud Moffett, 'no name', baby Cameron, baby O'Brian, baby 'Gray', John Brookland, Ethel Maud Hay, Florence Smith, Cecil Guilford, Arthur Wilson. Police failed to find: John Clark (Henry Cockerill), Cyril Scoular, Sydney McKernan. Fate unknown: eight infants (possibly including surnames Rainbow, Cherry and North).
24. See references to baby farming in Chapter XI.
25. Applicant had to be at least 18 years older than child if child and applicant of same sex; at least 40 years older if child and applicant of opposite sexes. Application required consent of both adopting parents, natural mother and district court judge.
26. See (20) above.
27. In the 1890s servants and dressmakers earned around 15s per week.

28. According to evidence given to 1912 Royal Commission on Cost of Living in New Zealand, in the 1890s a typical Auckland household spent about £1 16s 8d per week (or £95 6s 8d per year) on rent, food, clothing and other necessities.
29. *OW*, 16 May 1895.
30. *OW*, 16 May 1895.
31. MDLS.
32. In the December following Alexander Nicholson's last mortgage payment (in June 1888) ownership of The Larches reverted to the Invercargill mortgagees who received no income from it for nineteen months. The mortgagees must have assumed the property was unused, though Charles Dean was probably running stock and living there much of the time. Minnie and her brood joined him prior to 29 October 1889 (May Irene Dean's death certificate records that she died at The Larches on that date), but the owners were apparently unaware of their presence for at least three months.
33. Esther Wallis's birth certificate confirms that she was legally adopted by Minnie Dean.
34. MDLS.
35. *OW* 16 May 1895.
36. Inquest testimony, Bertha Currie, J46 Cor 1891/240 (NA).
37. MDLS.
38. MDLS.
39. See (20) above.
40. Receipt among material confiscated from MD in Chch, August 1893. P1 1895/845 (NA).
41. *Stone's Otago & Southland ABC*, Stone, Dunedin, (monthly) 1889–1895.

Chapter XIII

1. Files re claims for rewards following conviction of Mrs Dean. P1 1898/654 (NA).
2. Police records, Police Museum, Porirua.
3. MDLS.
4. Police telegrams. P1 1895/845 (NA).
5. MDLS.
6. MDLS.
7. MDLS.
8. Police telegram. P1 1895/895 (NA).
9. Bicarb. potash 1^1/$_2$ tsp, ipecacuanha wine 1 tsp, tinc. camphor compound 1^1/$_2$ tsp, spirits nitre 1^1/$_2$ tsp, syrup simplius 4 tsp, water 4 oz P1 1895/845.
10. Inquest into the death of Bertha Currie. J46 Cor 1891/240 Box 56 (NA).
11. MDLS.
12. Police correspondence. P1 1895/845 (NA).
13. Police correspondence. P1 1895/845 (NA).
14. *ST*, 22 June 1893.
15. Second police list. P1 1895/845 (NA).
16. Police correspondence and reports re John Clark (also known as Henry Cockerill) P1 1895/845 & MDLS (NA).
17. *ST*, 22 and 28 June 1893.
18. MDLS.
19. MDLS.
20. Correspondence re Mrs Dean in Christchurch. P1 1895/845 (NA).
21. *ibid.*
22. MDLS.
23. MDLS.
24. MDLS.
25. Chief Detective O'Connor's report makes his original intention clear: 'I then told her that I would have to take the child to the Police Station, and bring it before the court, under the Children's Protection Act 1890 Sec 3.'
26. Correspondence and reports re Mrs Dean in Christchurch, P1 1895/845 (NA).
27. Judge's notes *R. v. Dean*, J1 95/917 (NA), & MDLS.

28. She was right. Mr C. E. Rawson S. M. wrote: 'Mrs Dean's premises cannot be registered as they are not up to the standard required by the Act.' J1 94/1116 (NA).

29. Files re Mrs Dean's breach of the Infant Life Protection Act. J1 1894/1116 Box 486 (NA).

Chapter XIV

1. The events in Chapter XIV, XV, XVI and XVIII have been pieced together primarily from MDLS, Carter, Hornsby and skeleton inquest reports, Police and Justice Dept archives, Judge's Notes and items re the Dean case in newspapers 10 May–28 Aug 1895 *ST*, *SDN*, and *SC* , *ODT*, *OW* and *ES*, (Dunedin), *WS* and *BH*. The inquests, magisterial hearing & trial were covered in detail by reporters from *ST*, *SDN*, *SC*, *ODT*. The other papers added social comment & gossip to the NZPA account. The *ODT* reports were reprinted in full in the weekly *OW*. All the above newspapers were studied but for reasons of research convenience the OW is quoted most frequently in the text.

2. Her claims in her last statement that at different times she had placed John Clark, an unnamed child from Invercargill and Florence Smith in the care of other Winton women was confirmed by the police.

3. Report from Sergt Gamble, re working of the Infant Life Protection Act 1893. P95/845 (NA).

4. Corres. re Mrs Dean's breach of the Infant Life Protection Act. J1 1894/1116 (NA).

5. MDLS.

6. MDLS.

7. MDLS.

8. It was revealed at the inquest that Eva Hornsby's body was 22 inches long and 7^1/$_2$ lb in weight, Dorothy Edith Carter's body was 28 inches long and 14^1/$_2$ lb in weight. The hat box was 17 inches long, 14 inches wide and 10^1/$_2$ inches deep.

9. These words, written in Minnie's handwriting, were found by the police when they searched The Larches after her arrest (*ES*, 6 August 1895).

Chapter XV

1. For principal sources see Note 1 Chapter XIV.

2. A. C. Hanlon, *Random Recollections*, *ODT* and *OW* newspapers, Dunedin, 1939, p. 180. Hanlon's autobiography was actually ghost written by *ODT* reporter Ronald Jones.

3. The information about the Hall case in Chapters XV, XVI and XVIII came primarily from: *OW* 20 August 1886–18 March 1887: *Regina* v. *Thomas Hall*, Court of Appeal, V. 5, 1887; B. O'Brien, 'Hall, Thomas' in *DNZB* Vol 2; D. Gee, *Poison the Coward's Weapon*, Whitcoulls, Christchurch 1985; O. Alpers, *Cheerful Yesterdays*, Whitcombe & Tombs, Auckland 1932; D. Dyne, *Famous New Zealand Murders*, Collins, Auckland, 1969.

4. O'Brien, 'Thomas Hall'.

5. Reprinted in *OW*.

6. *SC*, 18 May 1895.

7. MDLS. *ST*, 14 May and *OW*, 13 June 1895.

8. W. R. Haselden, *New Zealand Justice of the Peace*, Government Printer, Wellington, 1895.

9. Quoted in *Coroners Act 1951 — A review with proposals for amendments*. Department of Justice, Wellington, 1984.

10. Hazelden.

11. Details of jurymen: *Stone's Directory*; *The Cyclopedia of New Zealand*, Vol. 4: Otago-Southland, Cyclopedia Co., Christchurch, 1905; obit. J. W. Bain, *ST*, 30 Sept, 1899.

12. *ST*, 5 June 1895.
13. Hazelden.
14. W. R. Cornish, *The Jury*, Lane, London, 1968.
15. Hanlon, p. 171.
16. *BH*, 21 May 1895.
17. Thomas Muir began his photography career with Burton Brothers, Dunedin. In the 1890s he had his own studio in Invercargill. In 1898, in partnership with George Moodie, he bought out Burton Brothers and returned to Dunedin. Scenic postcards, using their own work and collections bought from other photographers, were a 'Muir and Moodie' specialty (H. Knight, *Burtons Brothers Photographers*, McIndoe, Dunedin, 1980).
18. P1 1898/654 (NA).
19. *OW*, 30 May 1895.
20. *OW*, 30 May 1895.
21. *OW*, 6 June 1895.
22. Derek Dow, medical historian, ltr to the author.
23. *OW*, 6 June 1895, *ST*, 5 June 1895.
24. *OW*, 26 November 1886.
25. *OW*, 24 September 1886.
26. *OW*, 31 December 1886.
27. Hanlon, p. 319–332.
28. W. D. Stewart, *Portrait of a Judge*, Whitcombe & Tombs, 1945.
29. Descendant information, ltr to author.
30. J. Bassett, 'Williams, Joshua Strange' in *DNZB*, Vol. 2, p. 579.
31. O. T. J. Alpers, *Cheerful Yesterdays*, Whitcombe & Tombs, Auckland, 1927.
32. M. Cullen, *Lawfully Occupied*, Otago District Law Society, Dunedin, 1979.
33. Cullen, p. 45.
34. R. Cook (ed.), *Portrait of a Profession*, Reed, Wellington, 1969.
35. B. O'Brien, 'Robert Butler' in *DNZB*, Vol. 2, p. 69.
36. M. Bassett, *Sir Joseph Ward*, AUP, Auckland, 1993, p. 66.
37. M. Bassett, p. 74.
38. M. Bassett, p. 83.
39. Cullen, p. 162.
40. *The Supreme Court Act Amendment Bill, 1894. Remarks by Mr Justice Williams on the Proposal to Restrain a Judge in Charging a Jury from Commenting on the Evidence*, Conf. of Law Societies, Wellington, 1895.
41. MDLS.
42. MDLS.
43. Inquest on skeleton, J46 Cor 1895455 Box 119 (NA).
44. *ST*, 28 June 1893.
45. Ltr, MD to Mrs Olsen, 12 Sept 1893, court exhibit 34.
46. MDLS.
47. D. Hall et al., 'Post event information changes in recollection for a natural event' in *Eyewitness Testimony*, G. Wells & E. Loftus (eds.), C.U.P., London, 1984.
48. T. Butler, *Memory*, Blackwell, Oxford, 1989.
49. This letter, if Minnie really did write it, was probably as vague and unhelpful as the one she wrote to Colin Scoular's executor about Cyril Scoular's whereabouts.
50. MDLS.
51. John Irving, *Cider House Rules*, Morrow, New York, 1985.
52. *OW*, 13 June 1895.
53. *New Zealand Home Graphic*, 22 June 1895.
54. *SDN*, 11 June 1895.
55. *OW*, 28 January 1887.

Chapter XVI

1. '*Criminal Code Act 1893*, PART XLII — TRIAL. Sec. 390: (1) It shall not in any case be necessary to draw up any formal record of the proceedings on a trial for a crime; but the proper officer of the Court before which the trial takes place shall cause to be preserved all indictments and all depositions

transmitted to him, and he shall keep a book to be call the Crown Book . . . (2) In the Crown Book shall be entered the names of the Judge of the Court and of the grand jurors, and a memorandum of the substance of all proceedings at every trial and of the result of every trial.' In accordance with the legislation no 'formal record' was taken. The 'Trial File', supposedly containing the indictments and depositions, has vanished. The Crown Book, containing names of jurors challenged and empanelled, the duration of each court session, the verdict and a list of witnesses and exhibits, is still extant.

2. For principal sources see Note 1, Chapter XIV. The Judge's Notes (a complete record of the evidence transcribed from his own spidery handwriting) and *ST* coverage of the trial (a remarkable 478 column inches of painfully small print) provide a full record of the trial. Hanlon's 'Brief for the Defense of Minnie Dean' was also consulted.

3. *OW*, 20 June 1895.

4. *OW*, 28 January 1887.

5. Quoted in Simpson, p. 15.

6. The names were listed in *ST*. Their addresses and occupations came from *Stone's Directory.*

7. *New South Wales Reports*, Butterworths, Sydney 1893.

8. *ODT*, 20 June 1895.

9. Sgt Macdonnell's report of meeting with J. Hanan. P1 1895/1182 Box 214 (NA).

10. *ST*, 21 June 1895.

11. Const. King's report on Mrs Hornsby. J1 1895/862, attached to P1 1898/654 (NA).

12. Stewart, p. 54.

13. *ODT*, 21 June 1895.

14. Williams.

Chapter XVIII

1. Hall said he used antimony in his asthma cigarettes but Prof. Black's analysis proved this was not the case and another expert testified that antimony was never used for that purpose. Miss Houston said Hall used antimony in photography but the Crown established that it was never used for that purpose either.

2. *OW*, 28 January 1887.

3. New Zealand Court of Appeal, *R. v. Thomas Hall*, 1887.

4. O'Brien, 'Thomas Hall'.

5. *OW*, 18 March 1887.

6. Quoted in the *ST*, 21 March 1887.

7. *ibid.*

8. Alpers, p. 338.

9. New South Wales Court of Appeal, *R. v. Makin and Wife*, 1893.

10. These are the only records referred to in any reports or correspondence surrounding the trial, indicating that no official court transcript was taken.

11. G. McLauchlan (ed.), *New Zealand Encyclopedia*, Bateman, 1984, p. 183.

12. J1 1895/917 (NA).

13. *R. v. Dean*, murder. Judgments of Court of Appeal. J1 95/917 (NA).

14. J. Bassett, 'Conolly, Edward Tennyson' in *DNZB* Vol. 2.

15. J1 1895/917 (NA).

16. *OW*, 8 August 1895.

17. *New Zealand Graphic*, 22 June 1895.

18. *ST*, 6 August 1895.

19. J1 1895/742 (NA).

20. Outward Letter Book. J43 p. 494 (NA).

21. Laster.

22. Laster.

23. J40 PD Box 65 96/69 (NA).

24. J40 PD Box 65 96/69 (NA).

25. Outward Letter Book, March–Sept 1895, J5/76 (NA).

26. MDLS.

27. MDLS.

Bibliography

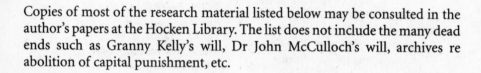

Copies of most of the research material listed below may be consulted in the author's papers at the Hocken Library. The list does not include the many dead ends such as Granny Kelly's will, Dr John McCulloch's will, archives re abolition of capital punishment, etc.

PRIMARY SOURCES

Unpublished

1.   NZ NATIONAL ARCHIVES, WELLINGTON
Note: Files related to Minnie Dean are scattered throughout National Archives. Some files listed below are attached to other files with different reference numbers.

J 46 Cor 1891/240 Box 56. Inquest into death of Bertha Currie.

J46 Cor 1895/455 Box 119. Inquest into death of skeleton.

J46 Cor 1908/1016. Inquest into death of Charles Dean.

J1 1894/1116 Box 486. Files re MD's breach of Infant Life Protection Act.

J1 1895/643. A large file including MD's last statement, Judge's notes & appeal judge's reports (J1 1895/917) and inquests into deaths of Eva Hornsby and Dorothy Edith Carter.

J1 1895/739. File re payment of inquest witnesses.

J1 1895/742. Appeal against sentence.

J1 1895/945. Complaint re 'sensational' newspaper accounts of execution.

J1 1895/978. Query re Cyril Scoular from executor of his father's will.

J1 1895/1006, J1 1895/1294, J1 1895/734, J1 1895/601. Files re lawyers' payments in Dean case.

J5/76 Outward Letter Book, J40 PD Box 65 96/69, J43 Outward Letter Book. Files re arrangements for hangman.

P1 1895/845. File re proposed amendments to the Infant Life Protection Act. Includes data re MD's Christchurch clash with police, searches for John Clark and 'no name', deaths of Bertha Currie and May Irene Dean II, first police list and earlier police surveys of baby farming (J 89/277, J 89/299).

P1 1895/1182 Box 214. Report of Sergeant Macdonnell's discussion with J. Hanan.

P1 1898/654. Files re claims for rewards following conviction of MD, earlier material re her arrest attached.

P5/11 Telegrams 1893-96 re Dean case: p. 424, 498, 530, 547.

PD 95/399 Notification of Minnie Dean's hanging.

2. OTHER
National Archives, Dunedin: Williams, J. S., Judge's Note Book, Invercargill, 1895.
Hocken Library: Hanlon, A. C., Brief for the Defence of Minnie Dean.
Invercargill High Court: Magistrate's Court Register, 1886–1895. Crown Book, 1895.
Police Museum: Nineteenth-century police service records.
New Zealand Registrar General's Office and regional offices: birth, death and marriage records.
General Register Office of Scotland: birth, death and marriage registrations and census returns.
West Parish of Greenock: Kirk session minutes, 1840–1865.
State Archives of NSW, Victoria & Tasmania: Birth, death and marriage registrations, shipping lists, convict lists and insolvency records.

Published

1. NEWSPAPERS AND PERIODICALS
Bruce Herald (Milton)
Evening Star (Dunedin)
Mercantile & Bankruptcy Gazette (Wellington)
New Zealand Gazette (Wellington)
New Zealand Graphic (Wellington)
New Zealand Mail (Wellington)
Otago Daily Times (Dunedin)
Otago Witness (Dunedin)
Press (Christchurch)
Southern Cross (Invercargill)
Southland Daily News (Invercargill)
Southland Times (Invercargill)
Sydney Morning Herald (Sydney)
Greenock Advertiser (Greenock)
Western Star (Riverton)

2. NEW ZEALAND STATUTES
Coroners Act 1867.
Juries Act 1880.
Court of Appeal Act 1882.
Criminals Executions Act 1883.
Criminal Code Act 1893.
Infant Life Protection Act 1893.
Amendments to the above up to 1895.

3. APPEAL COURT REPORTS
R. v. Thomas Hall, NZ 1887.
R. v. Makin & Wife, NSW 1893.

4. CONTEMPORARY (AND EARLIER) BOOKS AND PAMPHLETS

Electoral Rolls

Business and Post Office directories, Scotland, Australia and New Zealand.

Groomes Gazetteer of Scotland, 1905.

Cyclopedia of New Zealand, Vol. 4, Otago and Southland, Cyclopedia Co., Christchurch, 1905.

Hazelden, W. R., *New Zealand Justice of the Peace*, Government Printer, Wellington, 1895.

Scot, R., *The Discoverie of Witchcraft*, (reprint) Dover, New York, 1972.

Smith, J., *Our Scottish Clergy*, Oliver and Boyd, Edinburgh, 1849.

Taylor, A., *Poison in Relation to Medical Jurisprudence and Medicine* (Taylor on Poisons), Churchill, London, 1859.

Williams, J. S., *The Supreme Court Act Amendment Bill, 1894.*

Remarks by Mr Justice Williams on the Proposal to Restrain a Judge in Charging a Jury from Commenting on the Evidence, Conf. of Law Societies, Wellington, 1895.

Reprints (Local History Archives Project, Jorndanhill College, Glasgow): *Greenock — Housing, Health & Social Conditions 1860–1885. Greenock — Public Health 1800–1860. Reports on the Sanitary Conditions of the Labouring Population of Scotland, Greenock,* Clowes, London, 1942. *Shaws Water.* Wallace, J. *Observations on the causes of the great mortality in Greenock, Orr Pollock, Greenock, 1860.*

SECONDARY SOURCES

Unpublished

F. G. Hall-Jones notes.

Descendant information.

Oral and written folklore.

Published books and pamphlets

Alpers, O. T. J., *Cheerful Yesterdays*, Whitcombe & Tombs, Auckland, 1932.

Anderson, A., 'Tuhawaiki, Hone', in *Dictionary of New Zealand Biography*, Vol. 1, W. Oliver (ed.), Allen & Unwin/Dept. Int. Aff., Wellington, 1990.

Bassett, J., 'Conolly, Edward Tennyson', in *Dictionary of New Zealand Biography*, Vol. 2, C. Orange (ed.), BWB/Dept. Int. Aff., Wellington, 1993.

Bassett, J., 'Williams, Joshua Strange', in *Dictionary of New Zealand Biography*, Vol. 2, C. Orange (ed.), BWB/Dept. Int. Aff., Wellington, 1993.

Bassett, M., *Sir Joseph Ward*, AUP, Auckland, 1993.

Beattie, J. H., *The Southern Runs*, Southland Times, 1979.

Boyle, V. G., *Mossburn*, Mossburn Centennial Committee, Mossburn, 1987.

Butler, T., *Memory*, Blackwell, Oxford, 1989.

Catran, K., *Hanlon*, BCNZ Enterprises, Auckland, 1985.

Cook, R. (ed.), *Portrait of a Profession*, Reed, Wellington, 1969.

Cornish, W. R., *The Jury*, Lane, London, 1968.

Coroners Act 1951 — a review with proposals for amendments, Dept Justice, Wellington, 1984.

Cullen, M., *Lawfully Occupied*, Otago District Law Society, Dunedin, 1979.

Dyne, D., *Famous New Zealand Murders*, Collins, Auckland, 1969.

Eldred-Grigg, S., *Pleasures of the Flesh*, Reed, Wellington, 1984.

Gardner, W. J., 'A Colonial Economy', p. 78, in Oliver, W. (ed.), *The Oxford History of New Zealand*, Oxford, Wellington, 1981.

Gee, D., *Poison, the Coward's Weapon*, Whitcoulls, Christchurch, 1985.

Greenock Academy 1855–1955 (Centennial booklet).

Hall, D., et al, 'Postevent information and changes in recollection for a natural event' in *Eyewitness Testimony*, G. Wells & E. Loftus (eds.), C.U.P., London, 1984.

Hall-Jones, F. G., *Historical Southland*, Southland Historical Committee, Invercargill, 1945.

Hall-Jones, F. G., *Kelly of Inverkelly*, Southland Historical Committee, Invercargill, 1944.

Hall-Jones, J., *The South Explored*, Reed, Wellington, 1979.

Hamilton, T. W., *How Greenock Grew*, McKelvie, Greenock, 1947.

Hanlon, A. C., *Random Recollections*, ODT & OW Newspapers, Dunedin, 1939.

Hibbert, C., *The Roots of Evil*, Weidenfeld & Nicholson, London, 1963.

Holcroft, M. H., *Old Invercargill*, McIndoe, Dunedin, 1976.

Hughes, R., *The Fatal Shore*, Pan, London, 1987.

Irving, J., *Cider House Rules*, Morrow, New York, 1985.

Kingsford, P., *Victorian Railwaymen*, Cass, London, 1979.

Knight, H., *Burton Brothers Photographers*, McIndoe, Dunedin, 1980.

Kunze, M., *Highroad to the Stake*, U. Chicago Press, Chicago, 1987.

Laster, K., 'Frances Knorr' in *Double Time*, M. Lake & F. Kelly (eds.), Penguin, Melbourne, 1985.

McKenna, F., *The Railway Workers 1840–1970*, Faber, London, 1980.

McLauchlan, G. (ed.), *New Zealand Encyclopedia*, Bateman, 1984.

Milligan, D., *Moonlight Ranges*, Dipton Centennial Committee, 1977.

Monteith, J. & McCarroll, J., *Greenock from Old Photographs*, Vol. 2, Inverclyde District Libraries, Greenock, 1983.

Natusch, S., *At the Edge of the Bush*, Craig, Invercargill, 1986.

Norman, L., *Haunts of the Blue Whale*, OBM, Hobart, 1978.

O'Brien, B., 'Butler, Robert', in *Dictionary of New Zealand Biography*, Vol. 2, C. Orange (ed.), BWB/Dept. Int. Aff., 1993.

O'Brien, B., 'Hall, Thomas' in *Dictionary of New Zealand Biography*, Vol. 2, C. Orange (ed.), BWB/Dept. Int. Aff., 1993.

Olssen E., 'Towards a new society' in *The Oxford History of New Zealand*, 2nd ed., G. W. Rice (ed.), OUP, Auckland, 1992.

Philp, B., *Whaling Ways of Hobart Town*, Lindisfarne, 1935.

Pike, D. (ed.), *Australian Dictionary of Biography*, Vol. 3, MUP, Melbourne, 1969.

Preston, F., *A Family of Woolgatherers*, McIndoe, Dunedin, 1978.

Radznowicz, L. *A History of English Criminal Law*, Vol. 1, Stevens, London, 1948.

Rose L., *Massacre of the Innocents*, Routledge & Kegan Paul, London, 1986.

Scott, H. *Fasti Ecclesiae Scoticanae*, Vol. 3, Oliver & Boyd, Edinburgh, 1920.

Sheehan, J., *Famous Murders in New Zealand*, Waverley, Wellington, 1933.

Simpson, T., *Shame and Disgrace*, Penguin, Auckland, 1991.

Smith, F. B., *The People's Health 1830–1910*, Holmes & Meier, New York, 1979.

Smith, R. M., *The History of Greenock*, Orr Pollock, Greenock, 1921.

Smout, T. C., *A Century of the Scottish People 1830–1950*, Fontana, London, 1987.

Smout, T. C., *A History of the Scottish People*, Fontana, London, 1983.

Soper, E., *The Otago of Our Mothers*, Otago Centennial Historical Publications, Dunedin, 1948.

Stewart, W. D., *Portrait of a Judge*, Whitcombe & Tombs, 1945.

Westwood, J., *Albion*, Paladin, London, 1987.

Wohl, A., *Endangered Lives*, Dent, London, 1983.

Index